Saigon to San Diego

# Saigon to San Diego

*Memoir of a Boy Who Escaped
from Communist Vietnam*

*by* TRINH QUANG DO

McFarland & Company, Inc., Publishers
*Jefferson, North Carolina, and London*

LIBRARY OF CONGRESS CATALOGUING-IN-PUBLICATION DATA

Do, Trinh Quang, 1964–
    Saigon to San Diego : memoir of a boy who escaped from
communist Vietnam / by Trinh Quang Do.
        p.     cm.
    Includes index.

    ISBN 0-7864-1805-2 (softcover : 50# alkaline paper)

    1. Do, Trinh Quang, 1964–   2. Vietnam — Politics and
government —1975–   3. Political refugees—Vietnam —
Biography.   4. Political refugees— United States—Biography.
I. Title.
DS559.914.D6A3  2004
959.704'4'092 — dc22
                                    2004005131

British Library cataloguing data are available

*Cover photograph:* The author *(second boy from the right)* with
his mother and three younger brothers in front of his home in
Vũng Tàu three years before the fall of South Vietnam

Manufactured in the United States of America

*McFarland & Company, Inc., Publishers*
    *Box 611, Jefferson, North Carolina 28640*
    *www.mcfarlandpub.com*

# Contents

*Preface* . . . . . . . . . . . . . . . . . . . . . . . . . . . . . . . . . . . . . . . . 1

1. When the Guns Were Silent . . . . . . . . . . . . . . . . . . . . . . . 3
2. From Father to Son . . . . . . . . . . . . . . . . . . . . . . . . . . . . . 23
3. Wake Up to Darkness . . . . . . . . . . . . . . . . . . . . . . . . . . . 36
4. Back to School . . . . . . . . . . . . . . . . . . . . . . . . . . . . . . . . 54
5. The Competition . . . . . . . . . . . . . . . . . . . . . . . . . . . . . . 71
6. Against the Odds . . . . . . . . . . . . . . . . . . . . . . . . . . . . . . 85
7. Cháu Ngoan Bác Hồ (Good Children of Uncle Ho) . . . . . . . 106
8. The New Kids in School . . . . . . . . . . . . . . . . . . . . . . . . . 115
9. The Growing Pains . . . . . . . . . . . . . . . . . . . . . . . . . . . . . 130
10. The New Economic Zone . . . . . . . . . . . . . . . . . . . . . . . . 139
11. The Choices We Made . . . . . . . . . . . . . . . . . . . . . . . . . . 146
12. A Brief Moment of Glory . . . . . . . . . . . . . . . . . . . . . . . . 151
13. The Winds of War . . . . . . . . . . . . . . . . . . . . . . . . . . . . . 163
14. The Last Goodbye . . . . . . . . . . . . . . . . . . . . . . . . . . . . . 174
15. The Tango with Death . . . . . . . . . . . . . . . . . . . . . . . . . . 185
16. The Days of Waiting . . . . . . . . . . . . . . . . . . . . . . . . . . . . 212
17. Epilogue — After the Rain . . . . . . . . . . . . . . . . . . . . . . . 221

*Index* . . . . . . . . . . . . . . . . . . . . . . . . . . . . . . . . . . . . . . . . . 227

# *Preface*

"I came to America twelve years ago from Vietnam as a refugee and an orphan. When I was twelve, I didn't think I would get past ninth grade. When I was fourteen, I didn't think I would live to my twentieth birthday. For me to be here today is a dream beyond my comprehension."

When I was admitted to the MBA program at Stanford University in 1990, I didn't realize that I would be saying the words above many times. To lay bare the intimate details of one's past is not natural for a person born and raised in a Confucian culture. Yet, there I was among a group of curious first-year classmates taking turns needling me to divulge details about my mysterious background. The brief orientation sessions in the first week transformed into dramatic interrogations, with me under the glaring spotlight. Everyone wanted to know how a Vietnamese refugee had managed to escape death, poverty, Communist indoctrination, and hopelessness, and had against impossible odds now secured a spot to be among the selected company of Stanford MBA students.

What began as an uncomfortable impromptu autobiographical sketch later became a short story titled "Escape from Vietnam," which was published in the *Stanford Business Magazine* in 1991. Despite being taught to keep personal matters private, I felt a sense of responsibility in telling the story of my generation's coming of age in Vietnam during the brutal postwar period. But my story is more than just a harrowing narrative of personal tragedy and triumph; my experience is framed within a complex historical dimension. Apart from those who have suffered and endured the searing misery of Communist rule, I don't think it is possible for anyone living outside Vietnam to grasp the profound depth of pettiness and

1

vengeful spite displayed by the victors of the war. The Vietnamese Communists came down on their defeated brethren with all the merciless cruelty they could devise for the sole purpose of "internal security."

After graduating from Stanford, I went to work in marketing for the Procter & Gamble company in Cincinnati, Ohio. In 1994, I was sent by Procter & Gamble to an overseas assignment — first to the Philippines, then to Vietnam to help start up the company's business operations there. While moving between the various work assignments, I continued to write and expand on the original short story. The book would take ten years to complete.

There are many reasons for me to write this book. First, it is a tribute to my parents, whose sacrifices gave me the chance to come to America and whose irrepressible spirit and character were enduring inspirations that gave me the strength to face my darkest hours. It is also a tribute to my childhood friends, who went through the same hardships as I did but were not as lucky. Many are now dead or live in poverty and despair in Vietnam.

My story is not unique. It is the story of millions of people who made dangerous voyages to escape from Vietnam. Many succeeded, but many more perished silently in the cold depths of the South China Sea. Others survived the sea but met unspeakable horrors at the hands of pirates.

This book is written in part because I strongly felt a need to tell the truth, the cold hard facts about how my generation and our parents struggled against extreme prejudice and indiscriminate hatred in holding on to their last shred of humanity. Also, I cannot imagine a more fitting way to honor the memory of my parents and countless others who died trying to escape than to tell our stories.

Last but not least, if this book succeeds in instilling in my children or a disadvantaged child somewhere the belief that with courage, hope, and faith, one can overcome overwhelming odds, then my years of writing the book will have been well worth it.

# 1

# When the Guns
# Were Silent

*Vũng Tàu — April 29, 1975:* The explosion deafened my ears and almost sent my heart jumping out of my throat. This one hit too close. I thought that this shell must have landed within 500 meters of our hastily dug, pitiful hole in the ground. I looked at my mother, who sat across from me in the cramped space of this "dirt-fortified" bunker. Her face turned pale from fear. Both of her arms wrapped around my younger brothers. Every time a shell was about to hit the ground, my mother pulled my brothers close to her and bent her head down as if to use her body to shield my brothers from stray shrapnel.

I wanted so much to sit next to my mother, and bury my head in her breast to calm my fear. But there was no more room. Beside, I didn't want to make my fear too obvious and become the laughingstock of the people in this bunker. I turned to my left to look at my father. He seemed calm and unconcerned despite the sounds of explosions and gunfire in the distance.

My father patted my head and reassured me that everything was OK. Since there was no military installation within 5 kilometers, he said, there was no reason for the enemy to shoot at us. The last explosion sounded loud because it was one of their bigger shells, maybe a 175 millimeter cannon.

I knew that my father was just trying to calm me down. The North Vietnamese Army (NVA) did not have any qualms about shooting at civilians before, so why should they care now? I still remembered vivid images

3

of the massacres of civilians they carried out during the Tết Offensive of 1968 and the Easter Offensive (known in Vietnamese as "Mùa Hè Đỏ Lửa" or "The Summer of Fiery Red Fire") of 1972, that I had seen on TV. Nevertheless, I relaxed my tense muscles a little bit and told my father that I was not afraid.

My father nodded, and closed his eyes to get some sleep. I tried to do the same and thought of happier things to drive the terror from my head. At least it beat the anxiety of listening to the sound of an artillery shell being fired, the sharp, high-pitched noise of its flight through the air, and the dreaded explosion as it hit the ground. How many people out there were being blown to bits in these final, desperate days of South Vietnam? I hoped my family wouldn't be the last casualties of this war, whose ending was decided many days ago. I thought about the past few days. Slowly, the chain of events leading to this nightmare came back to my head.

It began several days before. During school recess time, my father came to pick me up. I was chattering with friends when he appeared out of nowhere and told me to pack up and go home. I knew immediately that something serious must have happened. When I asked him why, my father told me something that I never thought would happen. We were in danger as Communist troops were massing close outside Vũng Tàu. They would attack soon. It was only a matter of time before Vũng Tàu would fall.

Feeling apprehension welling up inside, I asked my father for reassurance that we would be all right. There was none. This time things were different, he said. The South Vietnamese Army was running out of ammunition and its generals kept ordering withdrawal. There was no sign it would make a stand. At the current rate, South Vietnam would crumble within a month. We needed to pack and move out of our home since our apartment complex, populated mostly by military officers and soldiers, might come under attack.

I shut up and thought about the dark days that were about to come. Though only eleven, I had learned enough. I knew that if South Vietnam were to fall to the Communists, the future would be as dark as a moonless, starless night for our family. The oppressive force of Communism that my parents fled from twenty years before was about to catch up with us.

My parents emigrated to the South from North Vietnam in 1954, when the Geneva Accord divided Vietnam into North and South. My father came from a landowner family in Nam Định province. My paternal great grandfather was a mandarin in the last imperial court of Vietnam, the

Nguyễn Dynasty. The mandarins, the nobility class in the old Vietnamese society, were officials and ministers of the king. Because of my great grand-father's position, his children were raised in the strict moral tradition of Confucianism. The education and the land my great grandfather owned and passed down provided my father and uncles a privileged life. The same privileges also made them into enemies of the Communists. Though his family had lived through the nine long years of the First Indochina War (from 1945 to 1954), my father and uncles were lucky to miss the Land Reform carried out by the Communists in 1952.

When they heard the news that Vietnam would be divided into two parts, my father and uncles quickly decided to head south. They had seen and heard enough to know what their future would be like under the Communist regime. My father told me many times the story of the dangerous journey he and my uncles' families took. They walked several hundred kilometers, from Nam Định to the port of Hải Phòng, to catch the last ship leaving for South Vietnam. They could travel only at night. In the day, they hid away to avoid Communist checkpoints. The checkpoints were set up on all the main roads to harass and stop people from emigrating to the South. With their background as the sons of "vicious, exploitative landowners," there was no telling what might have happened to them if they were caught at one of these checkpoints. At best, they could be beaten up badly and sent to prison. At worst, they'd be executed on the spot as an example for others who might be contemplating a move south.

Despite many close calls, they made it to one of the last ships leaving Hải Phòng full of refugees. While all the men in the family left, all of my father's sisters decided to stay back in the North with my grandmother (my grandfather had died a few years before). They wanted to stay to take care of the family land and our ancestors' graves. Since then, my father lost all contact with his family in the North.

My father was the youngest child in his family, being only 17 when he arrived in South Vietnam with only "hai bàn tay trắng" (two empty hands). For the first few years, my father lived with Uncle Tín's family, who sup-ported his schooling. They settled in Bàn Cờ, a section of Saigon popu-lated by refugees from North Vietnam. Uncle Tín supported his family and my father by working as a freelance nurse. His clients were poor neigh-bors who could not afford to go to a doctor. Since his clients were poor, he didn't make very much. The poverty didn't suppress Uncle Tín's gen-erous nature. He took care of anyone who came to him, regardless of whether they could pay him.

Uncle Tín barely earned enough to keep the whole family fed and clothed. They lived an extremely frugal life. Occasionally, to remind me how good I had it, my father told me the story of how he repeatedly wore the same shirt and pants for weeks since he didn't have any other clothes. Every day, he washed them at night, hung them in the back yard to dry, went to sleep without a shirt, and woke up early in the morning to get these clothes and wear them again. Each time that I was acting spoiled, refusing to eat because I didn't like my food, my father told me again the story of how he used to go on for days eating steamed rice with only salt or soy sauce. At first, I refused to believe that anyone could endure such a diet. I couldn't imagine myself eating steamed rice with salt once, let alone for many days. However, as I grew up and heard the story again from my mother, aunts, and uncles, I gradually realized that everything my father told me was true, and I saw how far he had come since this humble beginning. Out of respect for my father, I began to force myself to finish every meal, regardless of whether I liked or disliked the food.

Despite the hardships, my father studied hard and excelled. To help out Uncle Tín, my father worked as a private tutor for children of rich families. When he graduated from high school, my father was admitted to the Cao Thắng Technical College to study engineering. By then, Uncle Tín had built a steady, loyal client base and began to prosper. My father began to find better paying tutoring jobs. He started to date my mother and seemed on track to graduate as an engineer, a prestigious profession at that time. Then, his future suddenly took a different turn. He was drafted when the ARVN (Army of the Republic of Vietnam) began mass mobilization to fight the Viet Cong's insurgent activities.

After the second year of college, the ARVN sent my father to the Thủ Đức Military Academy. Because of his technical training, my father was assigned to the Communication Branch of the ARVN upon graduation. I never knew if my father ever faced combat in the front line. I didn't even know what he did, except that soon after graduating from the academy, he married my mother and was assigned to a post in Vũng Tàu. The assignment turned out to be a blessing because Vũng Tàu was the most peaceful city during the Vietnam War.

My mother also came from a well-off landowner family in Nam Định, North Vietnam. My maternal grandfather was an herbalist. During the 1930s and 1940s, many of my mother's relatives joined the Vietnam Nationalist Party to fight the French colonialists. In the days leading to the Japanese surrender in Vietnam in August 1945, Communist assassins murdered these relatives of my mother. The assassinations were part of the Communist Party's plan to eliminate all potential rivals vying for the power vacuum the Japanese would leave behind.

From these experiences, my mother's family knew well the truth about

My parents proudly showing off their children in 1966. Sitting at the far left, I was three at the time, unaware of the storms to come in the future.

the Communists' actions behind their patriotic propaganda. In 1954, my grandfather abandoned everything he owned and took the entire family to the South. He knew that as soon as they took over power in the North, the Communists would strip him of his possessions and persecute his family.

My grandfather soon prospered in South Vietnam while practicing medicine. My mother and her siblings lived a comfortable middle-class life. Many of my aunts and uncles went to college, and later worked for the South Vietnamese government. The association with the government further marked my family's obvious opposition to Communism.

Despite growing up during the Vietnam War, I had never seen the war's horrible destruction close to home, thanks to my father's good luck of being stationed in Vũng Tàu. The coastal city was a favorite vacationing spot for people from Saigon, foreigners, and American GIs. Surrounded on three sides by the sea, the city had only one main road to get in and out. Thus, Vũng Tàu was not a favorable military target.

My younger brother Truong and two friends and myself standing in the field of the
Đồng Đa military complex in 1967. I am on the left.

When I was growing up, the war always seemed to happen somewhere
else and to somebody else. I lived in blissful ignorance, thinking that life
would always be peaceful and happy. What I knew about the Communists,
I learned from watching TV or reading newspapers. Occasionally, I picked
up on pieces of my parents' conversation, or my cousins' and uncles' who
were ARVN soldiers fighting in places like An Lộc, Bình Trị Thiên, or
Laos. From the little that I heard, I learned enough to know that people
like my parents or my relatives would not be well treated by the Communists if they were to win the war.

Though my parents never intended it, I was exposed to the politics
and divisions of the war at an early age. When I was ten, I saw a classic
movie about the Land Reform carried out by the Communists in 1952. The
movie, *We Want To Live* (*Chúng Tôi Muốn Sống*), showed the systematic
persecution of landowners through carefully orchestrated steps by Communist cadres. The movie would have a lasting impact on me.

The year was 1952. Even though the first Indochina War against the
French was still raging, the Communist Party already embarked on the

plan to eliminate their potential enemies, the landowners. In rural areas where they had control, party cadres organized "Peoples Courts" to put landowners on trial. The trials were modeled after a similar "Land Reform" program going on at the same time in China, with the pretext of giving the land back to the people who actually farmed it. The landowners were tried in these "Peoples Courts" for supposed "crimes and atrocities" committed against poor peasants who worked for or rented the land from them.

Though some landowners were cruel to other peasants, most were innocent, kind people. Regardless, all were tried in the same kangaroo courts that Communist cadres set up. In these trials, there was always someone planted by the cadres to come forward and allege crimes against the luckless landowners. Inevitably, all were convicted and most were condemned to death.

The movie showed the process of these trials and many gruesome scenes of how the condemned were executed. Old men and women were buried with only their heads sticking out above the ground, left to endure the scorching sun without anyone giving them any water. After a few days of the torture, the Communists then drove tractors over the victims and decapitated them.

I was deeply disturbed and lost sleep for many nights. The movie troubled me as I couldn't imagine how people could be so cruel to each other. One day, I asked my mother if it was true that the Communists would kill all landowners if they were to control the country. Having seen the movie *We Want to Live*, I couldn't understand why people could harbor such deep hatred and do such terrible things.

Surprised by my inquisitiveness, my mother sat down to tell me what she knew. The Communists did kill many landowners in 1952. Many Communist Party members were poor peasants, who were exploited by cruel landowners for a long time. That's why they joined the Communist Party. The party promised them land and freedom if they were to control the country. The party worked up their hatred then manipulated other peasants to accuse landowners of crimes. No one dared to help the landowners. Anyone brave enough to do that would likely meet the same fate.

My mother was fortunate to not have to live through one of these "Land Reform" trials. In 1952, the Communists did not control all of North Vietnam. Had they controlled our village, my grandfather would have been put on one of those trials.

I was indignant. Did my grandfather ever do anything bad? How could the Communists think of putting my grandpa on trial? Laughing at my little show of righteousness, my mother told me that it didn't matter to the Communists. My grandfather was the kindest man she had known.

My mother holding my youngest brother, Tri, while I played with other kids in the Đống Đa complex field in 1968.

During the famine of 1945, when the Japanese burned our crops so that they could use our land to produce materials for their army, two million Vietnamese died of starvation in the North. People in my mother's village died like flies every day. My grandfather was the richest man in the village and the only one who had enough rice to last through the famine. He had a lot of rice cooked up every day to give to other villagers. Many people survived because of him. Grandpa had built a lot of good karma by saving other people's lives. That's why his family was able to move to the South safely and prosper, despite losing everything Grandpa owned in the North.

Yet, Grandfather's kindness and good deeds wouldn't save him from the Communists if he had stayed. They would make other peasants accuse him of all sorts of imaginary crimes. That was what they did to many people in 1952. Most people killed weren't vicious landowners. Their only crime was that they owned land and they were rich. The Communists hated all people who were rich, not just landowners.

If the Communists won the war, our future would look very ominous. Though our family didn't own land anymore, my father was an officer in the army that was fighting against them. Worse, both my parents fled from them in 1954. My mother didn't want to think about what persecutions they would have in store for people like us.

At the time, I wasn't concerned. I didn't think the South would ever fall. The war always seemed to be so far away, so it didn't seem real. All I heard on the news was that the ARVN was always able to push back major offensives by the North Vietnamese Army (NVA). Besides, I was a well-pampered kid. My main concerns were to study hard, make my parents happy, and play games with my friends. The war, for me, was a spectator sport. Able to read newspapers since I was eight, I scoured the daily papers *Chính Luận* and *Tin Sáng* every day for news about ongoing battles. The news always reported that the Communists were losing more soldiers than the ARVN. In my simple mind, the casualty report was the score for this war game. The "enemies" were losing more soldiers, so we must be winning the war. Thus, I became more convinced that the South would eventually win. It would take many years before I understood the terrible tragedies behind the casualty statistics that I innocently thought of as "scores" in this war game.

My father stopped going to work after the day he picked me up. My brothers and I also stopped going to school. We stayed home and helped our parents to pack food and clothing, as if we were preparing to evacuate. All this time, we were glued to the TV and the radio for the latest developments on the battlefront. Things continued to get worse. Communist forces started an offensive in March, the biggest campaign they had staged since 1972. This time, however, there was no stopping the NVA's onslaught. In early March, the news that the American Congress voted to stop providing military aid to South Vietnam dealt a death blow to the ARVN. The ARVN continued to retreat from the Communist offensive at a frightening pace. For several days, all I heard on the radio was that South Vietnamese generals had ordered another "tactical evacuation." These tactical evacuations soon turned into bloody retreats. Then, President Nguyễn Văn Thiệu went on TV to announce his resignation, saying that the withdrawal of American support tied his hands. He vowed to stay in South Vietnam and fight against the Communists to the last man. A few days after his appearance on TV, there were numerous rumors that Thiệu had already fled the country with many tons of gold on his own private jet. The title of president now fell into the hands of weak, aged Vice President Trần Văn Hương, who could do nothing to reverse the tide of events.

On April 25, 1975, a military Jeep pulled up in front of our home. A big man dressed in the uniform of an ARVN colonel and wearing sunglasses emerged from the car. He had a sinister-looking handgun on his right hip and two grenades dangling from his neck. Two soldiers, each with a rifle in his hands and a belt of grenades on his waist, came out of the Jeep and stood guard beside the colonel.

Walking up to me, the colonel asked to see my father. Though intimidated by his fearsome appearance, I managed to ask who he was. It turned out the colonel was Uncle Hướng, a second cousin of my mother.

My father heard the commotion and came out. He and Uncle Hướng recognized each other right away. My father invited Uncle Hướng in, asked me to prepare some tea, and called my mother and brothers out to greet him. The two bodyguards stayed outside our house, smoking cigarettes and keeping a watch over the neighborhood.

Soon, our family was sitting around Uncle Hướng in the living room, listening to his story.

A regimental commander in the ARVN, Uncle Hướng had seen his regiment melt away after 15 days of running from the Central Highland to Saigon. Half of his troops were lost to the NVA's ambushes. What he didn't lose to the Communists, he lost to desertion. By the time he got to Saigon, he had a tattered group of soldiers left. Only a quarter of the men who started with him in the Central Highland made it to Saigon.

Interrupting Uncle Hướng, my father asked why he didn't make a stand against the North Army's advance. Shaking his head sadly, Uncle Hướng said he couldn't as he kept getting orders to withdraw. He was told to get back to Saigon to defend the capital. By the time he got to Nha Trang, the morale of his troops was so low from the non-stop retreats that he was losing fifty men a day to desertion. There was a mad rush of both civilians and soldiers in Nha Trang to catch any planes, ships, or vehicles that could take them further south. The panic fed on itself. Soon, the ARVN was withdrawing from cities even at the slightest indication that any NVA units were near.

The South Vietnamese Army was now a snake without a head, Uncle Hướng told us. His regiment was not the only unit ordered to drop everything and withdraw nonstop to Saigon. None of his officers believed we had a chance anymore after the Americans decided not to give us military aid and they kept getting orders to retreat. If the officers didn't believe we have a chance, how could they rally the soldiers for a fight?

When he got to Saigon, there was already a line of troops at the outskirts of the city. He and his men were not allowed to go into Saigon, even if they dropped their weapons and came in just to see their families. His soldiers, already demoralized and disgusted after running for half a month, threw away their weapons and uniforms. Some bad soldiers threw away their uniforms but kept their weapons to plunder anybody they could. After seeing the situation in Saigon, Uncle Hướng left for Vũng Tàu to find a way to get his family out of the country. South Vietnam would last at most another 10 days. This time, the Americans would not come back to bail us out. Those who believed the Americans would come to the rescue were dreaming. The Americans didn't give a shit about us anymore, Uncle Hướng said. Nixon had sold us to the Commies when he visited the Chinese in 1972. Did my father remember the Paris negotiations in 1973? Did anyone act as if South Vietnam still existed at the time?

I could sense that the more he talked, the more Uncle Hướng was getting angry over events he could not control. My father just looked on and remained quiet, letting Uncle Hướng blow off steam.

His anger then turned on the American press. The "chó đẻ" (Vietnamese equivalent of "son of a bitch") American journalists, Uncle Hướng cursed, had always treated us as nothing more than American puppets. And the fucking American public believed them. Many times, he had wanted so much to blow their arrogant brains out. These assholes were the enemies he could not fight. In battle, at least he could respect the North Vietnamese soldiers. They were willing to shed their blood for what they believed in. The American hired pens acted as if they were our friends. They traveled with us, demanded our services and protection, then turned around and stabbed us in the back. With friends like that, who needed enemies? What did they believe in anyway? The NVA soldiers fought because they believed the Communist propaganda. They thought they were fighting to liberate South Vietnam from us and the Americans. We fought them because we wanted our children to have freedom. We wanted our kids not to have to go through what we went through with the Communists in the North. These fucking American journalists fought only for their fame and notoriety, at the expense of our blood. They claimed to report the "truth." What was the "truth" in this war?

My father finally interrupted Uncle Hướng's tirade. It didn't help us to talk about the American press, my father said. We needed people like Uncle Hướng to make a last stand to defend us. Why didn't he? Why was he trying to run away from his country?

All was already lost; Uncle Hướng shook his head vigorously. Our government's gamble to scare the Americans to come back failed. South Vietnam in 1975 was not the same as South Korea in 1950 to the Americans. By the time Thiệu and his cronies realized their mistake, the losses we had taken from these "tactical withdrawals" and the accompanying panic had exploded beyond their control. Then, they ordered us to withdraw to Saigon to make a last defense, right? No. They ordered us to hold off the NVA as long as possible so that they could gather their families and all the money they had made all these years on the blood and sweat of our soldiers to get out of the country.

In Saigon, Uncle Hướng told his soldiers to go home to their families. With the fall of South Vietnam now inevitable, they shouldn't be the last men to die in the war. The only thing left for Uncle Hướng to do was to find spaces for his family on any ships or planes leaving the country. Maybe my father should do the same while he still had time.

At this time, I got tired and went to sleep. While I remembered bits of the conversation between Uncle Hướng and my father, I did not understand most of it. When I woke up, Uncle Hướng and his soldiers were gone. My father told me he already went back to Saigon. That was the first and last time I saw Uncle Hướng.

In the last week of April, we started hearing the sounds of artillery fire in the distance. The explosions were the unmistakable warnings that war finally had come very close to peaceful Vũng Tàu. Thinking our military housing complex would soon come under attack, my parents took the family to an acquaintance's house in Bến Đình for refuge.

When we arrived, there were already families crowding in the small living room of the place. The house had a large back yard. The men were already working, digging two L-shaped holes in the ground. These holes would be our bunkers to hide from the shelling we knew was coming. My father and I joined the men to dig, while my mother helped other women to cook.

We stacked the sides of the bunkers with sandbags to keep the soft dirt from caving in. When we finished digging, we placed cot mats on the floor and used several layers of pressed wood and metal sheets to cover the bunkers. Despite knowing little about warfare, I knew the bunkers offered little protection from the coming attack.

The sounds of artillery fire got closer to Vũng Tàu as the days passed. By April 27, the city was under attack. We couldn't sleep the night before as the thumping sounds of heavy shells being fired became increasingly louder. My father told me that an NVA unit was probably about 10 kilometers outside the city. On the morning of the 27th, we all moved down to the bunkers, since the artillery shells seemed to explode so much closer. Together, sixteen people crowded into two small holes in the ground. We stayed there for the next three days, getting above the ground to take in a breath of fresh air whenever there was a break in the shelling.

No matter how hard I tried, I couldn't sleep. My nerves were raw from fear. The hot, humid air in the cramped bunker didn't help. There were ten of us, my parents, me, my brothers, and another family of four, crowding into this bunker. The artillery pounding had gone on for three hours, and I had not gone to the toilet for five hours. My bowel and bladder clamored for a revolution of their own. My parents wouldn't let me get out of the bunker to relieve myself until this barrage was over. Even if they had let me, I wouldn't have dared to. I gritted my teeth and hoped that I wouldn't defecate in my pants.

Today was April 29. I had finished three spy novels that I brought to the bunker and started reading the fourth one. My father didn't stop me from reading these novels as he usually did. He turned the radio on again to listen to news. There was nothing but bad news. The South Vietnamese government was turned over to General Dương Văn Minh as most top officials had fled the country. It seemed there were several NVA divisions massing outside Saigon. If Saigon fell, Vũng Tàu would follow the next day.

Exhausted and hungry, I fell into a fitful sleep. When I woke up, it was 9 o' clock on April 30, 1975. The artillery pounding had stopped. Yet now I could hear the sounds of gunfire. The Communist troops must already be in the city. By now, my bowel was ready to explode with all the wastes that my body accumulated during the past 18 hours. After asking for permission from my parents, I climbed out of the bunker and went straight for the toilet. With my bowel screaming to be relieved, I couldn't care less about flying bullets.

When I got back, everyone sat down to have a breakfast of rice and canned meats. After the meal, my father took out his handgun and unloaded all the bullets. When I asked him why, my father said wearily that the war was over and there was no more need for the gun. The radio news indicated that General Minh was trying to negotiate with the Communist commander on the terms of surrender. The surrender would probably happen in a day. The Americans had withdrawn all of their people, and we were left on a sinking ship.

The end came sooner than my father expected. At noon, April 30, 1975, the radio station announced the South Vietnamese government had surrendered to stop further bloodshed. Communist tanks began to rumble into the capital. Soon after, all the gunfire and artillery explosions that I had grown used to during the past three days went away.

We came out of the bunker and stretched ourselves. My father and other men went to gather all their military uniforms and burned them in the back yard. Afterward, they put all their guns and bullets into one bag. One of the men took the bag and rode off on his motorcycle to dispose of it.

At 2 o'clock, many people in the neighborhood began to go out to the street to take a look around. Everyone must have heard the surrender announcement on the radio. I followed Mr. Tám, one of the men who had hunkered down in the bunker with our family in the past week, to the street. The sounds of war had completely stopped. Surprisingly, the neighborhood seemed almost untouched. In the south, thick, black smoke was rising in the direction of the Junior Military Academy (Trường Thiếu Sinh Quân). The academy must have taken a beating from the Communist bombardment. Yet, many people in the neighborhood were rushing toward it.

Mr. Tám stopped and asked one of the men why he was rushing toward the academy. The man irritably pushed Tám off and said that he had to run to get his rice. The academy had a large rice storage, and the cadets defending the school were either dead or gone. The Communist army had yet to occupy the place. There was a short window of time to loot the place, and he was not going to miss it.

Winking at me, Mr. Tám asked if I want to go with him to the academy and join the fun. Knowing that my father would be furious if I did, I politely declined. Mr. Tám shrugged and sped off with the rest of the crowd.

Suddenly, the crowded neighborhood became deserted. Not knowing what else to do, I went in and told my parents what was happening. My father shook his head in disgust. We just lost our country and all people could think to do was loot rice. My mother, a practical woman, was more sympathetic. It was better that people loot the rice than let the food fall into the hands of the Communist troops. Who knew if the market would resume in the next few days so that people could buy their food? Those few kilos of rice they looted might mean the difference between life and death for some people.

An hour later, Mr. Tám returned with a happy smile, lugging a 50-kilo bag of rice. He told us of the mad stampede at the academy. People were cursing and trampling all over each other to lay claim to their rice. There were all kinds of people, from old men and women to adolescent kids, pushing and shoving. Mr. Tám was lucky. As one of the early arrivals and being strong, he easily pushed other people aside for his rice.

The rest of the day was quiet. In the afternoon, it appeared the Communists had taken over the government radio station in Saigon, because the radio now played Communist military songs. These songs were the most hideous sounds I ever heard. The singers sang with such high-pitched voices, my ear hurt when I heard them for too long. They were singing praises to Uncle Ho Chi Minh and the party, of whom I had no idea. My father turned off the radio after the second song and told us to go to sleep.

The next morning, May 1, 1975, I got my first look at the regular NVA soldiers. At about 10 o'clock, I heard loud cheers outside. I raced out to the street to see what was happening. My father and mother were already out there watching. People were crowding the streets and cheering a group of North Vietnamese soldiers. The soldiers marched by the side of a rumbling tank, heading north in the direction of the ARVN base that my father used to work at. Some of the NVA soldiers were so young, I thought they could not be older than seventeen. They were all wearing black rubber sandals.

Mr. Tám pointed at the sandals and told me that they were made from tires. The sandals were called "the rubber sandals of Bình Trị Thiên (the three provinces in Central Vietnam that experienced some of the heaviest fighting during the Communist Easter offensive in 1972)." They all wore simple green uniforms, with green hard hats emblazoned with a yellow star against a circular red background.

Some of the NVA soldiers seemed bewildered by the city, looking left and right at the streets, houses, and people. Other appeared to enjoy the cheering and attention they were receiving. I noticed that some of the sol-

diers were carrying rifles while others were carrying a long, wicked-look-
ing weapon with a big, sharp head.

My father told me that the weapon was a B40 rocket, often used by
Communist troops against tanks or armored vehicles. After the group of
NVA soldiers and their tanks had passed through, we went back inside. I
was deeply disturbed by the cheering I just saw. Weren't Communist soldiers supposed to be very bad people? Weren't they the same ruthless killers
that slaughtered hundreds of thousands of civilians who fled from them
during the 1972 Easter offensive on Highway 1 in Central Vietnam? Weren't
they the same NVA soldiers who would systematically kill all wounded
ARVN soldiers after a battle they had won, as my cousin Vũ, an ARVN
battalion commander, had often told me? If they were so cruel and ruthless, why were people cheering them?

Unable to contain my curiosity anymore, I asked my father about the
cheering. Shaking his head, my father patiently explained that things were
different now. No one would say anything bad about Communists publicly. It would be suicidal. People came out to the street to cheer for
different reasons. Some were just curious. They wanted to know what the
NVA soldiers look like. Some were Communist sympathizers who had
lived here for a long time, and now with the Communists winning the war,
they came out and showed their true colors. Many people were born and
raised in the South. They'd never lived a day with the Communists and
believed that they could not be as bad as the South Vietnamese government's propaganda portrayed them. Some were people who would lean in
whichever direction the wind blew, hoping to gain favors with the new
masters. And others didn't necessarily cheer the Communist soldiers. They
cheered the end of the war, which had claimed rivers of blood and mountains of bones from our people.

My father's explanation didn't clear up all my confusion. I wanted him
to tell me whether the Communists were good or bad people. Instead, my
father told me that things were not always as clear cut as black and white.
Back twenty years before in the North, he said, they were really cruel. They
were also extremely ruthless in the past 20 years of war. But the Communists weren't the only cruel and ruthless people in this war. Some ARVN
and American soldiers were just as cruel as the NVA soldiers. War changed
people. Someday, when I grew up, my father said, I would learn and understand for myself that there are good and bad people on every side.

The next day, May 2, 1975, a loudspeaker was set up near the neighborhood. An announcer with a gruff voice said on the speaker that the
"Giải Phóng Quân" (Liberation Army) was taking over Vũng Tàu and

putting out the last pockets of resistance by the "Ngụy Quân" (Illegitimate Army). He then said that all people who were displaced during the attack on the city must go back to their homes and prepare to register with the local "People's Committee." He further called for all "Ngụy Quân" and "Ngụy Quyền" (Illegitimate officials or bureaucrats) to drop all their weapons and register with the local People's Committee as soon as possible. "The party" assured that amnesty would be granted to those who complied quickly.

We packed up and returned to our home in the Đống Đa Officer Apartment Complex. When we left days ago, my father explained that staying there when the NVA attacked the city would be too dangerous. Most other families there thought the same way. When we got home, we found that many other families, who similarly had left to seek refuge elsewhere, were also returning.

I was surprised to find that the complex was pretty much intact. Our home was not damaged at all. The evidence of fighting, however, was all over the neighborhood. Two burned-out Jeeps, with the charred bodies of four ARVN soldiers with their guns still by their sides, laid in a crumbled heap on Trần Hưng Đạo Street in front of our complex. Light weapons of all sorts, from assault rifles, handguns, big and small bullet magazines, grenades of different shapes and sizes, to grenade launchers, were scattered everywhere. A big pile of ARVN uniforms in the middle of the complex served as an eloquent testimony to the panic and desperation of the last ARVN defenders as they threw in their uniforms to blend in with civilians.

Soon after settling back in to our home, I went to join other neighborhood kids to check out the area. Most families in the complex had returned. However, there were a few apartments where nothing remained. The people who lived in those apartments must have taken all their belongings elsewhere, possibly never to return.

After checking out the neighborhood, we followed Trần Hưng Đạo Street to the Bãi Trước beach, which was only half a mile away. When we passed by the Hòa Bình (Pacific) Hotel, we saw more evidence of fighting. The empty hotel was pockmarked with bullet holes. One of its corners was crumbling. There were many dead bodies of ARVN soldiers scattered around the hotel. The sights and smells of burned and mangled bodies were starting to make me feel nauseated. Other kids in the group must have felt the same way. All of us were well-protected children, growing up without ever seeing the horrors of war with our own eyes. The silent, broken corpses were scaring us witless. To calm my fear, I closed my hands together and prayed to Buddha for the salvation of these unfortunate soldiers. Other kids followed my example.

My three younger brothers and I standing in the Đống Đa military complex in 1972. I am on the left.

Dinh, the oldest kid in the group, told us that it might not be a good idea to continue to the beach. His parents had told him there were more corpses piling up that way. In the last day before the surrender, many people tried to get on the boats in Bãi Trước and Bến Đá. They hoped to make it to the sea and get picked up by American warships out there. Then, Communist soldiers set up gun emplacements along the beach, and started shooting. Many boats were sunk and thousands of people were killed. There were corpses floating all over the beach. We were better off waiting at least a month after the bodies were removed from the water. Otherwise, we could all get very sick.

Still feeling nervous from the sights of the dead soldiers, we agreed that seeing more dead bodies would not be fun. All the kids turned around and went back to the complex. Once back, we turned our attention to the guns and ammunition left behind by the ARVN. We collected the guns and magazines, put them in a pile and examined them, trying to figure out how they worked.

Tấn, a 13-year-old, held a rifle in his hand and pointed it at the sky, pretending he was shooting at an imaginary airplane. Not knowing the gun

My three younger brothers and I standing in the field of the Đống Đa military complex in 1974. I was the tallest boy, on the right.

was loaded, he squeezed on the trigger. The loud burst of fire coming from the gun's muzzle scared the wits out of all of us. We instinctively dropped to the ground, using our hands to cover our heads. Tấn threw the gun away immediately, his face pale with fear and incomprehension. Fortunately, none of us was hit.

The sound of gunfire startled the neighborhood, and many adults, including my parents, came out to look. Upon seeing a bunch of kids sprawling next to the pile of weapons and a standing kid frozen with fear, they immediately knew what had happened. All the parents came out to take their kids in. I did not know what punishment other kids received from their parents. Besides getting a long lecture from my father about the danger of guns, I also received a good spanking for my stupidity.

Despite the admonitions from our parents, we were still fascinated with the weapons. The next day, my brothers and I sneaked out again to play with other kids. We went back to the pile of weapons, still untouched from the previous day. Learning our lesson, we did not touch any guns or grenade launchers. We also left the grenades alone, knowing that these deadly metal balls could blow us to pieces. But the ammunition magazines and other loose bullets looked harmless enough. We took the bullets and magazines aside. After fiddling with them for a while, we figured out how to get the gunpowder from the ammunition round by using rocks, hammers, or any tools we had to pry loose the bullet head. Excited by this discovery, the kids competed with each other to see who could get more gunpowder than the rest.

We soon figured out how to use the gunpowder to make crude firecrackers. Our favorite game was to use the gunpowder to make a pile and a thin line. Covering the gunpowder pile with a metal can, we lighted the end of the line. The boys then stood near the metal can, waiting for an explosion. When the fire burned up the gunpowder inside the can and threw it high into the air, we all rushed after it, trying to catch the falling can. Despite my mother's repeated warnings to stop playing the dangerous game, we still found the thrill too exhilarating to resist. Being a kid, I didn't worry too much about tomorrow. The important thing to me was that I was playing games, having fun and my parents' love today.

While our parents worried about the future, we still reveled in our playful childhood. The first few days of May 1975 were some of my happiest days. My parents stayed home and spent more time talking to us. My father told me more about his life and taught me more things than he ever did. I listened with amazement to his stories about the starvation in North Vietnam in 1945 and his struggle to get a decent education in the South despite abject poverty. Deliberately, he taught me about ethics and perseverance through the stories of how hard he worked to gain the respect and love of everyone in my mother's family. Most people didn't think much of father at first because he was a poor orphan. What other people thought of him never shook his belief in himself. I took in every word, making note of all the lessons to be learned from his life. Little did I know at the time that later my life would be very similar to his and the lessons that I was learning then would be the most precious possessions my father passed on to me.

# 2

# From Father to Son

A few days after returning home, my father went to register himself with the City People's Committee (Ủy Ban Nhân Dân Thành Phố). The committee was the temporary governing body established by the North Vietnamese Army. The registration took him all day. When he returned, my parents had long talks after they had ushered us to bed. Two days later, my father, along with many other former South Vietnamese government officials and soldiers, attended meetings and study sessions for a week. Returning home every night after these sessions, my father became very quiet and much more contemplative.

One night after dinner, my father took me aside for a long talk. We walked out to our garden and sat down on the chairs that my father had placed there. The light of the half moon shone softly on the plants in the garden. The pleasant smell of the blooming flowers filled my nostrils. The air was cool with an occasional breeze. Everything was beautiful tonight. In the past, my father would invite his friends over for tea on nights like this, watching the moon and discussing poetry. But not tonight. He obviously had many things on his mind.

"How are you doing during the past few days?" my father asked. "Have you been studying at all since we returned home?"

"I am doing fine, Father," I replied, feeling a little guilty for playing too much in the past few days. "No, I haven't been studying during the past few days. School is out. I don't know when we will return. I don't have any homework, so why do I have to study, Father?"

"I know that school is out," my father shook his head with disapproval. "But you will return to it soon, probably in September, after the new government gets things under control. I don't mind that you play with your friends as much as you do, but I'd like you to study at least two or three hours every day. Do you remember the saying 'Let's live as if you will die tomorrow. Let's learn as if you will never die'? At times like this, when the last thing on any kid's mind is studying, you will get ahead of everybody if you are the only one doing it. Things in life will never be so desperate that you have to put off learning. Anyway, how far did you get with the novel *Kim Vân Kiều* that I gave you?"

I was not surprised with my father's question. Though he wore the rank of captain in the Army of the Republic of Vietnam, my father's real job was being an educator. He was the principal of the Trần Nguyên Hãn High School in Vũng Tàu. Besides running the school, he also taught classes in mathematics and, occasionally, Vietnamese literature. As for his military job, he spent two days a week working in an army camp near the school. I did not know what he worked on in the camp. What I knew was that my father was the scholarly type. One of his passions was studying and discussing literature. In our home, my father had a small library with his collections of poetry and novels. Influenced by my father, I became a voracious reader early. At eight, I read every newspaper and magazine that my father brought home. At ten, I finished most books in his library.

Because I read so much poetry and literary works when I was young, my vocabulary was rich and sophisticated by the time I turned eleven. This development often caused me problems in interaction with other kids my age. Many kids made fun of and taunted me, calling me names or saying that I spoke "funny language." After being picked on many times, I learned to walk away from these provocations, knowing that silence was my best defense. The more I talked or argued with them, the more reasons they had to continue picking on me.

*Kim Vân Kiều* (better known as *Truyện Kiều*) was the greatest classic in Vietnamese literature. Written by Nguyễn Du, a Vietnamese scholar who lived two centuries before, the novel was entirely in poetry, with more than 3,000 lines. *Truyện Kiều* told the story of Vương Thúy Kiều, a beautiful and talented young woman who became a prostitute in order to save her father from imprisonment. Nguyễn Du used the story to craft some of the most exquisite expressions in the Vietnamese language. He also embodied many profound Buddhist philosophies in the novel. For two hundred years after his death, Vietnamese scholars continued to discuss and debate the meanings of passages in his novel. The novel became required reading for all high school students in South Vietnam. My father bought me a copy of *Truyện Kiều* as a reward, after I had done well on my

**My three younger brothers and I standing in front of the Trần Nguyên Hãn High School in Vũng Tàu, where my father served as the principal.**

entrance examination to high school. I gobbled through the novel in two days, and had reread it many times.

"I've read it at least four times, Father," I eagerly answered my father. "I even memorized about 100 lines. Would you like me to recite them for you?"

"No, Son. I believe you. Do you know why Nguyễn Du wrote the novel?"

"Scholars have debated that question for centuries," I replied proudly. "Some believed that he wrote the novel to express his feelings. He was a mandarin who was loyal to the defunct Lê Dynasty but forced to work for the victorious Tây Sơn Dynasty. His situation was like Vương Thúy Kiều, who was always loyal to her lover, Kim Trọng, but was forced to work as a prostitute, being with many other men. He used Kiều to express his longing for the old Lê Dynasty and his sadness for having to sell his soul to the Tây Sơn Dynasty, just like Kiều, who had to sell her body. Other scholars believed that he wrote the novel as a moral admonition to people. The novel preaches the Buddhist philosophy of fate and the concept of 'nhân quả' (karma, the idea that what happens to you today or in the future is a result of something you've done in this life or in previous lives). It also extols the virtues of faith, loyalty, and perseverance while warning people not to be too proud or arrogant because of their talents or wealth."

"I see that you've done your study pretty well," my father laughed when I finished my little recital. "Well, those are the traditional interpretations of *Truyện Kiều*. Do you know how the Communists interpret *Truyện Kiều*? I had to attend several 're-education' sessions during the past few days with other former South Vietnamese officials and officers. A Communist political cadre led all of these sessions. He lectured us about the 'glorious liberation' of South Vietnam and the 'class struggles,' of how the rich and privileged have always exploited and oppressed poor people. He even cited Nguyễn Du as a visionary author. The way this man sees it, Nguyễn Du showed the exploitation of the poor people through *Truyện Kiều*. The story showed how the rich and powerful, such as the judge, Tú Bà, Hoạn Thư, and Hồ Tôn Hiến, always used their power to exploit and enslave weak people such as Vương Thúy Kiều and her father, Vương Viên Ngoại."

"How could they say that, Father?" I was flabbergasted by such a hideous interpretation of the classic that I'd come to love. "What idiots came up with such an interpretation?"

"Calm down, Son," my father patted my head gently. "These people are not idiots. And they are not supposed to be wrong. You'll have to remember that they are now the new masters of our country. No one can say that they are wrong. If you do that, you will be branded as 'anti-revolutionary' and bad things will happen to you. They interpret *Truyện Kiều* that way because they are Communists. The Communists preach that the injustices and sufferings of society are caused by the exploitation of the peasants and working class, and the exploiters, the capitalists and the landowners, must be destroyed to eradicate the sufferings. This is a foreign concept imported to our country by the Communist Party. This interpretation of *Truyện Kiều* is just the beginning. From now on, everything that you will learn in school, from classics to mathematics, will be given political interpretation. The reason I am telling you this is to make sure that you will always remember the way you feel and think today. I just hope that one year, two years, or however long from now, your mind will not be poisoned by the hatred and suspicions that they will try to program into you."

"I will never believe them, Father," I said emphatically.

"It's okay, Son," my father nodded. "You don't have to assure me. Now, do you still remember the story of Nguyễn Phi Khanh and Nguyễn Trãi?"

"Yes, Father."

"Tell me about it."

"Nguyễn Phi Khanh and his son, Nguyễn Trãi, were two scholars who lived 600 years ago," I said, reciting the historical legend that I knew so well. "Nguyễn Phi Khanh was a mandarin in the court of Hồ Quí Ly. When the Chinese army of the Ming Dynasty invaded our country in the 1400s and destroyed the Hồ Dynasty, Nguyễn Phi Khanh was captured and taken to China. Nguyễn Trãi followed his father as he was being dragged to the Vietnam-China border, crying and holding his father's hand. Nguyễn Phi Khanh, even though he was chained, turned to Nguyễn Trãi and said, 'Son, why don't you return home, plan to free our country and avenge me? Don't continue to follow me and cry like a woman.' Startled by his father's words, Nguyễn Trãi dried his tears and re-turned home. From then, he

My father, Mr. Đỗ Hữu Khánh, as a young captain in the Army of the Republic of Vietnam.

studied hard and started making friends with patriots all over the country. He later became a great military strategist and helped King Lê Lợi evict the Chinese from our country."

"Good, very good," my father nodded approvingly. "You don't disappoint me. Do you know why I ask you about the story?"

"No, Father!"

"Well, I did because I thought there are a lot of similarities between what I have to tell you tonight and what Nguyễn Phi Khanh told his son 600 years ago."

"What do you mean?" I asked with apprehension.

"Son, while I am not a man like Nguyễn Phi Khanh, and you might never be like Nguyễn Trãi, our situation and theirs are very similar," my father said calmly. "After tonight, you will not see me again for a long time, maybe never. Remember Nguyễn Trãi never saw his father again? Like Nguyễn Trãi, you will need a lot of courage and determination, not just words, to make something out of yourself."

"What will happen to you, Father?" I was at a total loss.

"Tomorrow I will have to report to the People's Committee of this neighborhood," my father said. "Then, they will take me, along with other South Vietnamese government officials and military officers to a re-education camp. There, they will make us study the Communist doctrine, cleanse ourselves of 'capitalistic, backward, and reactionary thoughts,' and work to make up for the 'crimes we have committed against the people of Vietnam.' They promised that we could be released in as soon as a month, depending on our cooperation and progress of 'political enlightenment.'"

"Then you will only be away for a month," I said hopefully. "Why did you say that I will not see you for a long time, maybe never, Father?"

"My son, you may be intelligent, but you are still too young and naïve," my father shook his head. "There are many things you still do not understand. The Communists put us in re-education camps, which are really prisons, so that there will be no one left who can or will have the courage to resist them. The people who are likely to want or have the ability to resist them are high-ranking officials, military officers, or former South Vietnamese politicians. The Communists are not stupid. They are not going to release those people quickly, no matter what they say. They will probably release some people in a month, but those are going to be lower ranking soldiers, like privates or corporals. I have no idea how long they plan to keep people like me in re-education camps. They know that people like me have been fighting them most of our lives, and we are not going to believe them, no matter what we may say. They may just keep us until we die in the camp or when our spirits are completely broken. Worse yet, they may just murder us in the middle of the night so no one would ever know."

I shuddered as I heard my father telling me the harsh realities about to come. My father had started to treat me like an adult several months ago. Yet, this was the first time he talked this frankly to me about the ominous future ahead of us.

"When we heard about this yesterday, other South Vietnamese officials and soldiers were so happy," my father continued. "They were glad because if the Communists keep their words, then the 'blood bath' that many people have been predicting will not materialize. They were even happier because they thought they only have to spend a month in camp, not many years in prisons as they previously believed."

"But isn't that what they promised?"

"Do you still remember President Nguyễn Văn Thiệu's favorite line?" my father asked. 'Đừng nghe những gì Cộng Sản nói mà hãy nhìn kỹ những gì Cộng Sản làm' (Don't listen to what the Communists say. Just watch what the Communists do). Mr. Thiệu might not have been a good president, and he has been wrong in many things. But he was completely right when he said that. Promise, to a Communist, does not mean anything. The ends to them always justify the means. They have broken their promises many times in the past, when they continued to attack the South even when they told the world they wouldn't. Your mother knows how much their promises are worth. Many of her relatives, who were members of the Vietnam Nationalist Party, were murdered because they believed the Communists' promise. It was a hard lesson that people like your mother and I, North Vietnamese who ran away from them in 1954, had to learn with the blood of our families. Despite fighting the Communists for 20 years, many South Vietnamese, who have never lived with them, are still naïve enough to believe their promises. It will not be long before they learn our lesson the hard way."

"Father, I am scared. What will they do to you? Are they going to kill you? What will happen to us when you are gone?"

"I don't know what they will do to me," my father replied wearily. "I guess that they will punish each person differently, depending on the 'crimes' that person has committed against them. Anyone who had worked for or was connected with the South Vietnam government already committed a crime against them. They have accused me of being a CIA agent while I was teaching and working in the Communication Corps. That is a pretty serious offense in their eyes. I don't know if it is serious enough for them to kill me, but it is certainly serious enough for them to keep me in jail for a long time, maybe until the day I die."

"But it is so ridiculous, Father," I said with exasperation. "Everyone knows that you are the principal of a high school, a teacher. How could anyone accuse you of being a spy? Who could you spy on?"

"I know that," my father replied patiently. "You know that. People who know us know that. But our words don't matter, Son. What matters is what those with guns in their hands now believe.

"But enough of that. All this doom and gloom is not what I want to talk with you about tonight. What I want to talk about is what you will have to do in the days ahead. Listen closely and remember well, okay!"

"Father, I want to ask you one more thing," I said. "If you know that they are going to put you in prison, why don't you escape right now? Why do you have to report to them tomorrow?"

"I had a chance to do that, but I decided not to do it, Son," my father shook his head sadly. "About a week before the South fell, I checked with many people to see if I could get spaces for us on a ship or plane that was leaving the country. I couldn't get enough spaces for all of us. A friend in the air force offered me a seat in his plane, but no more. If I had taken the offer, I would have to leave your mother and all of you here. I couldn't do that. I love you all too much to ever do so. What kind of husband and father would I be? Now, where can I escape to? The whole country already fell under their control."

My father took a sip of water, walked to a bush of chrysanthemum to smell its fragrance, then returned to me and continued. "I know you are a precocious kid. You learn faster and know more than other kids your age. But in the days ahead, you will need more than your intelligence to survive. You need to help your mother to take care of your younger brothers. You may be intelligent, but you are not yet smart. The road of life is full of traps and dangers for the unwary, the gullible, and the weak-willed. I have hoped that I can always be next to you to guide you past those dangers, but fate won't have it that way. Son, now you will have to go through all those obstacles by yourself. My last gift to you now is telling you all the lessons that I have learned in my life. Listen and learn them well. If someday you can use them and make something out of yourself, even if I die and never see you again, I will die a proud and happy man."

I felt a chill in my spine. My father had never spoken to me like this before. He was making me very afraid. Last week, I was the happiest kid in the world, enjoying my parents' love and all the fun games I played with my friends. Now, my father was telling me of an ominous future. I couldn't see how my future might change so quickly. But my father was being very serious. At the same time, I could sense from him a serene peacefulness and the quiet strength of a man who had come to terms with himself.

"But Father, I still have Mother to take care of me," I said while struggling to deal with the confusion and fear that knotted in my stomach. "And you will come back to us in one or two years. Why are you talking like this? Will something bad happen to us?"

"Tomorrow I won't be with you and the family anymore," my father replied. "A few days later, our family will have to move out of this home. The Communists already said they would take over this complex and kick everyone here out. This place is now declared 'government property.' I was told today we have to get out of here in two days. After two days, if we still don't move all of our possessions out, whatever remains in these apartments will belong to the government."

"Father, how can they do that? They are going to take you away. Then they are kicking us out of here in two days. Where can we go? Even if we have a place to go to, how can we move our belongings out in two days?"

"Oh, they sure can do that, Son," my father replied resignedly. "They have done worse things in the past. All of these events are just parts of their plan. The men of the families that live here will go to re-education camps tomorrow. There is no way the women and children can take all their belongings out. So, the state can confiscate our properties and yet still can blame it on us. After all, they give us some time to move our stuff out. If we cannot get all of it out in time, then it is our fault as far as they are concerned."

"Father, aren't they robbing us in daylight?" I asked with indignation.

"Yes, they are. But who will dare to say anything? Besides, we are nothing more than 'criminals' in their eyes. They will say that we owe 'blood debts' to the 'people,' so we deserve whatever that will happen to us. Anyway, you don't have to panic. Your mother and I have thought of this before today. We have learned our lessons about them 20 years before, and we know they didn't change much since. I have talked with Mr. Đa about renting a part of his house, the smaller side, and he agreed to let us move in. Your mother has already moved much of our clothes and kitchen utensils there during the past few days."

I was not thrilled about the idea of moving to Mr. Đa's house. Mr. Đa was the son of Mr. Chương, an acquaintance of our family. Mr. Chương came from the same village as my father in North Vietnam. Occasionally, my father told me the stories of how my paternal grandfather had done many favors for Mr. Chương in the North. When he moved to the South, Mr. Chương still kept in contact with my father and Uncle Tín because he was still grateful for what Grandpa had done. Now, in his late fifties, Mr. Chương recently married his fifth wife, leaving his first wife and Mr. Đa, his oldest son, to take care of his business.

Mr. Chương became prosperous in the South as a merchant. His family owned a small store selling books and other miscellaneous products on Lê Lợi Street. I had been to his house many times, as my father always stopped by his store after work to get the daily papers. I knew what my father meant by "Mr. Đa's smaller house." Initially, it was a storage room for Mr. Chương's inventory. Over the years, they expanded and added a small room to it. It was a cramped and filthy place. I shuddered when I thought about their outhouse, which was as filthy as any outhouse I'd ever been to.

Looking at my face, my father could tell I was not excited about moving to Mr. Đa's place.

"You should be glad that you will have a roof over your head," he said. "It was the best we could find. Things will be worse for our family soon. Despite planning ahead, we will not be able to move all of our belongings out in two days, and we will lose our refrigerator, TV, the chicken egg incubator that I built, all of the chickens that we have, and many other things to the 'government.' We can only move things that are absolutely critical for life out of this house. From now on, you will be poor. We won't have my monthly income anymore, and I don't know how your mother will be able to feed all of you when I'm gone. Our savings are not deep, but we'll have to make do with what we can."

My father paused for a moment, letting the words sink in to me, then continued. "Now you know the situation that you will be in, I want you to be a better son than you have been. With me gone, you will be the man of the house. You will have to do everything you can to help your mother take care of your younger brothers. You won't have money to spend like you're used to, and people will not be as nice to you as when I was still a respected principal. If anything, in the days ahead, people will harass, taunt, and bully you. You will have a rough road ahead of you, Son. Are you scared?"

"Yes, I am very scared, Father," I replied, not bothering to pretend to be courageous. "How can I do all of these things? I'm only a kid."

"It's okay to be scared, Son," my father patted my head. "But don't let it paralyze you. You are not as helpless as you think. If you can learn from my lessons and use them, things won't be all that bad.

He paced around the garden, collected his thoughts, then continued. "You know that I was very poor once. When you are poor, people tend to look down on you and bully you. That happened to me many times in the past. What happens to you will depend on how you take the insults.

"No matter how others may look down at you, ultimately what matters is how much respect you have for yourself. People can take everything from you, but they can never take away your self-respect, your knowledge, and your hope. When people insult you, they can only hurt you as much as you let them. Fighting them back with insults, arguments, or fists really doesn't do you any good. It satisfies your anger of the moment, but it doesn't improve the situation. If anything, it lowers you down to their level. If you can learn to take all the insults that people may heap upon you, and channel them into a source of energy to make yourself better every day, then you have won. The most eloquent answer and the sweetest revenge are to prove to people that they are wrong about you. It is a lesson as old as the earth. But it is still a very hard lesson to learn. I've learned it through many years of poverty. And I have faith that you can and will learn it, too. Do you understand what I am trying to tell you, Son?"

"A little bit, father."

"That's all right," my father nodded. "You will understand it all in due time. Remember that we come from an honorable family, well versed in the ways of Confucianism and Buddhism. Our ancestors had been scholars and mandarins for many generations. Your great-grandfather, grandfather, and I had always tried to help people in need and uphold our family honor. Now, it is your turn to uphold that honor. Do you still remember the saying, 'Giấy rách phải giữ lấy lề' (even the torn paper has to keep its edge)? Our family now has gone from being well off to being poor, just like the torn paper that was once clean and crisp. Even in poverty, we have to keep our honor and self-respect, just like the torn paper that still keeps its straight edge. No matter how poor and desperate you are, you should not cheat, beg, lie, or steal from others. Doing any of those things will damage our honor and lessen your self-respect."

My father took a break from his long lecture, got a sip of water, and walked over to the chicken pen in the back of the garden. Besides studying history and literature, planting flowers and raising chicken were his other hobbies. Most of the chickens, about 60 altogether, appeared to be sleeping. My father took some feedstock from a box and put it into the bowls inside the pen. He usually did this very early in the morning, when the chickens woke up, not late at night like today. It was as if he was afraid he would never feed his chickens again.

He let out a long sigh. "In two days, this beautiful garden that I've planted and all the chickens that I've raised will belong to the 'government.' While I know that these things are only worldly materials, they are still the works of my sweat and my mind. It is hard for me to accept that someone can just come in and take them away. What will the Communists do with these things? They probably will let the flowers wither away and kill all the chickens to eat. It has always been their way. They are much better at killing and destroying than building or nurturing something.

"Remember that well, Son. In the days ahead, they will try to plant hatred and suspicion into your mind. They will try to brainwash you with their ideology. They will tell you how 'glorious, just, and heroic' it is to destroy people whom they call their 'enemies.' Don't let the hatred and suspicions fester in your mind. If you do, you'll have let yourself become another cog in their machine of control and destruction. Open your eyes and ears wide and learn. They may make you say things that you don't believe in. But if you don't let them, they cannot read what you think and change your mind. Watch them closely and understand them well. Don't just react by hating them. If you do, you will only be as bad as they are. You have to find the guiding light within your heart to go on the right path.

Try to rise above your enemy. If their way is destruction, then your way is building. If their way is hatred, then your way is forgiveness, love, and understanding. If their way is suspicion, then your way is patience and perseverance.

"The Communists are not the only people you have to watch out for. You should also not let yourself be influenced by your peers. There will be times when you will be tempted to join your friends to do stupid things like smoking or doing drugs. They may tell you that it is the thing to do. They may tell you that you are a coward or a simpleton if you don't do it. Son, they don't know any better than you do. Nobody but your heart, your conscience, and your mind can tell you what the right thing to do is. In all the years I've lived, I've learned that most people are weak-willed and easily swayed. The masses are generally pretty stupid and ignorant. They let themselves be sidetracked by temptations, looking for easy ways out. Then, they try to convince others to do the same so that they can assure themselves what they do is right, taking comfort in the number of people like themselves."

"Yes, Father."

"It takes a lot of courage to resist peer pressure and do the right thing." My father pointed to my head. "You have a good head on your shoulders. Use it and think for yourself. Don't ever let other people think for you. Do you still remember what your name means?"

"Yes," I nodded. "My name is Đỗ Quang Trình. Đỗ is our family name. Quang means 'bright' or 'light,' and Trình means 'path' or 'way.' My name means the bright path or the path of light."

"Right. I named you that way when you were born with the hope that you will do many great things in life, that your path in life will be a path of light. I had hoped that you will always do the right thing, and take the right path, no matter how hard and lonely that path may be. If the South didn't fall, you would have had a good chance to do many wonderful things. You are a good student and I think it won't be hard for you to win a scholarship to study abroad when you finish high school. Now, with the situation that you are going to be in, that dream is just so hard to achieve."

"It's not that important, Father," I said. "I just want to be near you and our family."

"In time, it is, Son," my father replied. "You will grow up and do something with your life. And somehow, I still believe that someday you are going to do it. You are going to make something out of yourself. In the days ahead, there are times that it may seem your situation is so hopeless, so desperate and the whole world may come crashing down on you. It may seem that the odds against you are insurmountable and it is easier to give up and save your energy. Don't ever give up hope, Son. Don't ever let the dream die in you. As long as your heart still beats and your eyes still see, you will always have a chance to fight and win. Life cannot be unkind to you forever."

I felt confused and overwhelmed. My father was telling me too many things and predicting a hard, dark future ahead of me. He was asking me to be courageous, strong, and to think for myself. The most courageous thing I had done in my life to this point was to taunt the neighbors' dogs. I was not a strong and good-looking kid. I often lost in fights with other kids. Learning my lesson, I often walked away when other kids challenged me to a fight, preferring not to give them the pleasure of beating me up. My skin was very dark from the many hours I played in the sun. My dark skin made me the butt of many cruel jokes in school. To this point, I had had a pampered existence. Now, I had to shoulder a very heavy burden, helping my mother take care of my younger brothers and fulfilling my father's expectations. At the same time, the thought of losing my father, maybe forever, pained me deeply. It was very hard for me to make a brave face and listen to him all night long. It took all the self-control I had not to cry.

"But we are not going to lose you, are we, Father?" I asked in a whisper. "I do not understand many things that you told me. How can I do all of the things that you ask me to? I am still a weak and naïve kid."

"Don't cry, Son." My father pulled me into his embrace, and rubbed my head when he saw my red eyes and heard my near sobbing whisper. "You are now a man, and a man's tears are too precious to ever be shed lightly. You may not understand many things I tell you now. Just remember them. In time, they will make sense to you. I know you can do all the things I asked of you and more. The courage and strength you will need are not the courage and physical strength of a bully. They are your inner courage and strength. They are the courage and strength that grow on hope, faith, and understanding. You have them all within you. In time, you will learn how to use them, Son."

"It's already past midnight. Why don't you go to bed now? You'll need all your energy to help your mother move things tomorrow."

I said good night to my father then joined my brothers who were already sleeping soundly in our small bed. Exhausted from my emotions, I drifted into an uneasy sleep with many scary dreams.

# 3

# Wake Up to Darkness

Waking up late next morning, I jumped right out of bed to see if my father was still at home. Fortunately, he was. My brothers were already sitting at the family table with my parents. Seeing my hair still standing up on my head, my father told me to go wash up.

When I joined the family for breakfast, I noticed that my mother's eyes were red. She must have cried a lot during the past few days, but never in front of us. My three younger brothers, Trung, Bình, and Trị, were still too young to worry. They were only ten, nine, and eight years old respectively.

My father was telling my younger brothers to be good to Mom and study hard. He would be away for about a month to "study." When he came back, if anyone was lazy or disobedient, he would not be happy.

My mother had packed big bags of dried foods, toiletry, and a small bag of clothes for my father. After breakfast, he kissed each one of us on the forehead, hugged my mother, then took his bags to leave. When my father hugged me, he took a moment to look into my eyes. His eyes told me many things more than words. I could see a fire of defiance and hope in his eyes. At that moment, I thought I understood him more than I ever did. I was proud that he was my father.

My father carried the bags on his shoulder and walked the two miles to the People's Committee office. He occasionally turned back to look at us, then forced himself to continue on. He was not dressed in his military

*Opposite:* My mother, my younger brothers and I standing in front of our home in Vũng Tàu three years before the fall of South Vietnam. I am the tallest boy, second from the right.

uniform today, which always seemed to radiate strength. Wearing a plain white shirt, black pants, and rubber sandals, he looked as weak and ordinary as any other man. Yet, I knew that beneath my father's frail and ordinary exterior beat a heart of gold and a will of steel, which I would spend the rest of my life trying to emulate.

For the next two days, my brothers and I helped our mother to pack things and move them to Mr. Ða's house. My mother confirmed to us what my father already told me. The North Vietnamese Army would take over the apartment complex in two days, and use it as housing for their officers. Anything that wasn't moved in two days would be considered to be "the People's property." All other families in the neighborhood were also busy packing and moving. I felt a lump in my throat as I thought about not seeing the neighborhood kids, my childhood friends, again. They and their families, like ours, were looking for refuge somewhere else in the city.

My mother rented a Lambretta (a five-wheeled vehicle that people used as cab) to move our food, clothes, bicycles, and other belongings to Mr. Ða's house. She sold my father's Suzuki motorcycle to a neighbor. I almost cried when she told me about it. The motorcycle was our means of transportation all these years. It held so much of our family's memories. My father used to put my brothers and me on the little motorcycle and drive us all over town. Now, like my father, it would be just a memory, not to be seen again.

My mother tried to comfort me and told me it would be useless to keep the motorcycle. No one could ride it now, and we would not be able to afford the gasoline for it anyway. It was better to sell the motorcycle than to leave it to the "people."

By the second day, we managed to move the light furniture and miscellaneous appliances out. My mother also managed to sell our TV. Still, there were many big and heavy things that we could not move nor sell. We had to leave the refrigerator, the chickens, our big wooden bed, and all my father's bookcases behind.

On the second day, my mother told me to take my father's books into the back yard and burn them. I could scarcely believe my ears. My father loved these books more than anything else he owned. When I protested to Mom that I did not want to destroy my father's treasures, my mother told me that we had no choice. Many of the books contained strong anti–Communist materials and as such, they could become huge risks for us if the Communist soldiers ever found them in our place. We just lost most of our property. We couldn't afford to be thrown in prison now.

Even though I understood why my mother told me to burn the books, I still felt very upset. For the first time, I really felt angry at the Communists and the "people" they always hid behind. They had taken away everything that meant the most to me in my short existence: my father, our property, and now our books. As I leafed through each book before throwing it into the burning flames, I felt like I was abandoning an old friend. In the end, despite my mother's order to burn them all, I saved three books that I hadn't read and took them with me to our new dwelling.

It took me two weeks to adjust to my new home. Our family of five squeezed into two small rooms: one served as our bedroom and the other as a storage room. The kitchen, covered only with a metal sheet, was a four-foot-wide corridor between our storage room and the wall of the next-door neighbor's house. The kitchen had virtually nothing, as we had sold our gas stoves and electric rice cooker. The new stove was three pieces of red bricks arranged in the shape of an equilateral triangle. The bricks served as the stands for our pots and pans, while we fed firewood underneath. Our cooking fuel was firewood, dry leaves, papers, or anything we could use to burn. The new place also didn't have a room for a shower or bath. We had to haul water from a well across the street and took showers at night in the back yard.

My mother purchased a wooden bed from Mr. Ða for our bedroom. The bed served as the sleeping space at night, and as our reading, studying, and dining area in the day. The remaining space in the bedroom was taken up with my mother's inventory, things that she would take to the market to sell, and our two bicycles. The roof was made out of metal sheets, which made the house extremely hot during the dry season. There was only one electric light in the bedroom and nowhere else. A small electric fan made up the rest of our modern amenities.

The first two nights after moving in, I couldn't sleep because of the heat. Despite having the fan on all night, the heat and humidity were so stifling that I found myself soaked in sweat. My youngest brother, Trị, cried nonstop during the first night. He kept asking my mother to take us back to the old house, where our bedroom was always cool and spacious. My mother tried to tell him that we only had to stay in this cramped place for a short time and would return to our old home once our father came back. It wasn't enough to stop my brother from crying.

I closed my eyes and bit my teeth together to not cry when hearing my mother mention my father. I wondered where he was right now, and if the Communists had tortured him at all. To drive away all these unpleasant thoughts, I took out the books I saved and read until I felt asleep.

The next two days, my mother showed me how to do all the chores I was now responsible for: cooking, washing clothes, house cleaning, hauling water, feeding and watching my brothers, and finding firewood for fuel. In two days, I went from being a well-pampered boy to a maid and baby-sitter. Before, the most I'd ever done was to wash my own dishes or fold my own clothes. After two days, my mother left me at home alone to take care of my brothers. She had to go back to the open market to peddle her goods.

Before South Vietnam fell, my parents were well off enough to hire a maid. The maid came to our home daily to cook, feed us, and wash our clothes. My father usually didn't come home until late in the evening. Besides his regular jobs as a principal and an army captain, my father earned additional income by teaching private classes. My mother also was away most of the day, selling miscellaneous goods in the open market. The things she sold ranged from kitchen utensils to old army boots. She went to the market early in the morning and got home in early afternoon to relieve the maid. With hard work, my parents were able to provide us with a comfortable life.

With my father gone, our family income was cut by two-thirds. The eviction from our old home had taken away most of our possessions. My mother now faced an incredibly heavy burden: to keep all of us in school, fed, clothed, and to support my father in re-education camp. She would have to work much harder if we were to survive.

Knowing that peddling goods alone wouldn't be enough, my mother thought about applying for a job in any company. After much thought, she put the idea aside. Any hourly work wouldn't earn her enough money to support us. Furthermore, my mother knew the Communist government would soon nationalize all private companies. With her background as the daughter of a former northern landowner and the wife of a "Nguy Quân" officer (the Illegitimate Army, the Communist term for the ARVN), my mother would get fired if she already worked there, or would never get a chance if she applied. With no viable options, she went back to peddling her goods in the open market.

It took me a month before I could master all my chores. I had never cooked anything before with even gas stoves. Now, I cooked meals for my family using old steel pots, pans, a primitive stove consisting of three bricks, and fuel that ranged from dried leaves to tree roots. Within a week, my hands were covered with burns from fire sparks. My eyes were constantly in tears from the smoke. My clothes became stinky and filthy from the smoke, ashes, and black marks left by burned branches. Worse, my family had to endure many meals of burned rice and vegetables before I got my cooking right.

Cooking was the easy part. Our new home didn't have any running water. I had to get water from a well across the street, about 100 yards away. Every day, I hauled water from the well, poured it into two square metal buckets, and carried them on my shoulders using a balancing pole. The load weighed anywhere from seventy to ninety pounds, as each bucket was between five to seven gallons. The buckets felt like a ton on my five-foot-two, 100-pound frame. In the first day, I almost broke down in tears as it appeared I might have to take the whole day to fill our 200-liter barrels. I stopped every few yards to catch my breath, switched the load to the other shoulder, and went on again. My shoulders soon became red and painful from the heavy weight. Yet, I bit my teeth and forced myself to go on until our barrels were full. This water was used for all of our drinking, washing, and bathing needs. At night, I couldn't sleep from the intense, burning pain in my shoulders.

Then, there was the task of washing laundry. Daily, I handwashed all dirty clothes and hung them out to dry in the back yard. Squatting under the hot sun, I washed and squeezed out every drop of detergent and water. After a few hours, my back was stiff and in pain from the uncomfortable squatting position, my shirt was soaked in sweat, and my hands shook unsteadily. This simple task, like cooking and fetching water, became another test of my endurance and will.

On the second day that I took over cooking, my mother returned home to a ruined dinner of burned fish and rice. She started to complain, then noticed my disheveled hair, my smoke blackened face, my shaking hands with burns from fire sparks, and my red, blistering shoulders. She put down her bowl of rice, hugged me, and cried. Looking on with incomprehension, my brothers started asking why. I tried hard not to join my mother in crying, but the tears silently streamed down my face. I was feeling very sorry for myself. I felt worse that my condition was causing my mother pain. Yet, I also felt proud because I was able to help her and glad because I knew how much she loved me.

Gradually, I became stronger. The daily chores didn't appear as formidable as they were before. In a month, I was able to cook good meals for my family. I could carry the buckets of water from the well back to my home without having to stop. My washing chores became less monotonous as I tried to psyche myself up by singing or reciting poetry. In time, I no longer felt sorry for myself. I was a kid. My cheerful nature didn't allow me to feel gloomy for too long. Other neighborhood kids were doing the same things I did, and my ego didn't allow me to accept that I was any

The French cemetery across from our home on Lê Lợi Street. The cemetery is abandoned today.

less competent than they were. I even competed with them to see who could haul water home the fastest. As days passed, I could do my tasks faster and even had time to do something that I always enjoyed, reading and studying.

Our new refuge was located on Lê Lợi Street, across from two graveyards. A French cemetery sat directly across. I learned from the neighborhood kids that only French soldiers and civilians were buried there. The cemetery was well laid out and well maintained. The graves were lined up in straight rows and had marble plaques and tombstones. Several huge trees lined the cemetery, giving it plenty of shade and keeping the air cool. The tranquil atmosphere within made it feel like a park rather than a graveyard. Several graves had flowers planted near or on them. The French government paid a caretaker to look after the cemetery. The caretaker lived in a house in the back of it. He kept all the graves clean and the grass well cut. There was a long, flat dirt road from the entrance to the back of the cemetery where the neighborhood kids and I used to play soccer. As there were no French nationals living in Vũng Tàu after 1975, I never saw a funeral in this graveyard.

This shop was the little home that my family moved to after being kicked out of the Đống Đa military complex in May 1975. This picture was taken in 2003, when the old home, covered with corrugated sheet metal, was converted into a furniture shop.

Next to it was a Vietnamese cemetery, three times the size of the French one. In contrast to the well-kept graves in the French cemetery, many graves in the Vietnamese cemetery were simply dirt mounds with overgrown grass. A few small trees were scattered throughout, providing little or no relief from the hot summer sun. There was no caretaker for this graveyard. Families of the deceased were responsible for taking care of their graves. The families of many of the people who were buried here either had left Vietnam, or moved elsewhere, thus leaving many of these graves unattended. In many parts of the cemetery, large patches of green grass grew over these neglected tombs.

These grass patches became our favorite places to hunt fighting crickets during the rainy season. Several times when my brothers and I combed this graveyard for crickets after a summer rain, we came upon graves which were washed out by the rain, exposing the wooden coffins beneath. Occasionally, we caught glimpses of pieces of bone in some coffins that had been eaten away by termites and maggots. The sights and smells of these coffins made me sick and caused me to get out of the graveyard quickly. The huge contrast between the French and Vietnamese cemetery gradually made me think about the anguish of being citizens of a poor country. Even after death, we Vietnamese were not as well taken care of as the foreigners who were buried on our own land.

Mr. Đa, the owner of our dwelling and a former soldier in the ARVN, was just sent to re-education camp. After a month, he was released. The new government didn't think he could cause any trouble. Mr. Đa was a private who never had faced combat. Meanwhile, several months passed and I still had little news of my father. Once in a while, my mother would receive a short letter from my father, which simply told her where he was. The letters never told her when he expected to be released from camp, nor did they go into details about life in the camps. Slowly, I realized how prophetic my father was. He was right that the Communists would not release people like him quickly. While I prayed to Buddha for my father's safety and quick release, I did not believe my father would come home to us anytime soon.

The East Cloud Ice Factory sat a few houses to the right of our home. The factory manufactured huge ice blocks, which it sold to fishing boats in Vũng Tàu. The fishermen used these ice blocks to refrigerate their catches. The ice blocks were also sold to other small businesses. A four-story building, situated inside the factory, was both the house and office of the owner.

Yêng, a neighborhood kid I befriended, told me the factory owner was very wealthy. His family was the only one here that had a car and a chauffeur. Yêng also told me that the family had three children, two girls and a boy. The owner's children rarely, if ever, socialized with the neighborhood kids. According to Yêng, the owner's children were snobbish rich brats who felt it was beneath them to mix with the poor kids in the neighborhood. Though I didn't yet know the owner's children, I already felt a sense of antagonism toward them from Yêng's influence. I was conscious and sensitive of my newfound poverty. For the first time in my life, I suddenly became suspicious and disliked people who appeared to be well off. As for the rich kids from the ice factory, I was sure they would belittle me if I ever approached them.

From our back yard, I could see the balcony of the third and fourth floors of the building in the ice factory. The building was about thirty meters from our home. One morning, I caught a glimpse of a girl standing on the third-floor balcony and staring at me with curiosity when I was washing laundry.

Even from the distance, I could see that she was tall and had big round eyes. Her long, black hair was neatly tied behind her back. She was dressed

A view of Lê Lợi Street in Vũng Tàu. Our home is on the left and the wall on the right is that of the cemetery.

all in white, white flowery blouse, white pajama pants, and a white bow on her head. Looking at her clean, beautiful clothes and radiant features, I thought she look like a beautiful angel standing on a cloud and looking at the world below. Leaning against the railing with one hand on her chin, she apparently was startled and embarrassed as I suddenly looked up and caught her staring at me. She quickly shifted her gaze in another direction to avoid contact with my eyes, pretending to scan the neighborhood below.

Though I had never seen her before, I knew who she was. Yêng had told me enough about the factory owner's family, as gossiping about rich people was a favorite pastime of the poor neighborhood kids. I knew the girl must be Trang, the factory owner's oldest daughter. Seeing Trang for the first time, suddenly all my antagonistic feelings against the factory owner's children melted away. Trang looked so beautiful that I suddenly wondered how I could possibly hate someone like her just because of the words of another poor kid. At the same time, I felt embarrassed and was glad she was looking away. While Trang was beautiful and radiant, I was as dark and dirty as a boy could be. I was squatting and washing laundry with just my shorts on. My skin got darker every day from my labor in the sun. My hair was long and unkempt, as I hadn't cut it for four months. My face dripped with sweat from the summer heat.

Suddenly, I became more self-conscious than I ever was. I felt like a guilty criminal standing trial in front of a critical judge. *Boy, you must have looked like a filthy beggar to this beautiful girl!* Afraid that I might actually meet her eyes when she turned her gaze back in my direction, I looked down to concentrate on my bucket of dirty laundry. Furiously scrubbing and squeezing water, my mind was filled with two conflicting wants. On one hand, I wanted her to go back into her house and stop looking at me. On the other hand, I wanted her to stay there on the balcony a little longer, so that I could look up and catch another glimpse of her. Trying to control my curiosity the best I could, I kept myself from looking up until several minutes later. When I finally did, I was just in time to catch a look of her back as she turned to go inside. While I was glad that my uneasy ordeal was over, I regretfully wished I had looked up sooner.

When I went to sleep that night, my mind was filled with images and questions about the girl. I wondered what she was really like. *Is she nice or snobbish? How does it feel to live in her big house, eat good foods, and be served by servants? Where does she go to school? Would she talk to a dirty urchin like me?* Knowing that I was just fantasizing, I tried hard to push these questions out of my head, though without much success. I was a poor, dark, and dirty boy whose father was serving time in a re-education camp. She was a rich, beautiful girl who still had both parents and was living a well-protected life. The gulf between her and me was too great. Finally, I lulled myself to sleep after rationalizing that maybe our paths would not cross again after today.

One month after we moved, the Communist government had established sufficient control over Vũng Tàu and the rest of South Vietnam. Like many other Vietnamese cities, Vũng Tàu was divided into many smaller areas called "phường" (wards). Every ward in the city had a People's Committee set up. The People's Committee served as the local governing body. In our neighborhood, every family was required to register with the People's Committee. The People's Committee issued a "sổ hộ khẩu" (a registration file listing the name and information on everyone who legally lived in a household) to each family. Anyone not included in the "sổ hộ khẩu" was not allowed to buy his ration of food and fabric at the government stores. Additionally, they could be arrested by security agents if they were stopped in the street. The system was set up to flush out former South Vietnamese government officials and soldiers who were still hiding. Travel to other cities was severely restricted. To travel outside of town, people had to apply for permits from the People's Committee. Traveling without a proper permit virtually guaranteed an arrest and a few months in jail.

The People's Committees of the city and its wards quickly set up a huge police apparatus, which they called the Public Security Force ("Lực Lượng Công An"). The security agents were recruited from local youths who were anxious to prove their loyalty to the new government. The security agents lurked around the neighborhood to check people's identifications, spy on families they considered to be "phản động" (rebellious), and look for former South Vietnamese officials and soldiers who were still hiding. The security agents generally enjoyed unchecked power and many used their newfound power to harass people. Because of the abuses, they were soon widely hated and despised by most people.

The reason for the contempt for the security agents was simple. Before the fall of South Vietnam, many of these youths were either members of the South Vietnamese militia or draft dodgers. They had never fought a day in the war. Now, they bent with the new wind and joined the security force to earn favors with the new masters. To show their loyalty, they looked aggressively for any signs of subversion or resistance against the new government. They tried to prove that they were even more "Communist," more dedicated than the real Communists.

The security agents were hated and feared even more than the North Vietnamese Army (NVA) soldiers, who started coming into the city in greater number and became more visible. Most NVA soldiers were young men in their late teens or early twenties who came from impoverished regions in North Vietnam. They had spent the last few years of their lives fighting and hiding in the jungles and had never seen a real city before. For all their lives, these young men had been taught by their party leaders and political cadres that they were fighting to liberate the people of South Vietnam. They were taught that their South Vietnamese countrymen were suffering from the oppressive rule of the "South Vietnamese lackeys and their American imperialist masters." (Soon, I and millions of other Vietnamese students would be taught the same thing when we went back to school.) They were told the people of South Vietnam lived in utter despair and poverty, anxiously waiting for the "Giải Phóng Quân" (Liberation Army) to come to their rescue. When they finally came into South Vietnamese cities, these young men's visions of rescuing the South Vietnamese people were shattered by a bitter reality. South Vietnam's cities, particularly Saigon, were more beautiful and richer than any cities they had seen in their lives. While there were many poor people, even most of the poor people of South Vietnam had more money and material things than the NVA soldiers and their families ever had in the North. Additionally, not everyone in South Vietnam welcomed the "Liberation Army" soldiers with open arms. More often, they were greeted with fear and suspicion.

The contradiction between what they were taught and what the reality was caused great confusion for many NVA soldiers. They were bewildered by the wealth and the modernity of South Vietnam. While they struggled to adjust to the environment of South Vietnam's cities and tried to calibrate their ideology with reality, their superiors and political cadres worked hard to rationalize and explain away the inconsistency between the party propaganda and what the soldiers actually saw.

Because of their ignorance and confusion, the NVA soldiers were generally curious and inquisitive, but did not harass people. The security agents, on the other hand, were youths who had lived in the city all their lives. They practically knew everyone in the neighborhood. Their zealousness to prove their loyalty caused great discomfort for everyone. As the security agents normally wore light yellow khaki uniforms, which made them very visible and easily identifiable, many people contemptuously referred to them as "chó vàng" (yellow dogs) behind their back. The term quickly spread and became part of the vocabulary of every kid in the neighborhood.

After registering with the ward's People's Committee to get the registration paper ("sổ hộ khẩu"), every family was given a big portrait of an old, white-bearded man. The man was Ho Chi Minh, the late leader of the Vietnamese Communist Party. My mother was told to frame and put the portrait in a prominent place in our house. The People's Committee made it clear to her that if the security agents ever came into any house and were not able to find the portrait of Ho Chi Minh quickly, it would be taken as a sign of disrespect for "Uncle Ho" or discontentment with the party. These behaviors would not be tolerated and would be dealt with harshly. The threat was enough to make every family, however much they disliked the idea, do as they were told.

Putting up Ho's portrait was the most repugnant idea to my mother, but she had no choice. As she was putting it up, my mother mumbled curses under her breath. Not knowing who Ho was, I asked her why she had to put his picture up. My question opened my mother's bottled-up frustration. She burst into a tirade cursing the bastard Ho Chi Minh, the bearded monster that had caused her family to flee North Vietnam in 1954 and whose monstrous party had destroyed our family. Now, the yellow dog bastards forced her to worship this bastard in chief in our home. Wasn't there any justice in this world?

I had never seen my mother so angry before. She was shouting in my ears when she answered my question. I knew nothing of Ho Chi Minh other than that he was the founder of the Vietnamese Communist Party and he was long dead. I also knew that it was very dangerous for anybody to talk about him with even a hint of disrespect. If any of the hated security agents were lurking outside our home and heard my mother's shouting, she could be arrested immediately and sent to jail indefinitely.

Speaking softly, I tried to calm my mother's anger and reminded her of the danger if she was heard. My mother suddenly became very quiet. Tears slowly streamed down her face. Nodding slowly, my mother wiped off her tears and told me to not ask her about Ho Chi Minh again.

I knew how she must have felt. She was bitterly angry about what the Communist government had done to our family. She was more frustrated for not being able to vent the anger that built up inside her, even in the privacy of her own home.

After my mother finished putting it up, I couldn't help but look at the portrait whenever I passed by. If I didn't have any preconception about him, I would have thought Ho Chi Minh looked like a kind grandfather. He had a long face, white beard and sharp, penetrating eyes that seemed to reflect a keen intelligence. Yet, my mother made it very clear to me that Ho Chi Minh was anything but a kind grandfather.

Looking at his picture, I had an eerie feeling that this long-dead man might be watching my every move, reading my thoughts, and telling his henchmen to come and arrest me. I slapped myself in the face to shake off this irrational fear. I stared back at the picture and mumbled to myself, "I am not afraid of you. You might have killed millions of people when you were alive, but you are now dead. Your soul is burning in hell for all that you've done. I am not afraid of you."

Every day, the loudspeakers that the People's Committee had installed in every corner of the neighborhood bellowed out Communist songs, all of which praised Ho Chi Minh and the Communist Party as the "Pinnacle of Human Intelligence." Despite my trying not to listen to them, the repetition of these songs day after day caused me to memorize every word. At times, I even found myself humming along to the song "Uncle Ho is here in the day of our victory":

"Như có Bác Hồ trong ngày vui đại thắng
Lời Bác nay đã thành chiến thắng huy hoàng
Ba mươi năm đấu tranh giành trọn vẹn non sông
Ba mươi năm dân chủ cộng hòa kháng chiến đã thành công
Việt Nam, Hồ Chí Minh muôn năm, muôn năm
Việt Nam, Hồ Chí Minh muôn năm, muôn năm"

(Uncle Ho is here in our joyous day of victory.
His words now had become our glorious victory.
Thirty years we fought to win back the whole country.
Thirty years of democratic resistance, now we have succeeded.
Viet Nam, long live Ho Chi Minh.
Viet Nam, long live Ho Chi Minh.)

Catching myself singing along with these songs many times, I often had to remind myself that I may sing their songs, but I would never let them brainwash me. Little did I know that the songs were just the beginning of the intensive political indoctrination that I and every kid in my school would go through.

In July 1975, the Communist government announced that all currency issued by the former Republic of Vietnam (South Vietnam) would be converted to a new currency to be issued by the Socialist Republic of Vietnam (the new name of the now "unified" Vietnam). The official purposes of the plan were to establish a single currency throughout Vietnam and to eradicate all remnants of the former South Vietnamese government. Another objective of the scheme, which was never mentioned officially, was to strip away the wealth of the rich and the middle class in South Vietnam.

The plan achieved the hidden purpose by limiting the amount of money each household could convert. The limit was set on a per-capita basis (both adults and children had the same limit). Each household could convert at most the amount of money equal to the number of people in the household multiplied by the per-capita limit. The limit was set so low that most households could not convert all their South Vietnamese money into the new currency. All South Vietnamese money became worthless after the conversion date.

The currency conversion was a key piece in the Communist government's plan of taking away the wealth of the "tư bản mại sản" ("capitalists"), a Communist word for anyone who had anything worth having. Several days prior to the date of conversion, bands of security agents went into the home of any families that appeared to be well off. The security agents took inventory of these families' belongings to make sure that they didn't hide or scatter their wealth by temporarily distributing it to their poorer relatives. Often, the security agents requested these families to "donate" or "lend" properties such as TVs, refrigerators, typewriters, phones, or anything else of value to the state. Once something had been "loaned" to the state, it would never be returned. People who refused to

comply with the security agents' request faced threats of imprisonn
or outright confiscation of their properties.

The Communist government and their security agents justified thei.
daylight robberies as "asking the people to contribute their fair share to
the revolution." The people whose properties were seized were labeled as
"exploitative capitalists who grew fat and rich on the sweat and blood of
the working people." Anyone who dared to voice any opposition to the
actions of the security agents was arrested and put away.

The conversion plan and the accompanying activities by the security
apparatus had a devastating effect on commerce in the few days prior to
the conversion date. Most people had more South Vietnamese money than
the maximum amount they were allowed to convert. As a result, people
tried to get rid of their excess cash by buying anything they could. On the
other hand, people who had goods to sell would not do so. The sellers all
knew that if they did, they would be stuck with worthless money they
couldn't convert. Merchants hoarded and hid their inventories, hoping to
survive this first wave of attack.

The result was easily predictable. Prices for basic goods such as rice,
food, clothing, and coal skyrocketed. Even at stratospheric prices, it was
nearly impossible to find and buy these goods in the market. The Communist government's drive to eliminate the capitalists ("tư bản mại sản")
hurt everyone in South Vietnam. Even poor people who did not have more
money than their maximum conversion limit were badly hurt. They could
not find or afford to buy basic goods in the days leading to the currency
conversion.

The rush to hide wealth from the marauding bands of security agents
and to get rid of excess South Vietnamese money was frantic. Some people whose houses had yet to be searched dug holes in their back yards to
hide anything of value. Some tried to move valuables to the homes of their
poorer relatives, hoping the security agents wouldn't look there. Well-off
people desperately looked for poorer people who could help them to convert excess money at a price. Other tried to buy gold and dollars at any
price.

Knowing people were hiding their wealth, the security agents also
tried their best to restrict people's movement and discover the hidden
wealth. They looked in every nook and cranny in people's houses to find
dollars and gold. They looked for signs of freshly dug earth in people's back
yards to find hidden treasures. They stopped people occasionally in the
street to see if they were moving valuables or money. If caught, these valuables and money would promptly be confiscated. The chase was on. The
predators and the prey were trying their best to outfox each other.

My mother stopped peddling her goods in the market the day she heard the announcement of the currency conversion plan. Despite having most of our possessions confiscated by the Communist government when we were kicked out of our old house, my mother still had more South Vietnamese money than she was allowed to convert. She joined our neighbors in the frantic game of trying to get rid of the soon-to-be-worthless money. She also buried all the gold taels that she had saved and her goods under a tree next to the outhouse (toilet). Her rationale was that even the security agents would not think that people might actually hide their valuables near such a dirty, stinky area. Additionally, my mother also made our rooms look as bare as possible. Fortunately for us, my mother's plan paid off. The security agents who searched our house did not look too hard for anything. Our rooms looked so bare and dirty that the agents quickly got out to find more promising targets.

While my mother succeeded in keeping the security agents from taking our valuables, she didn't have much luck getting rid of the excess South Vietnamese money. Like millions of other South Vietnamese, we saw our tiny savings, already depleted from the original confiscation, reduced even more after the currency conversion. I had thought our lives could not be any more miserable after we were kicked out of our home. I was wrong.

The stress on my mother was visible. She ate less and lost weight rapidly. At night, she slept very little as she constantly thought of ways to keep the government from taking away what little money we had left. In these days, all I could do was to watch as events happened. There was not much I could do to help my mother.

Frustrated, a quiet but intense anger slowly penetrated my soul. I never knew how to hate anyone or anything so badly before. Even though I had grown up hearing horror stories about the Communists all my life, my feelings toward them had always been fascination, curiosity, and fear, not hatred. Now, after what they had done to my family in the past few months, I suddenly felt hatred so deep that I sometimes wondered what I had become. If I could have killed one of those hated security agents to let out my anger, I would have. Now, I fully understood all the stories my parents had told me all these years. I also finally understood how people could hate each other so deeply. It was easy to be righteous when I was at a safe distance from events. Now that my family was a victim of the Communist policy, it was nearly impossible for me to keep my primordial feelings of hatred and anger from overwhelming my consciousness. For me, things now appeared in black and white. I knew that for as long as I lived, I would never forget what they had done to my family.

The loudspeakers in our neighborhood dutifully bellowed the party propaganda every morning, noon, and evening. By now, I had memorized all its lines, particularly Ho Chi Minh's favorite saying, "There is nothing more precious than independence and freedom" ("Không có gì quý hơn độc lập tự do"). For me, only the first part of the statement, "There is nothing" ("Không có gì"), was true.

# 4

# Back to School

By September, schools were reopened. I was excited when the loudspeakers in the neighborhood announced the reopening of schools. Separated from my classmates for four months, I did not know what happened to them and their families. I also missed my teachers. Most of all, I missed the joy of learning.

For months, I had nothing to read and study, except for some textbooks that I convinced my mother to let me keep. When the security agents were about to search our home for valuables, I had to burn many of my father's books that I saved before. My mother didn't want to take the risk of the agents finding anything in our house that could be used as evidence of "anti-revolutionary sentiments."

The neighborhood loudspeakers became the only source of news. We no longer had a TV or a radio. Buying a newspaper was out of the question, as we did not even have enough money to buy rice. Besides, all independent newspapers in South Vietnam were shut down as soon as the Communist government established its control. All TV and radio channels were now run by the state. The red curtains had fallen over South Vietnam, totally covering our eyes and ears.

Mr. Đa, our landlord, was still well off enough to have a radio. Every time he turned it on, I ran over to catch whatever was on. Most of the time, the stations regurgitated ad nauseam the party propaganda. On the few occasions they actually broadcasted some news, the stories were always about how steady the Socialist Republic of Vietnam was advancing on the road to socialism. Other times, the broadcast droned on about how great "our brother Communist countries, the Soviet Union, China, and Cuba

54

were doing" and reassured the listeners of "the ultimate triumph of Communism in the world."

On rare occasions, the radio news broadcast mentioned how "the American Imperialists are still reeling from their defeat, but we still had to maintain our vigilance against their agents and saboteurs." The broadcasts reassured the listeners about the steady decline of the American Imperialists and ground being gained by our socialist brothers every day.

I rarely heard any news about other regions of Vietnam. The little world news that got through was always filtered and altered to fit the official party interpretation. Every day, the party propaganda filled the airwaves to the point I memorized it by osmosis. The Red Curtain had now completely shrouded our world. Resigned to the reality that our eyes and ears were controlled by the government, I stopped listening to the radio. The neighborhood loudspeakers, the mouthpieces of the ward's People's Committee, now provided us with the necessary information for our daily lives: when to buy our rations, when to go back to school, and when to report to the People's Committee for various meetings and political rallies.

The Vũng Tàu High School had too few classrooms to accommodate the number of enrolled students. The school day was divided into two separate sessions, one from 8 A.M. to 12 noon and the other from 1 to 5 P.M. The division allowed students from different levels to use the same classroom by attending a different session. My classmates and I, now in seventh grade, shared the same classroom with an eighth-grade class. This year, we were assigned to the morning session.

On the first day, things didn't appear to change much versus before. I saw many familiar teachers coming back while hearing rumors that some other teachers had left the country. I soon learned the ways the classes were conducted wouldn't change. When school abruptly ended five months before, I was in my last few days of sixth grade. Thus, I started the new school year as a seventh-grader. Most of my classmates from sixth grade also returned and we were all grouped in the same class as before.

In our school, students in a class were assigned to the same classroom. When a period ended, teachers moved from one classroom to another to teach their subjects. All students in the same class advanced together to the next grade. Rarely did a student transfer from one class to another. There were few opportunities to mingle with students from other classes except for the mid-day recess. As classmates, we spent every hour of the day in the same classroom, for the entire school year. Further, if we stayed in school, we would spend four years of high school together. As a result, we got to know our classmates much better than our own brothers or sisters.

When I entered high school the year before, I chose English as my foreign language. The choice put me in a class of the A group, where A stood for "Anh Văn" (English). The other choice for foreign language was French. Students who chose French were placed in classes of the P group, where P stood for "Pháp Văn" (French). I didn't know at the time whether it was my luck or misfortune that I was placed in class 6A3, an all-boys class. Now, we were all automatically advanced to seventh grade, as all records of our previous school year were lost. Our new class would be known as class 7A3.

I was happy to see many familiar faces in class 7A3. There were also many new faces. The first period teacher was a familiar face, Ms. Huyền Trân. She welcomed us back for the new school year, then paid a perfunctory tribute to the "great victory of the people and Communist Party of Vietnam." Ignoring the surprised looks on our faces, Ms. Huyền Trân went on to tell us how fortunate we were to soon be "educated in the school system of the Socialist Republic of Vietnam, under the always correct and brilliant guidance of the Vietnam Communist Party." On this first day, the boys in my class were unfamiliar with the new school administration to know how to react to the first wave of propaganda that came our way. Their behaviors would soon change dramatically.

I sensed that Ms. Huyền Trân was forced to say these things. It was hard to believe that these words come easy for her. Last year, I heard rumors that she was engaged to an ARVN officer. I wondered what had happened to her fiancé and her family. Regardless of what had happened to her during the past four months, Ms. Huyền Trân did her job admirably. She regurgitated the now-familiar propaganda quickly, then went on to tell us about changes in our new school year.

We were to be relocated to the buildings of "Trường Thánh Giu Se" (the St. Joseph High School), a private school across the street from our high school. Classes from 10th to 12th grades were to stay in Vũng Tàu High School. The St. Joseph High School now would be named as the Châu Thành High School.

Our class took in many students from the former St. Joseph High School. In a few months, some North Vietnamese students would join us, too. A complement of North Vietnamese teachers would come later to round out the northern influence in our southern school. These students and teachers would bring fresh ideas and the party's teachings to enrich our education. At this announcement, the quiet class suddenly became noisy as many conversations erupted. Trying her best to keep us quiet, Ms. Huyền Trân went on to tell us that a new class, the political class, was to be added to our curriculum.

When she was done, Ms. Trân left us a few parting words, exhorting us to "Học Tập Tốt, Lao Động Tốt" (study well, labor hard), "to be good children of Uncle Ho and the party," then left the class. As soon as she exited, the class was buzzing with noise. We all looked around the room, trying to figure out who from 6A3 returned and who was missing. With no other classes scheduled for the day, I joined the old boys from 6A3 to catch up with events in the past four months.

Dropping the first bombshell, Cải, a short, well-built kid, told us that Ms. Kim Ánh, one of our teachers from previous years, was dead. During the attack on the city, an artillery shell landed on the hole her family was hiding in. Afterward, no one could find any whole body parts. The flesh and blood were scattered all over the back yard. Cải lived only two blocks away from her house. That was the first thing he learned when the war was over.

All of us were shocked. For me, it felt as if someone had taken a knife and stabbed me in the stomach. Ms. Kim Ánh was the nicest teacher we'd ever had.

Defusing the tension, another kid, Chiêm, asked about other kids who didn't show up today. We speculated that they either were dead or had left Vietnam already. Thành, a friend who lived in the same military complex as I did before May, knew some kids whose families left on boats to make it to American warships along the coast of Vũng Tàu. These families either had the money to buy or the power to get passages out in the last days. Only those of us whose fathers didn't have money or connections were still here.

Our chattering then turned to what happened to each of us. Like my family, Thành's family also got kicked out of the apartment complex. Like my father, Thành's father also went to a re-education camp. Cải's father, a policeman, met the same fate. None of us had any idea where his father was. All of us struggled to help our mothers dealt with the new hardships. Cải became more emotional as we talked. He started swearing at the "sons of bitches" Communists, wondering what harm his father could have done them that they put him in jail.

I was startled to hear Cải swearing at the Communists. He could get us all in the principal's office with serious trouble if we were heard. My effort to calm Cải down drew a defiant shrug from him. The Commies were not everywhere, he said. Why were we so afraid of them? If we didn't tell them, how were they going to know? He couldn't care less if he were kicked out of school. What were we going to learn under the "socialist" school system? How to praise Uncle Ho and the party until our tongues broke?

Trying a different tack to get Cải to shut up, Chiêm told us about Trí, another kid we knew, who was now dead. His father was an ARVN major. The day after the South Vietnamese government surrendered to the NVA, his father poisoned his entire family, shot everyone, then blew his own brains out. The neighbors didn't know the whole family was dead until a week later, when the smell of the corpses became unbearable. We all should be thankful that our fathers didn't do that to us.

I felt sick. Hearing that people I knew were now dead was not what I expected to find out when I came to school today. First, it was Ms. Kim Ánh then it was Trí. Trí was a good friend and a funny kid. I thought my father knew his father, too. I even saw him two days before my father took me from school in April. Five months later, I found out that he and his entire family were long dead. I couldn't comprehend why the tragedies happened.

"Why did Trí's father do it?" I asked Chiêm, feeling numbed from the news. "The war was over. Why did Trí's family have to die?" Chiêm could only shake his head. The only person who knew was Trí's father. If I wanted to know, I had to go to hell to ask him. If I wanted his guess, Chiêm said, the reason is that Trí's father didn't want his family to have to live with the Commies. He probably thought that they would be tortured and persecuted. It was better to die than to face vengeance from the Commies. Trí's father wasn't the only one who did it. There were also other ARVN officers and policemen who committed suicide when the South Vietnamese government surrendered.

The group's mood slowly swung from anger to gloom, then self pity. "Who is better off, Trí or us?" Thành asked. "We are alive but our families are miserable. Our fathers are in jail, and our mothers barely scrape enough money to feed us. May be Trí is somewhere in heaven feeling sorry for us. He doesn't have to deal with all this shit any more."

Thành's question turned the conversation into a gripe session. We all had endured miseries in the past few months with no one to tell to. When we ran out of things to complain about, the topic turned to what would our school be like this year. It could be nothing good, we all agreed, not with the North Vietnamese students and teachers joining us. Worse, students from the former St. Joseph High School had reputations as being lazy, rowdy, or even violent. Putting the North Vietnamese and the St. Joseph students together in the same room would make it into a powder keg. We were all going to be in for a fun ride.

When there was nothing left to do or say, I picked up my book bag and headed out. On the way to my bicycle, I walked past class 6A2. Class 6A2, a co-ed class, was next to ours. The students in this class were also heading out. I recognized many faces I knew from last year. Suddenly, I caught the look of a girl also heading for her bicycle. Something about this girl nagged at me until I realized who she was. She was Trang, the girl who lived in her castle, the ice factory in my neighborhood. She apparently didn't see me. Like all other students, she was in a hurry to get to her bicycle.

I waited until she had taken off before getting my bicycle. My mind was filled with confused and incoherent thoughts. I had thought about her for a few days after I caught her staring at me doing the laundry in my back yard. I had wondered how nice it would be to talk to such a beautiful girl. At the same time, I could not understand why the image of this girl kept staying in my head. She was rich and I was poor. She was beautiful and I was dark and dirty. If she knew I existed, she probably thought I was just a little better than a beggar any way. Why did I keep thinking about her?

Not seeing her since for two months, I began to forget the incident. Now, suddenly I found out that my path and hers would cross again at least twice a day. We both rode our bicycles on the same road to school daily. How was I going to act when I rode past or next to her on the way to school? It would not take long for her to know the poor boy next door was in the class next to hers. Was I going to ignore her forever when I was dying to talk to her? My peace of mind was now shattered by this discovery.

Though only twelve, I was familiar with the concept of love from reading many romance novels. Could it be that I somehow was in love with this girl, Trang? But the idea was impossible. I was just a kid. I couldn't possibly understand the feeling of love. I knew little about Trang and had always thought if she had any feeling about me, it would be at best curiosity and at worst contempt. I thought about asking my mother to help me explain this weird feeling, but quickly brushed the idea out of my mind. My mother was preoccupied with so many things, she would not have time to deal with this silly feeling I had. I would have to learn how to deal with the uneasiness by myself.

We spent the first week to get used to our new school and classmates. My class, 7A3, now totaled 60 students. Half were from St. Joseph High, or from other schools nearby. Some were strange characters with outrageous behaviors. It took me some time to know and adjust to them. It took all of us a lot longer to adjust to new political activities now being imposed by the school administration.

Our class had a "political" advisor, Mr. Trần Quang Diệu. At 21, Mr. Diệu was an alumnus of the Vũng Tàu High School. He never had done anything with the Việt Cộng before the fall of South Vietnam. In fact he

The St. Joseph Church in Vũng Tàu. The old Châu Thành High School, where I spent three years from 1975 to 1978, is hidden behind the trees on the left of the church.

was nearly drafted into the ARVN. Yet, Mr. Diệu somehow managed to be one of the earliest recruits of the Young Ho Chi Minh Communist League ("Đoàn Thanh Niên Cộng Sản Hồ Chí Minh") from our school. Because of his dedication and service to the Young Ho Chi Minh Communist League, Mr. Diệu was given a job to be a teacher. He didn't know how to teach. In reality, his main job was to establish and recruit members for the Young Communist League branch in the school. His other responsibility was to set up and manage branches of the Ho Chi Minh Avant Garde Youth (Đội Thiếu Niên Tiền Phong Hồ Chí Minh).

On the second day of school, Mr. Diệu and his assistant, Ms. Trần Thị Vân, another recent high school graduate, came to our class in the first period. Their arrival was pre-arranged, as our first period teacher didn't show up as he should have.

"Welcome back to school," Mr. Diệu promptly got into his prepared speech after we had settled into our seats. "I am Trần Quang Diệu, a member of the Young Ho Chi Minh Communist League, and your political advisor. I will also advise all other classes in this school. I am here to educate you about our great Communist Party, and the path the party will take to lead our country quickly, strongly, and firmly to Socialism. In other words, my job is to help all of you to be politically enlightened and to become good, model Communist youths, worthy to be children of Uncle Ho and the party."

The good Communist wannabe stopped, stared at us to let the words sink in, then continued with his well-rehearsed monologue. He introduced Ms. Vân, his assistant, who would manage us on a daily basis. Her job was to set up a sub-branch (Chi Đội) of the Ho Chi Minh Avant Garde Youth (Đội Thiếu Niên Tiền Phong Hồ Chí Minh) in my class. Every class would have its own sub-branch of the Youth. We were all " strongly encouraged" to join and participate in activities of the Avant Garde Youth.

Diệu droned on about administrative details. Each week, we would endure him for two hours in the political class. Vân would lead our class activities during the first period each day. Our cooperation with Vân was expected and we should all strive to be good children of Uncle Ho. Those who refused to participate or tried to disrupt the class would not be tolerated.

Diệu turned the stage over to Vân and exited from the class. As Diệu left, my group of friends erupted into a buzz. "Do you guys know who this pompous asshole is? Is he a Việt Cộng or something?" Cải asked.

Laughing, Chiêm told us that Diệu wasn't a Việt Cộng. Rather, he was one of the "ba mươi" (thirty) guys. The label drew loud chuckles. After the fall of South Viet Nam on April 30, 1975, many young men and women in South Vietnam worked hard to ingratiate themselves with the new regime. These people hoped to achieve a better future for themselves under the new government than their less-than-"revolutionary" background might allow them to get. They promoted themselves to the new masters, Communist political cadres, by volunteering to work as security agents or to carry out any errands. The reward for their hard work was to be admitted to the Young Ho Chi Minh Communist League. Many South Vietnamese contemptuously referred to these ambitious young men and women as the "ba mươi." The name referred to the perception that these South Vietnamese zealots suddenly and conveniently saw the light of Communism after the thirtieth of April 1975. The term quickly spread and became synonymous with "traitors" or "scum."

It took Vân several minutes to quiet us down. A short, plump woman with long hair and brown skin, she appeared to be no older than twenty. Her face was round and pleasant. She wore the same uniform as a schoolgirl: black pants and white shirt. The one difference was the red kerchief on her neck.

"Welcome back to school," she looked at us for a moment, then restating the obvious. "My name is Trần Thị Vân, and I will be working with your class this year. I'm excited to get to know all of you and to plan all the activities that we will have for the coming year. I will interact with you in the first 15 minutes each day. I will also organize a sub-branch of the Ho Chi Minh Avant Garde Youth in your class. Together, we can make this the best sub-branch in the Châu Thành High School."

A kid in the front row, Kiệt, asked Vân, "What is this Ho Chi Minh Youth that you keep talking about? Mr. Diệu said that he is a member of the Young Ho Chi Minh Communist League. What is that league? Are you a member of the league, too?" Kiệt was asking the same questions we were all dying to ask. These strange words Diệu and Vân were throwing around—the sub-branch, the Young Ho Chi Minh Communist League, and the Ho Chi Minh Avant Garde Youth—were foreign to us. We didn't know why these people made them sound so important.

"Very good questions," Vân answered calmly. She used Kiệt's question to launch into a full-throttled pitch. "Now that our country is finally unified under the leadership of the glorious Vietnamese Communist Party, there will be organizations for every Vietnamese, for all different age groups. All these organizations will be working under the guidance of the Vietnamese Communist Party. These organizations aim to help everyone understand the party's policies, to be enlightened politically, and channel their energy, under the leadership of the party, to reconstruct our country and propel it forward on the road to Socialism. The Ho Chi Minh Avant Garde Youth is the organization for all children from 7 to 15. All children are eligible to join. The Youth will teach children the ideology and policies of the Party, its history, and the long struggles to evict the French and American imperialists from our country. The youth will organize public work projects so that all children can contribute toward the rebuilding of our country. The youth will also train bright, promising leaders and provide recruits for "Đoàn Thanh Niên Cộng Sản Hồ Chí Minh" (The Young Ho Chi Minh Communist League) by the time these children reach fifteen."

The words flowed out from Ms. Vân as effortlessly as if she were a tape recorder. For the first time, we heard the party propaganda from a real person instead of the ubiquitous, obnoxious loudspeakers in our neighborhood. After the first few minutes, a few students began to get tired and started whispering. Ms. Vân ignored the noises and went on with her prepared speech. The Young Ho Chi Minh Communist League, she said, was the elite organization for young men and women between the ages of fifteen and thirty-five. The league was dedicated to serving the Communist Party, leading other organizations to defend and rebuild our country, and helping other organizations to understand the ideology and policies of the party. The admission criteria to the Communist League were strict. To be admitted, one must have a distinguished record of service to the party, demonstrate a high level of ideological enlightenment, and have an absolute commitment to be willing to sacrifice everything, including one's own life, for the party. Thus, membership in the league was both a great honor and a great responsibility. The Communist League, during its 50-year history, had produced many great heroes and leaders for our country. The league provided the sole source of recruits for the Communist Party. All leaders of our country had come and would only come from the party. Thus we should all join the Youth and strive to achieve a distinguished record of service to the party so that one day we would have the honor of being admitted to the Communist League."

"Do we really have to join?" Kiệt asked again. "How do you know who is a member and who is not?"

The reply was another long lecture. We should think of joining the Ho Chi Minh Avant Garde Youth as an honor, not as something that was forced on us, Vân said. Admission to the Youth was open to everyone, and everyone was strongly encouraged to join. Those who joined the Youth would wear the red kerchief on their shirt in school or in the Youth's gatherings. Joining the Youth was not mandatory, but it was absolutely critical to our academic success. Part of our grade would be based on our participation in the Youth and on our ideological enlightenment.

The kids shut up to ponder Vân's implied threat. Pulling out a sheet of paper, Vân asked the students to come and sign up for the Youth. We also were asked to fill out our "lý lịch" (background) according to a specific format. The reason, Vân said, was that the school, the Communist League, and the Youth did not have information on everyone. In addition, many student files were destroyed or lost during the liberation of the city. The background files helped the school in monitoring our ideological progress. It helped the school and its cadres to focus energy on those students who needed the most help in understanding our party ideology.

The class became quiet again. Vân turned to the blackboard and began writing all the background information that we had to provide: our name, addresses, place and date of birth, our parents' background and occupation prior to and after April 30, 1975. In addition to these details, a student also had to list out the name and occupation of everyone in his family, whether his parents immigrated from the North in 1954, and what his grandparents' occupations were.

A chill went through my spine as I slowly understood what Vân's words really meant. She didn't ask for our background for benevolent reason. Rather, the information would help the school and the Youth to identify who might be troublemakers and resistant to the party's ideology. Maybe the information would help them to identify and keep an eye on those of us whose parents were former South Vietnamese government officials or military officers. I didn't like the idea of having someone keeping a close eye on me, but I didn't have any choice. Reluctantly, I filled out my background paper and turned it in.

When I returned to my seat, my friends were hotly debating whether to sign up for the Youth. Chiêm thought Vân was full of shit. She couldn't be serious about the school failing us if we didn't join the Youth. I took the threats more seriously. Though Vân was just a mouthpiece, the Communist government she represented had clearly demonstrated in the past few months it had little patience for dissent or disobedience. Besides, even if we decided not to join the Youth, we couldn't avoid studying the ideological bullshit any way.

After a long discussion, we reluctantly signed up for the Youth while other students still debated the issue. In the end, half the class signed up and the other half decided that they weren't going to be scared into joining. Ms. Vân collected the background papers and the sign-up sheet then left as our first period began.

Diệu, Vân, and the teachers who taught class 7A3 soon found out how frustrating and difficult it was to deal with our class. When it came to being mean-spirited, the Vietnamese had a saying: "Nhất Quỷ, Nhì Ma, Thứ Ba Học Trò": (First is the devil, second is the ghost, and third are the students). We, the students of 7A3, would more than prove the validity of this statement.

Despite the obedient appearance of my class on the first day, the student composition and the changing environment of the school made class 7A3 a powder keg waiting to explode. Most students had fathers who were former South Vietnamese government officials or military officers. Their fathers were now incarcerated in re-education camps. Others had parents who were merchants or street vendors. These kids had seen their houses raided and part of their property confiscated by the hated "yellow dogs," the security agents. These experiences, coupled with the dislike and distrust of the Communists inherited from their parents, made the kids restless, cynical, and angry. As a result, they always looked for ways to vent their anger. On the other hand, there were a few students whose parents were Communist sympathizers or who just simply wanted to do well. Whatever their reservations might be, these students always went along with the class' mischievous acts, for fear of being alienated, ostracized, or even beaten by their classmates.

The lax discipline of the new school administration also helped to make us a more rebellious bunch. The students who came from class 6A3 in the former Vũng Tàu High School were accustomed to much stricter discipline. Before April 30, 1975, we had to wear school uniform (blue pants, white shirt, belt, and a name tag) to be admitted to school each day. Those students who didn't wear the complete uniform, or were tardy, or had long hair, would immediately be sent to the disciplinary officer to be punished. Profane language was not tolerated. Anyone caught uttering profanity would face detention after school or a few days of suspension.

We didn't have the same strict discipline in Châu Thành High School. Long hair and profanity were rampant. Our uniform consisted of a white shirt and any pants we could afford. There was no longer a disciplinary officer. The enforcers of discipline now were members of the Young Ho Chi Minh Communist League such as Diệu, who were only concerned about acts of disrespect for the Communist Party or Ho Chi Minh. Noting the lax discipline, many students, who to this point were good-mannered kids, were tempted to push the limits of what they could get away with.

The students from the former St. Joseph High School provided another reason for the deterioration of discipline. These students attended St. Joseph before because they failed the entry examination to Vũng Tàu High School. They generally were lazy and addicted to all kinds of bad habits. Many smoked cigarettes and spent much time talking about sex. The parents of some had opened bars and brothels catering to American soldiers prior to the fall of South Vietnam. As such, these students were familiar with prostitutes and what they did. They took delight in talking about these activities in gory, explicit details to other wide-eyed, naïve students. These students couldn't care less if they were expelled from school. Their main thing was to have fun and to try to attract other students to be like them.

Our class showed its rebelliousness quickly. In the first two weeks, Vân came in at the beginning of each day to teach us many "revolutionary" songs. Two songs we had to sing every day were the new Vietnamese national anthem and a song praising Ho Chi Minh, "Last night I dreamed of Uncle Ho" ("Đêm qua em mơ gặp Bác Hồ"). When we had memorized the songs, Vân turned the responsibility of directing the singing in the first fifteen minutes of class over to Hường, our elected head of class, and Chính, the vice head of class. Every day, Vân came in during the first five minutes to get things going, then went to other classes.

One day in the second week, sheets with revised lyrics of all the songs we had learned were passed to all students in my class. There was a simple note on the sheets: "Memorize, then burn this. We will sing these songs after Ms. Vân leaves class tomorrow." I had no idea who had revised the lyrics and passed them out. Regardless, I broke out in delirious laughter after reading the revised lyrics. I couldn't wait to sing them the next day.

When Vân came in the next morning, she gave us the singing assignment for the day. We were to sing the national anthem three times, then the songs "Last night I dreamed of Uncle Ho" and "Uncle Ho is here with us in our day of victory." When Ms. Vân was still in the class, we dutifully sang the national anthem, "Đoàn Quân Việt Nam đi" (The March of the Vietnamese Army), as we were taught:

> Đoàn Quân Việt Nam đi
> Sao vàng phất phới
> Bước chân dồn vang trên đường gập ghềnh xa
> Cùng chung bước góp sức xây đời mới
> Đứng đều lên gông xích ta đập tan
> Từ bao lâu ta nuốt căm hờn
> Quyết xây nền đời ta tươi sáng hơn
> Vì nhân dân chiến đấu không ngừng
> Tiến mau ra sa trường, tiến lên
> Cùng tiến lên
> Nước non Việt Nam ta vững bền

> (The Vietnamese Army marches,
> Our proud yellow star flag flying overhead.
> The strong footsteps echo loudly on the long, rough road.
> Together, we join our strength to build a new life,
> Together, we stand up to crush the chains that tie us.
> For so long, we have swallowed our anger,
> Now we are determined to make our lives better.
> For the people, we will fight tirelessly.
> Advance quickly to the battlefields. Advance.
> Together, we'll advance.
> To make our country, Vietnam, strong and stable.)

Satisfied that we had learned the song well, Vân left, turning the responsibility of directing the class over to Hường. We continued singing the national anthem as before. After Vân left, Hường winked and told us, "I will have to go to the rest room, you guys go on." As soon as he left, the kids in the first five rows started bellowing the revised lyrics of the national anthem with delight. The rest of us gleefully followed.

Đoàn quân Việt Nam đi
Như lũ chết đói
Cả một bầy lang thang trên con đường xa
Cả một lũ đầy tớ cho Tàu Nga
Chúng cùng đi tàn phá nước Việt Nam
Từ bao lâu chúng sống trong rừng
Chỉ mong ngày được ăn hai bữa cơm
Vì Đảng đi chém giết không ngừng
Máu xương ôi tuôn tràn núi sông
Cả Bắc Nam
Nước non Việt Nam ta thảm sầu

(The Vietnamese Army marches
Like starving beggars,
A ragtag bunch wandering on the long road,
A bunch of servants for China and Russia.
Together, they march to destroy Vietnam.
For so long, they live in the jungles
Just hoping to have two meals a day.
For the Party, they will kill tirelessly
To make blood flow all over our rivers and mountains
From North to South
To make our country, Vietnam, drowned in sadness.)

Once we finished with the national anthem, we began singing the song "Last night I dreamed of Uncle Ho." The original lyrics portrayed Ho Chi Minh as a kind grandfather, so loved and revered by all the children of Vietnam that they often dreamed of him.

Đêm qua em mơ gặp Bác Hồ
Râu bác dài tóc Bác bạc phơ
Em sung sướng em hôn má Bác
Bác mỉm cười Bác bảo em ngoan
Bác mỉm cười Bác bảo em ngoan.

(Last night I dreamed of Uncle Ho
His beard is long, his hair is so white
I'm so glad, I kissed his cheek
Uncle Ho smiled and told me I'm a good kid
Uncle Ho smiled and told me I'm a good kid.)

We sang the song with its original words once, then changed to singing the revised lyrics with great relish. I didn't know who wrote it, but the words portrayed an entirely different image for Uncle Ho.

Đêm qua em mơ gặp Bác Hồ
Chân Bác dài, Bác đạp xích lô
Em thấy Bác, em kêu xe khác
Bác gật đầu "Học tập nghe con"
Bác gật đầu "Học tập nghe con"
Đêm qua em mơ gặp túi tiền
Trong túi tiền có bốn ngàn đô
Em sung sướng em đem khoe Bác
Bác mỉm cười "Đưa hết cho tao"
Bác mỉm cười "Đưa hết cho tao."

(Last night I dreamed of Uncle Ho
His legs were long, he was pedaling a cyclo
I saw him, I called a different cyclo
Uncle Ho nodded at me "To re-education camp you go, son"
Uncle Ho nodded at me "To re-education camp you go, son."
Last night I dreamed of a money bag
In the money bag, there were four thousand dollars.
I was so glad, I told Uncle Ho
Uncle Ho smiled, "Give all the money to me"
Uncle Ho smiled, "Give all the money to me.")

We sang loudly and laughed uproariously. Our singing, the combined noise level of 60 boys yelling at the top of their lungs, drowned out the singing from the two neighboring classes, 7A1 and 7A2. As soon as we finished the second repetition of "Last night I dreamed of Uncle Ho," Diệu and Vân rushed into our classroom, their faces reddened with anger. Coincidentally, Hường walked in a few seconds after Diệu's and Vân's arrival.

"Where have you been?" Mr. Diệu stopped Hường and yelled at him. "Aren't you the one responsible for directing this class? Do you know what they did?"

Putting on his best innocent face, Hường pretended to be scared. He stammered that he just went to the bathroom and did not know what happened. In the last rows, my friends and I kept our heads low, trying hard to keep our laughter from breaking out. We all knew there wasn't much Diệu could do to Hường. Hường had a family background ten times more "revolutionary" than Diệu himself. Hường's father died many years ago.

His mother was a Communist agent, planted in Vũng Tàu for many years. After the fall of South Vietnam, his mother had expected to get a good position in return for her years of service for the National Liberation Front. Instead, she got a ceremonial post in the local ward People's Committee while the Communist government filled all powerful positions with party members from the North. By late 1975, we didn't hear of the "Mặt Trận Giải Phóng Quốc Gia" (National Liberation Front) or the "Chính Phủ Cách Mạng Lâm Thời" (Provisional Revolutionary Government) anymore. Rumors were rampant that these "southern" organizations were dissolved by the northerner-dominated Vietnamese Communist Party. Many members of these organizations were given ceremonial posts with no real power, while many others were sent to re-education camps with former South Vietnamese government officials and military officers. Hường's mother must have been disillusioned with the "revolution" and the "party" and passed this disillusionment on to him. Not only he didn't stop us from singing these outrageously disrespectful songs, he also became a willing accomplice in our mischievous activities.

Hường was a tall, big kid of seventeen in a class of twelve and thirteen years old. He started school late, and was stuck in a class with much younger kids. He was as tall as Diệu and more muscular. Knowing that he could not punish Hường without getting some retribution from Hường's mother later on, Diệu angrily told Hường to go back to his seat. Then, he turned his attention to trying to find the culprits.

The investigation quickly turned into a comedy. Diệu tried to find out who was responsible for controlling the class when Hường was out. The blame was placed on Chính, the vice head of class. Not knowing who Chính was, Diệu ordered him to stand up. When a student finally informed Diệu that Chính was absent, the kids could no longer contain themselves and broke out in delirious laughter. Embarrassed, the red-faced Diệu shouted at the top of his lungs "Shut up all of you! You think this is funny? You all will be punished for what you've done today. Just wait until I get my hands on the ringleaders."

Changing his tactics, Diệu started questioning several kids, trying to get them to point a finger at the culprits. The answers he got were all the same. The kids in the front row thought the ones in the back rows did it. The kids in the back row thought the singing started from the front rows. None really knew who started the whole thing. All denied that they participated.

Diệu became more frustrated as his questions were leading him nowhere. By the time he finished questioning the kids in the last row, the activity period was over. Mr. Sanh, the literature teacher came in, ready to start the new period. Not knowing what happened, Mr. Sanh was surprised to see Diệu and Vân still in the class, questioning the students.

After telling Mr. Sanh about our heinous crime, Diệu declared that our classes would be cancelled today until the perpetrators were found. Shrugging, Mr. Sanh packed his books and left, while Diệu returned to his futile interrogation. An hour later, he had finished asking every student and still hadn't gotten anywhere. We all gave the same answers. We didn't sing the rebellious lyrics and we didn't know who sang them. Though realizing the futility, Diệu wasn't any less angry. I didn't know whether his anger was because we defied him or he was scared that what we did could hurt his chances of advancement in the Young Ho Chi Minh Communist League.

"All right. I know that you have lied to me," he finally said while still trying to regain his calm. "You either sang the rebellious songs yourself or know who did it, but won't tell me. Well, if you want to protect your friends, then all of you will get the punishment together. You will all kneel on the ground from now to the end of the day. This class will be suspended three days and this transgression will be recorded into your files. If any of you change your mind and want to tell me who did it, you could come down to my office to let me know, and you will be spared this ordeal."

Finishing his verdict, Diệu angrily stormed out, leaving Vân to carry out the order. We knelt on the ground from 9 A.M. until noon. After an hour, our knees were numb and sore, yet no one left to report to Diệu. Being restless, we still talked loudly with each other while kneeling.

Vân tried hard to keep the class quiet, but she didn't have Diệu's intimidating meanness to shut up the sixty loud mouths. The kids were so noisy that the teachers in the neighboring class, 7A2, came over to yell at us. As soon as they left, the cacophony began again. Vân became so frustrated, she almost broke down in tears, not knowing what to do with these mischievous devils. As for us, we were so happy Diệu didn't catch anyone and we were able to make other people pay for our deeds as well. When school ended at noon, we finally were allowed to stand up. After stretching to let blood circulate through our bodies again, we happily planned to play soccer the next day, our first day of suspension.

# 5

# The Competition

Despite much exhortation from Diệu and Vân, only thirty students in my class signed up for the Ho Chi Minh Avant Garde Youth. The number was enough for Vân to form Chi Đội (sub-branch) 7A3. It was her task to form a sub-branch for each seventh-grade class. True to form, our sub-branch was the smallest in the school, reflecting the stubborn resistance of the students to conform to this strange new order.

All the sub-branches, from sixth to ninth grades, together formed a branch (Liên Đội) of the Youth in Châu Thành High School. The members had to wear red kerchiefs as part of the uniform for school and all gatherings. At first, having to wear the red kerchief caused me much uneasiness. I felt like I had betrayed my father by not having the courage to resist joining. To soothe my troubled conscience, I kept telling myself that though I might appear to be a Communist kid, deep down inside I would never buy its ideology.

Our curiosity about the Youth was answered in the first meeting, which took place one week after my class' suspension. On a Sunday, all the sub-branches held their first meeting to elect officers and to interact with other groups.

When I arrived at the meeting, my fear about being brainwashed diminished somewhat when I saw other classmates also had that cursed red kerchief around their necks. Yet, they seemed totally unaffected by it. They appeared to be as rowdy and mischievous as ever.

Vân gathered the students in the schoolyard and asked us to form a circle. Other Chi Đội's (sub-branches) were doing the same thing and occupying areas next to ours. The sub-branch standing next to us was

7A2. The largest sub-branch in the school, it had well over 50 students, nearly double the size of our rogue group 7A3. I could hear the whispering of the 7A2 students about our class suspension last week. By now, the reputation of my class as the most unruly was well known.

I suddenly felt a nervous, tingling sensation as I saw Trang standing in the middle of sub-branch 7A2. She looked as beautiful as the last time I saw her. Her long hair was neatly tied behind her head and her clothes looked so clean and well pressed. I quickly turned my eyes back to my friends in sub-branch 7A3. I was worried one of my classmates might figure out that I was staring at a girl who also happened to be my neighbor. I knew my classmates well. They were always looking for things to gossip about. If they were to find out that Trang was my neighbor, it would be enough for them to fabricate and perpetuate all kinds of imaginary stories. Even if I were to hide under the ground, I would never hear the end of it.

Vân was busily running through three sub-branches 7A1, 7A2, and 7A3, trying to get the students organized. Our group was the first on her list. She directed us to elect the officers for our sub-branch, then ran off to 7A2. Our tasks were to select five officers: sub branch head, sub branch vice head, chief of academic activities, chief of work activities, and chief of sport activities.

None of us wanted to run for the posts. The main reason most of us joined the Youth was so that we would not get low marks in school. Others joined because it seemed fun to belong to an organization that was going to do something. None of us wanted more work. Therefore, all the 7A3 kids figured they just do the minimum to get by. After 30 minutes of arguing and volunteering someone else for the officer posts, we still did not get any candidates.

When Vân returned, she gave up and appointed the officers herself. Chiêm was appointed sub-branch head since he was the oldest kid at thirteen. I was appointed chief of academic activities, as everyone pointed to me when Vân asked who was the most studious. Cường became chief of labor activities since he was the most muscular and Phước was appointed sport activities chief because of his undisputed soccer talent. The appointed officers looked at each other and winked. We all knew how difficult it would be to lead the other thirty restless and mischievous kids in the sub-branch. On the other hand, we didn't care. We all adopted the "wait and see" strategy.

We didn't have to wait long. After the democratic appointment process was finished, Vân doled out the tasks we were supposed to do for the day. "We will spend the morning to learn more revolutionary songs,"

Vân said matter-of-factly. "Then, we'll learn about the historic struggle of the Vietnamese Communist Party to regain our country's independence, and the great life story of Uncle Ho. There will be a brief period when our sub-branch will join sub-branches 7A1 and 7A2 in games. Afterward, we will have a "Đố Vui Để Học" (trivia pursuit) competition between all the seventh-grade sub-branches. The topic of the competition will be the history of the Vietnamese Communist Party and the biography of Uncle Ho. We'll have a full, fun day ahead. Before we start, we need to find three members who will represent this sub-branch in the competition this afternoon. So, which of you volunteer to represent sub-branch 7A3?"

We all looked at each other. None of us knew any thing about the party or Ho Chi Minh other than that we were supposed to treat them as deities. How were we supposed to compete in trivia pursuit on a subject that we did not know? The kids' answers to Vân's question were only curious stares. Undeterred, Vân asked the question again.

"Chị (older sister) Vân, I don't think any of us can volunteer to represent 7A3," Chiêm stood up to answer as all the eyes turned to him. "We do not know any thing about the party nor Uncle Ho. If we compete, we will just make fools out of ourselves."

"Oh, you don't have to worry about that," Vân held up a book and waved it in front of our faces. She was obviously prepared for Chiêm's little show of objection. "We still have four hours before the competition starts. I have four copies of this book. It covers everything you'll need to know about the party and Uncle Ho. If we can select the three representatives for 7A3, they can read the book and will know enough by the time of the competition to play. Come on, the students in other sub-branches don't know more than you do."

We all looked at each other again. Reading a book in four hours was a tall order for anyone. Memorizing it to compete in the trivia pursuit was far too much to ask. Besides, we had no incentives to want to play. What did we have to gain in this competition? All of us paid lip service to the party and Uncle Ho because we had to. Trying to cram all these "facts" about these beings that we did not particularly love into our heads was more than any of us wanted to do. We all stared back at Vân with blank looks.

Seeing our stares, Vân tried a different tactic. She started suggesting that we didn't want to compete because we were scared of the girls in the other classes. The boys of 7A3 were good only for pranks, but really were no better than simpletons and cowards. The girls would laugh in our faces for the rest of the year.

Vân finally hit on our soft spot. Her challenge was the ultimate insult.

None of the boys wanted to be told that we were not as smart as the girls or scared of them. As soon as she finished, we all spoke at once. Chiêm stood up to quiet the group down and told Vân we would compete. Instead of asking for volunteers, he would ask the group to nominate the best students to represent the group.

Satisfied that we took the bait, Vân stepped back to watch the boys noisily arguing who should represent the class. Striking a quick blow, Thành loudly suggested my nomination, "Trình is a bookworm and a reading machine. He will do well for us." Before I could even object, other kids in the group raised their hands and echoed their agreement with Thành's suggestion.

I was dumbfounded. *Damn, what was Thành trying to do? I was just trying to do the least to get by just like everyone else. If Thành was so hot about beating the girls, why didn't he volunteer? Hell, this guy wanted me to make a fool out of myself for his own enjoyment, I bet. I am not going to let him get away with this.* I gave Thành a dirty look. He winked back at me and smiled, ignoring my threatening glance.

"Chị Vân, I am a poor choice for this competition," I objected with a growl. "I don't know any thing about the party and Uncle Ho. I never competed in a Đố Vui Để Học competition before. I think Thành or Chiêm can represent the class better than me."

Shaking her head, Vân said that since all the boys had confidence in me, I must be good enough. She then turned to ask the group to nominate two more members.

I almost blurted out that I didn't give a damn about the party or Uncle Ho. No one should force me to study about them. Fortunately, I was able to control myself. Meanwhile, the group was busy nominating and electing the two other members. After 10 minutes, Chiêm and Thái, a new student in our class, became the other unwilling volunteers.

Handing each one of us a book about Ho Chi Minh and the Communist Revolution, Vân told us to find a quiet room to study in and come back at 2 o'clock for the competition. The rest of the kids would stay to learn more revolutionary songs.

We took the books and walked upstairs to our classroom. Thái and Chiêm were not concerned. They laughed and joked about putting on a comedy in the afternoon in front of the other students. Seeing the frown on my face, Thái told me to cheer up. We were not attending a funeral, he said.

Still irritated, I growled at Thái, "What is there to be happy about? If we read this stuff, we are brainwashed. If we don't, we make fools of ourselves."

"Hey, you are not going to be able to avoid it, so why not have fun doing it anyway?" Thái shrugged. "You worry too much. We are not going to make fools out of ourselves. Think about those poor souls representing the other classes this afternoon. They don't know any better than we do, so do you think they are going to humiliate us? I don't think so. If we read this book well and try to remember as much as we can, I think we can kick some ass."

Thái's attitude was infectious. I shook my head to ward off my surly mood, while still wondering how Thái could appear to be so happy.

He was a new student in our class, as his family just moved from Saigon to Vũng Tàu a few months ago. Thái and I got along real well and became good friends only a few days after school started. I started to think that it might not be so bad to compete after all.

For three hours, we sat in different corners and read the book in silence. Despite my dislike of the Communist Party and Ho Chi Minh, I found the book interesting. It was well written and talked about many events in Vietnam's history that I had not learned. At the same time, I thought that the book's propagandistic language was too offensive. Nevertheless, I gobbled through the book in an hour and a half, using my pencil to mark many details that I wanted to memorize. Thái and Chiêm were doing the same thing. By noon, I had read through the book twice. Our classmates came to give us some sandwiches then left us alone to continue the study.

I knew my motivation was nothing other than pride. I disliked the idea of losing more than anything. I was always competitive at anything I did. In addition, I didn't want to look stupid in front of the girls in other classes. My recent poverty somehow boosted my sensitivity at being slighted by anyone, real or imagined.

At 1 o'clock, we joined our group in the schoolyard. At 1:30, Vân came to tell us about the arrangements for the competition. We would meet sub-branch 7A1 in the first round. Other matches were 7A2 versus 7P2 and 7P1 versus 7P3. The winners of the three first-round matches would face each other in a single final match for the championship. Our team would have the benefit of watching one match, 7A2 versus 7P2, before we were due up.

The rules were simple. There were twenty questions for each first-round match. Each question was worth one point. When the moderator, Diệu, finished reading each question, the team that raised its hands first would get to answer the question. If a team could not answer a question within 30 seconds, the other team would get the chance to respond. Vân and Liên, the advisor for the 7P's sub-branches, were the referees.

Their jobs were to keep scores and to determine which team got to answer first.

At 2 o'clock, all the sub-branches gathered in the middle of the school-yard to watch the game. The students sat on the ground in rows, while the moderator, referees, and the competing teams sat in the front, facing every-one else. I suddenly felt a rush of adrenaline. This was it. I knew we had to win this competition for the bragging rights of every boy in 7A3. When the chips were down, I would play hard.

The team members of sub-branches 7A2 and 7P2 moved to the front. They went through the formality of introducing themselves before the game began. I felt a tinge of excitement as I saw Trang on the team for 7A2. She looked beautiful and confident. Now, I had one more reason to want to win this competition. I did not know if Trang recognized me, but she would know I was her neighbor sooner or later. For my own pride, I had to win this competition so she would not look down on me. My teen-ager's rationale was simple: I might be poor but I can show you how much smarter I am.

The match between sub-branches 7A2 and 7P2 started out slowly as both teams were tentative. I could tell that the students on both teams had never competed in a trivia pursuit game before. They appeared nervous, took too long to answer, or raised their hands too slowly to answer ques-tions. At the end of the game, 7A2 won by a modest margin of 9 to 7.

"Look, as soon as Diệu has finished reading, we will all raise our hands and yell "7A3," regardless of whether or not you know the answer, all right?" I told my teammates. The strategy became obvious to me from seeing the slow reaction of the other teams.

"What are you trying to do, Bookworm?" Thái stared at me. "We will look pretty stupid pulling a stunt like that then turning mute."

"Trust me," I replied confidently. "Just raise your hands then let me take care of the rest. I could answer every question he just asked in the last game. Even if we could not answer, at least we had the first shot at the question. The team that is faster will win. I just want to make sure that we are the fastest team."

"You are sneaky, man," Chiêm nodded. "I think that is smart. Hey, we are depending on you to carry us through here, Bookworm."

When it came our turn, we took our places in the center of the cir-cle. After introducing ourselves, we sat down on the ground facing every-one else. I glanced quickly at our competition, three girls who represented sub-branch 7A1. They looked more nervous than we did.

"Hey, look at those girls," I whispered to Chiêm. "They looked pretty scared. If we can get the first three questions, it's over."

"Okay. Here we go," Chiêm nodded. "Just make sure you can do what you said. I don't want to be the butt of jokes for the rest of the year, man."

I nodded, while listening to Diệu reiterating the rules of the game. After taking his sweet time repeating himself, Diệu started reading the first question.

"What is the real name of Uncle ?"

Before Diệu even finished with the word "Uncle," I raised my hand and yell out "7A3." My yell was so loud it startled everyone. Hundred of pairs of eyes looked at me as if I were crazy.

"Team 7A3, I did not even finish reading the question yet," Diệu looked at me with irritation. "Are you sure you are ready?"

"Yes," I said quickly. "The question was 'What is the real name of Uncle Ho?' While Uncle Ho had taken many other names such as Anh Ba, Nguyễn Tất Thành, or Nguyễn Ái Quốc, his real name when he was born was Nguyễn Sinh Cung."

Diệu couldn't conceal his surprise. He didn't expect us, the rowdiest kids in the whole school, to come out strong in the beginning.

"Correct. One point for team 7A3," he conceded reluctantly.

"Good going, Bookworm," Thái winked.

"Name three French generals who had commanded the French forces against the People's Army of Vietnam…," Mr. Diệu started to read the next question.

Again, I raised my hand and yelled "7A3" before Diệu finished reading. Chiêm and Thái looked at me as if I was crazy.

"Look, you should wait until I finish the question," Diệu said while giving me his coldest stare.

"I know, but the rules didn't say that I have to wait for you to finish reading the question," I protested. "Besides, I had a greater chance of answering wrong by not waiting for you to finish. That will be our penalty."

"All right! All right! Answer the question then," Diệu snapped.

"The three French generals who had commanded French forces against the People's Army of Vietnam during the nine-year resistance against the French colonialists from 1946 to 1954 were Jean de Lattre de Tassigny, Raoul Salan, and Henri Navarre," I replied easily, ignoring the threatening edge in Diệu's voice.

"Correct. Another point for 7A3." Diệu resigned to the fact that once again I was correct. Despite his obvious dislike of me, he had to give us the point.

My classmates in the audience all stood up and cheered loudly. They were getting excited that our team jumped to a quick two and zero lead.

Mr. Diệu became even more irritated. He had never liked us or all the trouble we had caused him.

"Sit down, sub-branch 7A3," he shouted at the cheering kids. "Because of your disturbance, team 7A1 will get to answer the next question."

The kids sat down, but not without loudly booing his decision. Ignoring the booing, Diệu returned to reading his question. I looked at the girls of the 7A1 team again. They looked shaken up after my blitzes of the first two questions.

Despite getting the first shot at answering the third question, the girls could not answer it within the 30-second time limit. Diệu was forced to pass the question to us, which I promptly answered correctly.

The game quickly turned into a rout. Thái and Chiêm simply followed my strategy of shooting up their hands before Diệu finished the questions and letting me answer. The girls of team 7A1 became more demoralized as the game went on. They tried to imitate our strategy twice, but ended up giving the wrong answers. When the match ended, we had won easily with a score of eighteen to two.

Despite Diệu's stern face, the lopsided victory caused my classmates to cheer uproariously. Our opponents, the girls on the 7A1 team, were embarrassed and angry. When we walked past them on the way back to our sub-branch, one of the girls sniped at me, "Show off." Thái and Chiêm heard the remarks and gleefully looked at me, expecting me to lash out a nasty response. They didn't get their wishes. Pretending not to have heard the taunt, I shrugged, looked at the ground, and continued walking back. I had achieved what I set out to do: not to look stupid in front of everyone. The girls from sub-branch 7A1 were unfortunate victims of my pride. I had embarrassed them enough, and I did not want to rub it in any further.

I looked in the direction of sub-branch 7A2 until I found Trang staring at me. There was a look of amazement on her face. I quickly turned away as soon as our eyes met. That look was all the reward I needed.

We sat down next to our classmates to watch the next match between sub-branches 7P1 and 7P2. This contest was more exciting and evenly matched, with the girls of 7P1 winning with a score of nine to eight.

"Hey, Bookworm," Thái whispered in my ears when the match ended. "We are depending on you to win this championship. I want you to continue doing what you did, blasting everyone else away. Don't have mercy for any teams, particularly 7A2. If you do, I'm going to tell all the animals of our class about your secret."

I was startled by Thái's statement. *What secret was he talking about?* Giving him a quick elbow, I asked Thái, "What the hell are you talking about?"

"Nice try, Bookworm," Thái winked mischievously. "You don't think that your big brother here would be watching, hey? During our match with 7A1, you kept looking at a particular pretty face in class 7A2. Hell, you looked at her more than at Diệu himself. What's her name? Thu Trang, right? When we walked back here, you looked at her again and she was staring at you. I caught you red-handed, Bookworm. You know what would happen if the animals of our class got wind of something like this, don't you? If I was not wrong, wasn't she your neighbor, too?"

"Hey, Thái Giám, I thought you were one of my best friends," I protested. "Friends don't blackmail each other like this. Besides, I was checking out several girls. You can't accuse me of looking at this particular girl. I didn't do anything different than what you did."

"You can't pull that one over me, Bookworm," Thái shrugged nonchalantly. "I kept seeing you staring at her. Anyway, it doesn't matter whether or not I was right. If I leaked out that Trang is your neighbor, it is enough for the animals of our class to cook up juicy stories to spread around. You know how they are. But I will be nice. You are right. It's not nice to do that to your friend. I just want to make sure we win. Don't have a faint heart now, okay?"

I nodded and walked with our team up for the final match. I wondered who else besides Thái had noticed my behavior. If the kids of our class even had an inkling that Trang was my neighbor, they could manufacture all kind of gossip. Even if I had ten mouths, I still could not defend myself against these vicious gossips.

The students in my class all had active imaginations. Unfortunately, their imaginations were not channeled into useful learning or creation. For the first three weeks of school, we were inundated with political lessons about Communism and how great, wise, and brilliant the Vietnamese Communist Party and Uncle Ho were. Our teachers were obviously instructed to incorporate the political messages into their subjects. All the kids had gotten sick of hearing these propagandistic statements day after day. The repetition of these messages got to the point where we could recite them even in our sleep

Many kids in my class quickly lost interest in studying. Most, if not all, found it difficult to get any substance out of the lessons other than the political messages. I knew even this trivia pursuit competition was just another brainwashing tool in the Communist kit. I found myself torn between two opposing forces. On one hand, I didn't want to appear stupid in front of all my schoolmates. I wanted to prove that I was one of the best students and I could learn and win in any academic competition. Unfortunately, this first academic competition I found myself in was about the Communist Party and Ho Chi Minh. If I were to win, I would appear to be a Communist convert to know the subject so well. If I lost, I would look incompetent in front of my classmates and everyone else.

Bored with the political indoctrination, my classmates turned their imagination and creativity into pranks and gossiping. They gossiped about anything or anybody. At the adolescent age of twelve or thirteen, they were fascinated with girls and dating. They created stories about relationships between the boys and girls in our school and spread them as if they were the truth. So far, I had managed to stay out of their unwanted attention and I wanted to keep it that way.

The three winning teams sat down to prepare for the championship. The final match was to be a three-way competition, with the same simple rules. The team with the fastest hands and the most points would win.

Our team was placed directly across from the 7A2 team, with the 7P1 team sitting in the middle of a semicircle. Thái's warnings before the game caused me to keep my eyes away from the 7A2 team.

I didn't concentrate well on this match as I was still bothered by Thái's observation. At the same time, my conscience was greatly troubled. I wondered if I had broken my sacred promise to my father. On one hand, I wanted to win this competition for my own pride and the bragging rights of every kid in class 7A3. On the other, my father's words to me before he left for re-education camp kept echoing in my head: "Don't let them plant the hatred and suspicions in your mind." I had dutifully promised my father I would not let the Communists brainwash me. *What am I doing up here? I am speaking and acting like a truly zealous Communist kid. Am I taking the first step of allowing them to plant their ideology, their hatred, and suspicions into my head? What will my father think of me if he sees me here now? Will he be sad to see that his son did not have the courage to keep his promise? What happens to my honor and integrity? What kind of person am I?*

These conflicting, troubling thoughts distracted me completely from the competition. Before I knew it, team 7A2 had jumped to a three-point lead over our team and team 7P1. We still had yet to score.

"Wake up, Bookworm," Chiêm whispered in my ears while giving me a hard pinch in the back. "You can't sleep in this match here."

The pinch startled me into realizing that we were trailing. I nodded to Chiêm. "All right, let's get them."

"Comrade Nguyễn Thị Minh Khai was one of the ...," Diệu read the next question.

Chiêm and Thái yelled "7A3" when Mr. Diệu just got to the word "the...." Diệu's irritation was written all over his face at our team's latest gambit. He hadn't read enough for us to even know what the question was about.

"Team 7A3. You got the chance to answer this question now," he nodded after shooting us a murderous glance. "If you cannot answer it, I will read the complete question for the other two teams to answer. You won't have another turn at this."

Every pair of eyes stared at me. I felt like cursing. In their excitement, my teammates had put me in a tough spot. I had no idea what the question was about. Neither Chiêm nor Thái would know. They were expecting a miracle from me.

"Comrade Nguyễn Thị Minh Khai, the wife of Comrade Lê Hồng Phong, was one of the early Vietnamese Communist Party members to sacrifice her life for the revolution," I collected myself and composed a catch-all answer. "She was captured by the French Secret Service and imprisoned in Côn Sơn. While in prison, she composed the following poem to encourage all her comrades to be courageous, have faith in the ultimate victory of the party, and not succumb to the torture of the jailers:

Vững chí bền gan ai hỡi ai
Kiên tâm giữ dạ mới anh tài
Thời cuộc đẩy đưa người chiến sĩ
Con đường cách mạng vẫn chông gai

(Hang tough, my comrades
Keep your faith. Hold your heart. That's the hero.
Time pushes and shoves the fighters.
The path of the revolution is always hard and dangerous.)

No one could tell whether I had answered correctly. All the eyes now shifted to Diệu, waiting for his decision. Meanwhile, Diệu stared at me as if I was a monster.

"You did not answer one question, but three," he said after a momentary silence. "Fortunately for you, one of your three answers was the correct answer for this question. The question was, "What was the poem that Comrade Nguyễn Thị Minh Khai wrote when she was imprisoned by the French colonialists?" I will give you the point for this answer. However, next time, you can only give one answer for each question, not three. If you don't, you will not get any point even if you answer correctly."

As soon as Diệu finished speaking, the kids in my class jumped up and down, cheering uproariously for our first point.

"Good job, Bookworm," Chiêm wiped away the sweat on his face. "I have no idea how you do that."

"You can thank me by not jumping the gun so early," I retorted. "Shit, that was just a lucky guess."

With the momentum of our first point, we went on the offensive and got to answer nine of the next ten questions. By then, the competition quickly turned into a rout. We won easily with a score of twelve points. Team 7A2 got only six and team 7P1 only two points. My classmates hugged each other when the game was finally over. Meanwhile, everyone else was stunned. No one had expected us, the kids from a class with the reputation of being the most undisciplined and the laziest, to win this competition so convincingly.

I tried hard not to look at the 7A2 team and Trang when the game was over. I wondered how she felt. Was she really going to hate my guts now? I had made every one of them look bad. While I was the star of this competition, I didn't feel elated as I should, just an empty feeling. I set out to prove myself as one of the best students in this school. In doing so, I had acted and spoken as if I was a true, dedicated Communist. What would my father think of me if he saw me now? While I knew that deep down inside I did not believe in anything I studied about today, I wondered if other kids in school would privately jeer at me as a spineless, shameless convert to Communism. The way I memorized and answered the questions with such standard propagandistic language, I probably didn't appear to be any different from Diệu or Vân, whom my classmates had so much loathing for. I wondered if I did the right thing, making a name for myself by humiliating other kids, including the girl that I had such a strong feeling for.

The prize for our victory was another blow to my already troubled heart: many more propagandistic books about Communism, the party, and Uncle Ho. I wondered what I would do with them.

"Bookworm, you are a real hero today," Thái slapped me on the shoulder when we lined up to receive the "prize." "The girls of 7A1 and 7A2 could never call us stupid again. Aren't you proud of yourself?"

I growled in Thái's ears while making sure that no one else was close enough to hear me. "What the hell is there to be proud about? To show that we were more fucked up, more brainwashed than the losers?" Thái turned quiet. He nodded his head and left me alone.

The trivia pursuit competition was the last event of the day. After singing a few more songs, the students disbanded. When I went to get my bicycle, I was in time to see Thu Trang rode past me on her new bicycle. Though she must have seen me coming, she didn't even look in my direction.

"Hey, Bookworm," Thái chuckled and slapped my shoulder when he caught up with me at the bicycle rack. "It looks like người đẹp (the beauty) Thu Trang is upset at you."

"Shit, why do you keep insinuating about things that aren't there, huh?" I shook my head helplessly. "What does she have to do with me?"

"Jeez, don't get too sensitive now. Hey, I am sorry for saying what I said before our final match."

"All right," I nodded. "Apology accepted. Just don't get on my case about Trang again."

"Deal!"

We got on our bicycles and started riding out to the street. I remained sullen for several minutes until Thái made another peace offering. "Hey, do you want to come to my house for some chè (sweet soup)? My mother just cooked some last night."

"Okay."

"Bookworm, I know how you feel," Thái continued. "You made me think when you said that there was nothing to be proud about in showing we were more deeply brainwashed than others. I know your father is in re-education camp, and it hurts you to have to learn this propaganda bullshit about the same assholes that put your father there. It's all right. You don't have to feel bad. We do it because we have no other choice."

"Do we really?" I asked. "Or are we just cowards for not having the guts to say no?"

"Hey, there is a difference between being courageous and being stupid, Okay," Thái laughed. "The smart man lives to fight another day. It's not smart to show how tough you are, and then get kicked out of school. Then, who are you going to show off your courage to?"

I shrugged, but didn't bother to answer Thái's question. Thái nodded. "I am a little more fortunate than you are. My father was stranded in America when South Vietnam fell. He went there for a six-months training in electronics equipment with the U.S. Army since December last year. I don't think he'll come back to this country. I don't know when we will see him again. We were kicked out of our home in Saigon, too. That's why we moved here and you have me for a pal. My grandmother has a house here. Otherwise, we wouldn't have a roof over our heads. Shit, I hate these Communist bastards as much as you do."

"Cool down, will you? You can curse them until your saliva dries, and none of them will even lose a hair. I just don't want to get carried away and start to believe what they are teaching us, that's all."

"You worry about a stupid thing," Thái said seriously. "You and I are twelve now, too old to ever be brainwashed. The Communists aren't worrying about brainwashing us. They just make sure that we'll never denounce them in public, that's all. If you worry about brainwashing, take care of your younger brothers and teach them. They are still young and naive enough to absorb this propaganda bullshit."

Thái and I got along better as we continued to talk for the rest of the ride. After having chè with him at his home, I went back to my house to begin my daily labor. The day's events caused me to be in a reflective mood. I realized that I had learned an important lesson today: that winning was not everything. Every victory has its costs, and sometimes the costs of the victory outweigh the benefits. My performance in the competition had caused my conscience to be troubled. I wondered if I had trampled on other people's pride to protect my own. *Had I also sacrificed my honor, integrity, and my solemn promise to my father just for my stupid pride?*

# 6

# Against the Odds

A few months after the currency conversion, my family's financial situation became more desperate. My mother never made much money peddling her goods in the open market. Now, she was quickly running out of cash to cover our basic necessities. The Communist government, determined to bring South Vietnam into a centralized, planned economy, started to crack down on the black market in 1976. The state security agents stalked the open market places. Their task was to seize the goods of any vendors whom they considered to be doing business illegally. My mother never had it easy earning our livings, as she had to squat all day in the hot sun of the muddy, stinky Vũng Tàu open market to sell her goods. Now, she faced the constant fear of the security agents springing on her, confiscating all her goods, and sending her to prison.

Despite the risk, my mother had no choice but to go to the open market to face this danger every day. If she didn't, we would not have food to eat. My mother had many close calls. Many times, she barely escaped from the security agents, but lost all her goods in the process. Whenever she came to the market, she always looked out for undercover agents, ready to run at the first sign of danger. I didn't know what would have happened to us if my mother were to be caught. With my father in jail, if my mother were caught, what could I, 12 years old, do to feed myself and my three younger brothers? The prospects were too frightening for me to think about. Each night when my mother came home, we had won another victory — we had survived another day!

Further, the basic necessities of life, food and clothing, were getting more expensive. Soon after establishing control in South Vietnam, the

Communist government began to form co-operatives in the rural areas. All peasants were required to belong to these co-operatives, and had to sell a major part of their rice production to the government at cheap prices. After setting aside enough rice to feed their own families, the peasants had little or no rice left to sell in the market.

The government became the de facto controller of rice in the entire country. By controlling the rice supply and making people constantly worry about feeding themselves, the government achieved its political objective of minimizing resistance to its control. People spent all their energy just to fill their stomachs, and had no strength or courage left to contemplate opposing the government.

The cheapest rice people could buy was sold in the "cơ sở quốc doanh" (government-owned stores). Subsidized by the government, the prices in these stores were several times lower than on the black market. However, the quantity any household could buy was severely rationed. Each person in our family was allowed to buy only 3 kilograms of rice per month. Eating as little as we could, our ration still lasted us only two weeks. To make up for the shortfall, we had to buy rice from the black market. The high prices my mother paid for the black market rice drained her of any money she could make.

Prices also escalated for other commodities such as fabric, sugar, cooking oil, coal, and gasoline. Vietnam was essentially bankrupt after the "glorious victory" of the Communist army. While people struggled to find enough rice to eat from day to day, the government had plenty of surplus rice that it had bought, or more accurately, extorted, from the peasants at dirt-cheap prices. In my hometown of Vũng Tàu, I repeatedly heard the popular rumor about the surplus rice being shipped to China and the Soviet Union. The rice was payment for the military aid North Vietnam received from these countries during the war. No one knew whether the rumor was true or not. Nevertheless, my classmates and I strongly believed this explanation for the ever decreasing supply and increasing prices of rice in South Vietnam.

We were old enough to see and understand what was happening. Soon, we became very bitter and cynical of the Communist government's policies and propaganda. We knew we were paying for the Communist Party's debt to its brother countries of China and the Soviet Union. We also knew the "precious freedom and independence" that Ho Chi Minh preached and was faithfully repeated every day by the government's mouthpieces was nothing more than empty words. Growing up, I came to understand "freedom" and "independence" very cynically. "Freedom" meant being free to praise the party and Uncle Ho publicly and incessantly.

"Independence" meant we Vietnamese no longer depended on American aid for our livelihood, but now depended on the availability and prices of rice on the black market for our survival.

By early 1976, the little money that my mother had managed to save was depleting quickly. Knowing she could not afford to buy more than half of our supply of rice in the black market much longer, my mother decided to produce a substantial portion of our food supply ourselves. She borrowed money from my grandfather and wrote to my uncles and aunts abroad to ask for help. With the money, she bought a piece of land in the "Núi Nhỏ" (Small) mountain, which sat behind the French cemetery in front of our house. We planted yams and bananas on this piece of land to supplement our diet. Within a week of buying the land, I took on the additional task of tilling it with my mother. My hard daily routine now got harder.

Every day, I went to school in the morning and came home at noon. After cooking lunch and dinner for the family, fetching water, and washing clothes, I took off with an ax, a hoe, and a sack to the mountain to work on our land. While there, I also gathered firewood until dark.

To this day, I believe that working on the land was another test of perseverance that God made me go through in my young life. In the first few days, my mother showed me what I needed to do: digging up and removing all the huge rocks on the land, planting the yams and the bananas, and digging up tree roots to use as firewood. When I had learned how to do these things well, my mother went back to selling goods in the market and left me alone with the mountain.

When I realized the monumental task I had to do to make the rocky land produce the food that would nourish us, I never thought I could do it. The plot was two acres, with thousands of huge rocks buried in the ground. The rocks weighed an average of over a hundred kilograms, with some as heavy as three or four hundred.

The previous owner had planted some bushes of yams and some bananas in a small area. However, the rest of the land was covered with large rocks. The existing few bushes of yams and bananas were not enough to feed our family for more than a few weeks. To provide a sufficient supplement, we had to cultivate as much of the land as possible.

To make the ground arable, I had to dig up all these rocks and roll them into a corner with my puny ax and hoe. Even with my mother helping me in the first few days, I was barely able to move some of these huge rocks. At night, my back ached and my hands were full of painful blisters from the hard labor. I thought about complaining of my aches and pains to my mother, but stopped since she was in as much pain as I was.

My mother could tell how much pain I was in. Looking at me limping, she could only shake her head. Then, she gave me a lesson I would not forget.

"Son, I know how hard the labor has been for you," my mother told me the night before I had to work alone. She held my hands to look at the blisters and calluses, then sighed deeply. We had nothing to soothe the pain. I could only hope the calluses would harden quickly.

"I know how much pain you are in. Just hang on, OK. If anything, I love you very much. You know how desperate our situation is. I can't make enough money to feed all of us. No one can or will help us except for ourselves. That's why you have to work on the land no matter how much pain you are in. I'm hurting to see you in so much pain, but there is not much I can do. I can only tell you to be courageous. Maybe some day God will hear our prayers and save us from this. Right now, we have to work and survive until the day God hears our prayer."

"I have to go back to selling tomorrow. We didn't make any money in the past three days and I cannot afford to be at home any more. From now, you have to work the land every day by yourself. You have to work hard even though I won't be there. If you don't, not only you, but all your brothers and I will be hungry. You know I could not buy enough rice for all of us. If we can't produce any food from this land, we won't survive for long. Do you know how important your job is?"

"Yes, mom," I promised. "Don't worry, I'm not a slacker. I'll grow enough food on this land to feed all of us."

It was easy to assure my mother with bravado when I was home with her. It was a different matter working under the relentlessly scalding sun the next day, with all the huge, stubborn rocks staring insolently at me. It took me half an hour to dig up and move a rock to a corner. Then, I had to rest for several minutes before I could start working on the next one. I almost broke down and cried. There were thousands of these rocks on our land. At the rate I was working, I wouldn't be able to plant anything for a few months. My mother and brothers would be hungry, and it would be my fault. What could I, a weak kid with puny tools, do to conquer this hard land? May be I should quit and tell my mother I couldn't do this work alone.

I sat down to rest and started thinking about what my father told me before he left. His last words still echoed in my head: "In the days ahead, there are times that it may seem your situation is so hopeless and desperate. It may seem that the odds against you are insurmountable and it is easier to give up and save your energy. Don't ever give up hope, Son."

Suddenly, I felt ashamed of myself. My father had told me to face the "insurmountable odds" with courage and never give up hope. Yet, here I was ready to cry at the first problem I ran into. Worse, the problem was inanimate rocks that could not fight back at me. If I couldn't even deal with these stupid rocks, then how could I possibly think about overcoming other insurmountable odds that would come my way? If I gave in to these rocks now, I would never have the courage to face up to other obstacles. I would never learn to fight and win.

The thoughts brought renewed energy to my tired body. I stopped feeling sorry for myself and started digging and moving one rock after another. I stopped thinking about how long it would take to clear all the rocks. Instead, I focused on moving them one at a time. I worked steadily, taking breaks as needed. The rocks no longer looked like immovable objects any more. They were just simply opponents I had to beat. Engrossed in my task, anxious to vanquish my silent foes, I forgot how much time had passed. If the sun didn't set in the horizon, I would not know when to stop.

My body was exhausted from the long hours of hard work. But unlike the days before, I no longer felt dejected. I was very happy when I saw what I had done. I had moved more than twenty rocks, cleared a large area of grass and bushes, and dug up many tree roots that I was going to use as firewood. It was more than I ever thought that I could do. Slowly, I realized the power of the simple lesson my father tried to teach me. I could never have done it if I continued to feel sorry for myself or waited for a fairy materializing out of thin air to solve my problems. For the first time, I understood what my father meant when he told me about the "inner courage and strength, nurtured by hope, faith, and understanding." Despite being exhausted, I felt extremely excited. My hard work today had finally made me understand and believe the simple truth my father tried to impart: that I could always fight and win against tough odds if I didn't give up. The lesson would serve me well for the rest of my life.

I kept up my hard work for the next six months, and gradually had results to show for my labor. In two months, I had cleared the rocks off most of the land and started planting more yam bushes. In six months, the land was covered with green bushes of yams and bananas. I had done what my mother asked me to do. Not only had my hard work resulted in food for my family, it also made me into a stronger kid, physically and mentally. The painful blisters on my hands turned into tough, hard calluses. Carrying the daily load of yams, bananas, or tree roots from the mountain was my weight training. Gradually, I developed a tenacity when faced with any tough problems. I no longer became discouraged at the first sign of difficulty. There were many days when the sky became cloudy and rain was imminent, but I refused to quit working until I finished what I had set out to do that day. I never thought that I had the perseverance in me until I was forced to work on the land.

Every night, after a hard, exhausting day of labor, I stayed up late to study by candlelight. Electricity became a luxury, as all the power plants were nationalized and poorly run by the state. Power was cut often as power plants suffered from lack of fuel, spare parts for equipment, and qualified technical personnel. In school, the use of electricity was reduced to a minimum. The lights were never turned on in class. At first, it was difficult getting used to not having enough light. Gradually, we all resigned ourselves to our situation. We all had learned to accept our harsh lives in Vietnam's "Socialist Paradise."

As the school year progressed, it became more difficult for me to stay focused on learning. Teachers and students alike were struggling to feed themselves. The teachers received monthly salaries that were barely enough to buy their families a two- or three-week supply of rice. As a result, they had to find additional means of making a living. Many teachers made and brought food to school to sell to students during break time. Others worked as cyclo drivers after school hours or grew vegetables to sell in the market. These activities kept the teachers from devoting their energy to teaching. As they struggled to survive, they could not find the motivation to teach, let alone motivate the students to study.

Halfway into the school year, the school administration brought in many teachers from North Vietnam and laid off several South Vietnamese teachers. Despite their distraction and struggle for survival, the South Vietnamese teachers we had were still far better than the new northern teachers we had to suffer through. The northerners sent to my school were poorly trained and knew little about the subjects they were supposed to teach. Their introduction to the school brought more pranks and resentment from my restless classmates.

Our class got two North Vietnamese teachers, one in history and one in chemistry. The history teacher, Ms. Chiên, a woman in her mid-thirties, looked like a peasant who had just come from the countryside. She always wore the same white shirt and black pajama pants, the same uniform that all North Vietnamese teachers, both male and female, wore whenever we saw them. There was nothing feminine about Ms. Chiên. Her face was angular. Her chest was flat and her arms were as big as a man's. Her walk was as stiff and awkward as a soldier's march. The only thing about her that let us know she was a woman was her long hair which was tied into a bundle.

Ms. Chiên did not make up for her ungainly physical appearance with either a gregarious personality or sharp intelligence. On her first day, she immediately earned our silent contempt with her dictatorial style, her boorish vocabulary, her self-importance, and her poor grasp of history, the subject she was supposed to teach. She spent the first twenty minutes of class talking about her fifteen years of service to the Communist Party, and how proud she was to be admitted to the party recently. Acting with the imperious attitude of the victors that so many Northerners displayed, she went on to demand absolute obedience from everyone. With her authority as a Communist Party member, she threatened to expel any student who dared to cause trouble in her class. Ms. Chiên had yet to learn how tough and stubborn the kids in class 7A3 were.

We got an inkling of her intelligence once Ms. Chiên opened the history book and began the lesson of the day. Her lecture was the worst I ever heard. It was not a lesson, as all she did was to read off the first sentence of each paragraph in the book and write it on the board. She did not discuss what any paragraph meant or add any information that was not in the book.

The lesson of the first day, Emperor Quang Trung's victory over the invading Chinese army in the spring of 1789, happened to be a subject that I knew well. I had read my father's history books years ago and knew Vietnam's ancient history better than all my classmates. Hearing Ms. Chiên's lecture, I sensed that she knew little about what she was teaching. She was trying to bluff her way through the class and cover her ignorance. To test my suspicion, I asked her a question, the answer to which I knew was not in the book she had.

As I expected, she looked in the book for the answer, and when finding it was not there, promptly declared that my question was irrelevant. She chided me for wasting the class's time and ordered me to be quiet. The action was all that I needed to judge her competence. When I sat down, I could see several classmates winking at me, signaling that they knew as well as I did how ignorant our new history teacher was.

"Hey, Bookworm, that woman didn't like you too much," Thái said when class was over. "You made her look really bad today."

"Hey, I didn't make her any worse than she already was," I shrugged.

"Shit. I really hate that bitch," Công, one of the craziest kids in class, jumped in. "Do you remember what she said? 'I am going to expel anyone who dares to cause trouble in class.' What the shit does she think she is? I wonder if the bitch ever looks at herself in the mirror. She looked to me like an insect becoming human. I'm going to make her pay for all the bullshit she gave us today."

Công's last statement got our attention. He had the reputation of being the most reckless kid in class. He was also cunning. From what he said, it was obvious that he was up to something no good for Ms. Chiên. Thái and I could not contain our curiosity. We prodded Công to tell what he planned to do but got only a useless reply that when it happened, we would know.

For two weeks, Công did nothing. Just when I had forgotten his threat to do something to Ms. Chiên, Công came to class one day carrying a small, old metal milk can. Before class started, he came up to the teacher desk. Using a piece of cloth to take something from the metal can, he spread it all over the teacher's chair. There were many students in class when he was carrying out his task.

When we saw Công spread something over the teacher's chair, we crowded around him to find out what he was doing. He told us to stay away and avoid touching the teacher's desk and chair. He had them covered with "mắt mèo" (a type of poison ivy) pollen. The "mắt mèo" pollens came in small furry balls with numerous tiny, sharp filaments. These filaments are poisonous and nearly invisible in daylight. It we touched them, the filaments would stick to our skin. If they got stuck to our clothes, they would eventually get through the fabric and prick the skin. The poison on these filaments caused the skin to be irritated and itch very badly. Scratching could only make the itch worse as the action would spread the filaments to other parts of the body.

When we understood what havoc these tiny filaments could wreak, we could not contain our laughter in anticipation of what would happen shortly. Thái tried hard to keep his voice low and said, "Man, so Ms. Chiên is going to scratch her butt until it doubles in size? I think that is a great idea. A bigger butt can only help her look more like a woman."

"That is the idea," Công grinned. "Hey, you all keep quiet about this, all right! That idiotic woman can be very vengeful and dangerous. If she finds out I did this, she could have my head for dinner."

In unison, we all promised our complete silence. The drama didn't take long to unfold. At 8:15, Ms. Chiên walked in with her customary swagger. She set her books down on the table and immediately sat down on the chair. Then, she took out the class list and began calling roll, as she had always done. As Ms. Chiên stuck her nose to the list and called out our names, the kids winked at each other with anticipation. Sitting in the furthest back row, Công was calm as he pretended to look at his note. So far, so good. The trap had been sprung and the quarry remained unsuspecting.

When she finished calling roll, Ms. Chiên picked up her book, walked toward the blackboard, and began writing the first sentence of each paragraph in the book, as she had always done. She was halfway through her first sentence when she began to feel the itch. The sixty pairs of eyes staring at her behind could see her body tremble slightly as she tried hard to control the urge to scratch herself.

It was a futile attempt. She walked back to sit down on the chair before she got through with the second sentence. Using the desk as a shield against our prying eyes, she stuck one hand in her pants to furiously scratch her itching bottom. Attempting to cover her action, she called on Thái to recite the details of the last lesson. By the time Thái finished his answer, it was apparent that Ms. Chiên did not hear even one word he said.

Her scratching became more furious than before, to the point that we now could see and hear it. The filaments got on both arms, forcing her to take her hand out of her pants and scratch her arms. Then, she stuck her hand back in her pants and scratched her bottom again. Soon, all her self-control was gone. Wanting only to relieve herself of the maddening itch, she did not know nor care what an embarrassing spectacle she was acting out in front of the gleeful eyes of sixty kids. We tried hard to keep ourselves from laughing. Since she did not tell Thái to sit down, he remained standing.

"Ms. Chiên, I have answered the question," Thái finally said, pretending to be oblivious to Ms. Chiên's troubles. "Can I sit down?"

"Oh, mother! I'm itching so bad," Thái got a surprising answer back from Ms. Chiên. "I am going crazy."

We could not contain ourselves any longer. The kids broke down laughing uncontrollably until our stomachs were aching. Hearing our laughter, Ms. Chiên finally snapped out of her misery and realized what a scene she was making. Her face, which was never a pleasant sight, reddened with embarrassment and rage. She picked up her books and ran out the door, sprinting down the stairs to the empty teacher's lounge.

We did not know what she did afterward or how she finally got rid of her itch. We were too busy laughing and chattering. All we could talk about was how stupid and comical she looked scratching her butt like there was no tomorrow.

As soon as Ms. Chiên left, Công went up to the teacher's chair and used a cloth to pick up all the "mắt mèo" filaments that remained. Then, he dumped the cloth in a trash bin. Since he had gotten rid of the incriminating evidence, there was little chance that Ms. Chiên could figure out what or who had caused her misery.

Our next three classes of the day proceeded without any further incident. The teachers in these periods didn't have a clue of what happened to Ms. Chiên. They came in and sat on the teacher's chair without any hesitation. They didn't experience the same maddening itch. Thus, they became potentially favorable witnesses for us, as they couldn't suspect foul play by the students.

When our last class was over, Diệu came in and ordered us to stay put. He waited until the teacher in the last period had left the class, then cleared his throat. In his now familiar self-important way, he pronounced, "Something very unfortunate happened in this class today. Your history teacher, Ms. Chiên, got some bad allergic reactions which forced her to be hospitalized. Her condition is serious and she likely will be out at least two weeks. I will take her place during the time that she is out."

He stopped and searched our faces for some reactions. We all put on our most innocent looks while fighting hard to control the urge to laugh. Seeing no clues from our stone faces, Diệu continued, "How she got her allergy was suspicious. She was fine today until she came to this class. The school administration, including me, suspects that there is foul play by some students in this class. If we determine that indeed someone has done something to cause Ms. Chiên's allergy, I can assure you we will spare no efforts to find out who those individuals are. The guilty will be punished. Now, I do expect some cooperation from all of you. If none of you come forward to tell me who did this, the whole class will be suspended for two days. Further, you will have to clean up all other classrooms in the school for a month. You have fifteen minutes to think this over. If I do not hear anything at the end of the fifteen minutes, your suspension will begin tomorrow."

The students looked blankly at each other. Diệu reverted to his threats again. By now, he should realize that threats did not work with the kids in our class. I couldn't even remember how many times we were suspended for all the troubles we caused the faculty. In fact, the kids loved being suspended. Instead of going to school, they would spend the days playing soccer. Yet, other than suspension, Diệu had no other ways to punish us. Neither he nor any other teachers had ever been able to pry a confession or allegation from any kids. There was an unspoken code of honor among the students: we would not tell the school or any teachers who started the trouble in the class. It was much easier to take the punishment they gave out to the entire class than seeing the school expel any of our friends. Besides, the usual punishment, suspension of the entire class, gave us the opportunity to play soccer. Those who dared to come forward and tell on their classmates would be regarded as traitors. At best, they would become pariahs, rejected and scorned by other kids. No one would talk to them. At worst, they could be beaten. Thus, our class remained the biggest headache for the school administrators as they had yet to find a way to bring it under control.

Diệu probably knew it was futile. He had threatened us many times before, so none of the kids took his threat seriously. Besides, we knew he was just guessing that we did something to Ms. Chiên. He had no proof. Yet, he had to show his masters, the North Vietnamese party members who were the school administrators, that he was doing something about our problem class.

Hường, as the class head, stood up to protest. There was no proof anyone caused Ms. Chiên's problem, he said. His face darkened, Diệu brushed Hường's argument aside. It was too much of a coincidence that Ms. Chiên got her allergy in class 7A3, the largest collection of devils in the school's history. Reverting to being a dictator, Diệu told Hường to sit down and shut up. For the rest of us collaborators, if we didn't tell him who did it, our class would be suspended tomorrow.

We all remained quiet despite Diệu's threat. We had been suspended too many times to care about another one. Despite all the suspensions we had received, the school could not expel all of us. Frustrated by our obstinacy, Diệu stomped out of the class after giving his last threat. "Fine. If you don't want to tell me who did it, then stay home. If I find out you knew the culprit but didn't tell me about it, you will be punished just as harshly as the culprit himself."

After Diệu left, we all looked at each other and laughed behind his back. We never had any respect for him. Once again, he proved to be an ineffectual bully, who could do nothing more than dish out meaningless threats. We left class feeling satisfied and happy, knowing we had made life miserable for the two people we hated so much.

Despite the occasional joy of playing tricks on teachers whom we didn't like, the numerous suspensions and the declining quality of teaching were making it much harder for me to learn. Most of my classmates had lost their motivation to learn since the year started. All our families were getting poorer and more desperate. All the kids had to work after school to help their families. Many of my classmates also had fathers who were in re-education camps and their properties had been confiscated by the government. Their strong dislike of the Communist regime caused them to hate anyone who represented the government or tried to ingratiate themselves with it.

To add more fuel to this fire of hatred, we had to listen to and repeat the same political indoctrination from the school faculty day after day. The incongruence between the virtues of a "Vietnamese Socialist Paradise" and the harsh realities of life we faced made the students very cynical. As the school year progressed, I could sense the anger and frustration building up inside myself and my classmates as our families were having less and less to eat. Meanwhile we were forced to praise the "brilliant guidance of the party" incessantly. Worse, we all had to denounce the former South Vietnamese government, which our parents were a part of.

The political class we had to take was just sheer torture. The purpose of the class was to ingrain in our minds the "supremacy of Marxism-Leninism," the "brilliant and always correct guidance of the party," and the "ultimate victory of Communism." In the class, we had to go through the practice of "criticism and self-criticism." Diệu, our hated political teacher, often forced us to confess in front of others our behaviors, thoughts, or acts that were in any way inconsistent with the characteristics of a "good Communist." After doing this self-crucifying act, we had to take criticism from others of our thoughts or behaviors and promise to correct them. Usually, kids with parents who were former officials and officers of the South Vietnamese government took the most heat. We had to grit our teeth and listen to others denouncing our parents as "the bloodhounds of the imperialists," "enemies of the people," or "cold blooded criminals."

Diệu and his political masters knew exactly what they were doing. By making the kids criticize each other and denounce their parents publicly, they were sowing the seed of suspicion in all of us. They figured if they kept up the pressure of "criticizing and self-criticizing" long enough, they could break our bond of unity and make everyone inform on others. Those who informed on or criticized their classmates were rewarded and praised as being "politically enlightened." Those who remained silent were pressured relentlessly by Diệu to come up with something to criticize about themselves and others. Even if the kids had nothing to say, they were still forced to invent or confess some token thoughts to satisfy Diệu. The ultimate goal of the practice, to turn each one of us into spies in the Communists' fearsome instrument of control, gradually became very clear to me.

Despite trying hard not to criticize any of our friends, we often had to say something about each other to get Diệu off our back. The criticism, no matter how slight, easily caused tension between the kids. We often talked to each other after these sessions to try to mend the fences that Diệu was trying to get us to tear down. Yet, it was very difficult to take public denunciation of our parents from other kids and forgive them afterward. Day by day, Diệu and his Communist masters were getting closer to their goal of creating divisiveness between us.

Looking back, I believe these were the most trying days of my life. Difficult as it was, I thought the experience taught me, in a very tough way, a great sense of self-control. It also taught me, at an early age, to identify for myself who I was and where I fit into the great scheme of things. To control the anger and the frustration I felt after the political classes, I often ended up mumbling to myself that "I am much better than these Communists and nothing they do to me could ever convince me otherwise."

My classmates relieved their anger in different ways. Often, they turned their energy into pranks on teachers they didn't like or vandalizing school property. The results were almost always suspension for the class. Many teachers, other than Ms. Chiên, had gotten a taste of the "mắt mèo" filaments these kids brought to class. The portrait of Ho Chi Minh in the center of the room was replaced many times as it became a target for the kids to practice their dart-throwing skills or was smeared by ink. The school administrators treated the desecration of Ho Chi Minh's portrait as the worst offense committed by our class. For this, we got suspended and had to clean up the entire school for weeks. Despite all the threats and punishments we received, the portrait still had to be replaced once a month.

Lacking any motivation to study, many kids began to pick up bad habits such as smoking cigarettes, drinking, and fantasizing about sex. Hường was the first to start the trend. At seventeen, he was the oldest student and the only one who claimed to have slept with prostitutes. He often boasted about his sexual exploits, attracting a big crowd of wide-eyed boys who were hungry to absorb every gory detail. Another kid, Phương, whose parents owned a bar catering to American GIs before South Vietnam's fall, brought pornographic pictures and magazines to class. He charged other kids money to see the pictures. Other students brought cigarettes to class and smoked incessantly. While there were many good kids who still wanted to study, boys like Phương and Hường began to attract their own followings and actively tried to convince other kids to join them.

When some of my closest friends and I resisted their invitation, they made fun of us as cowards and simpletons. As days went by, it became harder for me to concentrate, as these kids became more rambunctious and disrupted just about every class, including those taught by competent teachers whom I respected.

My attempt to resist brought me unwanted attention from my unsavory classmates. They soon noticed my concentration on studying. At first, they peppered me with questions on why did I bother to study so hard. Later, our differences escalated to physical confrontations.

It all began on the day Phương offered me a cigarette. Phương was a character that I loathed. He always came to class wearing tight jeans and three-inch-high sambos (a strange footwear that was a hybrid between a shoe and a sandal). Apparently, it was a popular American fashion that he picked up. He smoked so much that his lips were black and his breath was too foul to stand close to.

"Hey, why don't you join us at my house for a party tonight?" Phương pressed on despite my refusal. "We can buy some beers and I have more new provocative magazines to show the guys. Man, you got to see the nude pictures of these women. They'll make your saliva drip all over."

Disgusted, I told Phương I had to study. My continued refusal drew a contemptuous laugh from him. "Why the hell do you waste your time studying so hard for?" Phương asked. "With your background, you'll be lucky if they let you get into high school after ninth grade. It would be a miracle if they ever let you get into college. Haven't you heard of the phrase "Học tài thi lý lịch" (Study with talents, take exam with background)? The Communists don't give a shit about talents. They don't give a shit about "reactionaries" like you and me. They care about those who are loyal to them. They know people like you will never be loyal to them. Do you see Hường there, telling dirty jokes and talking about fucking prostitutes? The guy doesn't study much. But you know what? He will get admitted to high school, and then to college, because his mother is a Commie spy. And you, do you know where you will end up? You will end up tilling your land or working as a coolie three years from now, because your father was an ARVN officer. So, why the hell do you study so hard if you are not going anywhere? Why don't you mellow out and be like us, enjoying your life when you still can? Who knows how long you will live? Heck, you and I may die tomorrow. At least I am enjoying every moment of my life right now so I won't regret it if I die tomorrow. And you, keep working hard until the day you die, boy, and all your life will be nothing but fucking misery."

Phương's words infuriated me. Here was this loathsome bastard making justification for his decadent lifestyle and trying to convince me to be like him. Yet, he did have a few good points in his arguments. He obviously knew as well as I did the reality of the future we faced.

I snapped angrily at Phương. "It's my life, and if I live in misery because of what I do, then it's me who pays the price. I don't need your sympathy." Unruffled, Phương shrugged and walked away.

The conversation with Phương still bothered me several days later. He had made me face a question I had consciously avoided for the past year: why did I work so hard if I knew my life was going nowhere? Hell was going to freeze over ten times before the Communist government would allow people like me to go to college. The scenario Phương had painted for my life was very real and most probable. For so long, I had put off thinking about the future so that it would not distract me from doing my best in the present. Thinking about a depressing future could only sap my strength and courage to face the harsh life my family was living. I was at least occupied and relatively unconcerned before. Now, that bastard Phương had to wake me up from my blissful ignorance. The more I thought about my future, the more I became unsure as to why I had to work so hard.

I struggled with my own thoughts for several days and still was unable to come to an answer I was satisfied with. One night, I ventured to ask for my mother's opinion at supper. "Mother, do you think that I should continue to go to school? Maybe I should stay at home to work on the land and help you earn more money for us?"

My mother was so startled she stopped eating and stared at me for a while before responding. "Son, why are you asking this? Do you want to quit school?"

"No, Mother," I said slowly. "I am just wondering whether it would be better for us if I stay home and help you earn more money. I know how hard it is for you to work and feed all of us. Maybe instead of going to school, I can work more on the land and do other things to help you support our family."

"And exactly what other things do you think you could do to earn money, eh?" my mother asked.

"I don't know exactly, Mother, but there has to be something I can do, like driving a cyclo, selling our crops in the market, or working on a fishing boat, or something else."

"And is that, working like a coolie, what you want to do for the rest of your life, Son?" my mother frowned.

"No, Mother. But what choice do we have?" I struggled to come up with my best answer. "I am not learning much of anything in school. All they do is brainwash me with propaganda. My teachers aren't teaching me. They are busy trying to survive themselves. If I continue to go to school, it will cost you more money to pay for my books and school expenses. If I don't, not only can we save the money but I can also help you more with things at home. I can do something else to bring in more income."

"Do you know that if you quit now, you will have no chance of getting to high school and then college later?" my mother shook her head. "Do you want to waste the intelligence and talent that God has given you?"

I could sense that my mother was not pleased with my thinking. She was always so proud of my achievements in school. The fact that I was even thinking about quitting must have been a devastating blow to her. Yet, I had to try to defend my thinking.

"But Mother, there is little chance I will ever get to high school, let alone college. You know the Communists hate people like us. No matter how well I do in school, when I take the exam to get to high school two years from now, they will certainly fail me. Mother, everybody knows of the system 'Học tài thi lý lịch' (Study with talents, take exam with background). They will only pass those students with 'revolutionary' family backgrounds or those who didn't do anything against them in the war. With our family background, North Vietnamese refugees who ran away from them in 1954 and then soldiers in the South's army, they will never admit me to high school."

"That is something we will worry about two years from now," my mother replied, her face visibly calmer after she heard what I had to say. "Right now, you still have a chance to study as much as you can. I see no reason for you to quit. Son, in life there are not that many opportunities to learn and to better yourself, so why do you want to give up the opportunity before you have to?"

"But Mother, what I am doing in school now is not something I would call an opportunity," I protested. "I am wasting my time. My teachers aren't teaching me anything. The South Vietnamese teachers are not teaching well any more. They are as strapped to make ends meet as everyone else. Some of my teachers even have to drive cyclos after school to make a living. The North Vietnamese teachers are idiots. They know less about the subjects they are supposed to teach than I do. Then, my classmates are smoking, drinking, and forming bands to loiter around. They even try to get me to join them. Mother, how can I learn anything if there isn't anyone who can or wants to do it well? How can I study in peace if other kids always pick on me and tell me I am an idiot for even trying? Mother, you don't go to school these days like I do, so you don't understand all these things that I have to put up with."

I nearly sobbed when I got to the end of telling my mother about all the hassles I faced in school. At the same time, I felt better as I was able to release the frustration that had built up inside for a long time. Listening intently, my mother's face softened as she heard about me being picked on in school.

"My poor son! Did they beat you up because you refuse to be like them?" My mother gently rubbed my head when I finished.

"No, mother. But they make fun of me and call me names everyday. They call me names like 'idiot,' or 'sleepwalking fool.' Yet, when there are exams, they always want to look at my answers to cheat. If I don't let them, they say that I am selfish. Then, they would look for any opportunity to put me down."

"Well, are these kids someone whom you could consider to be your friends?" my mother asked. "Do you have any real friends? Do your real friends pick on you?"

"No. These guys are not my friends. But they bug me so much."

"Well, Son, they should be the least of your worry. So, let me make sure that I understand what you are telling me. You want to quit school because you think you don't learn much right now. Even if you do, the Communists won't let you get to high school anyway. So why not quit now to save your energy and help me to support our family, right?"

"Yes, Mother" I nodded slowly. "Mom, it hurts me to see you have to work so hard. I can see that you are losing weight and getting weaker every day. I want to do more to help you. Mom, how long can we keep this up?"

"Son, I love you very much," my mother said, unable to stop the tears that slowly rolled down her haggard cheeks. "But it hurts me just as much to see you giving up hope for a better future. I work hard because I want my sons to have a chance. My life and your father's life are over. We experienced everything there is in life: joy, happiness, sadness, success, failure, love, hope, and despair. If I were to die tomorrow, I won't miss very much. You and your brothers are what I live for now. I'll do anything I can to make sure you and your brothers have a chance for a better life. But you have to help yourself, too. To do that means doing anything you can right now to prepare yourself well. That way, you can take advantage of opportunities when they come your way. You will have so much ahead of you, you cannot give up hope now no matter how bad the future may appear to be. If you give up hope, it means that your spirit is broken and you are nothing more than a walking corpse. Do you still remember what your father told you before he left?"

"Yes, Mother," I replied. "He told me to be courageous and to help you to take care of my brothers. He also told me to always study hard, Mother."

"He also told you to never give up hope until you die, didn't he? I heard that point from him so many times, I was sure he would tell you that before he went. He learned the lesson from a lifetime of struggling to make something out of himself. When he told you to never give up hope, he wanted you to take it very seriously and to think about it long and hard. And yet, here you are, talking about quitting school. Do you know how sad your father and I would be to see our oldest son quit? You still have me, and no one kicks you out of school yet. So why do you have to write yourself off?"

My mother was stopped by a hacking cough. She took a deep breath then continued. "You still can learn a lot in school even if your teachers don't teach you well. Even if no one will teach you, who is stopping you from teaching yourself? You still have all the textbooks. You are smart enough to read these books and learn the lessons, aren't you? If there are parts that you don't understand, you can at least ask me. If I cannot answer them, then you should read those parts over and over again. If you think about them long enough, eventually something will click in your head and you'll understand.

"Didn't you read your father's books about the lives of great men and women of the world several times? Do you remember that many of these famous people, like Abraham Lincoln or Thomas Edison, were self-taught? If they sat and waited for some great teachers to come around to teach them, they would never make something out of themselves. There is something to be learned from the lives of these great men, Son. If you believe in yourself, you can teach yourself a lot of things. If you have enough confidence in yourself, you never have to rely on anyone else. You've read and known all of these things before. It's time to put your knowledge to some use, all right?"

"But Mother, even if I teach myself for the next two years, they won't let me get into high school," I objected. "Then, how am I going to learn anything? What I learn now will not be of any use to me. Why do I have to waste my time and energy to do this, Mom?"

"You are assuming that two years from now, things will be the same for you as they are now," my mother shook her head emphatically. "You don't know that for sure, Son. That's why you have to have faith. You have to believe that God will eventually hear our prayers and help us. But for God to help you, you have to help yourself first. What if two years from now, somehow you will be allowed to get into high school, and then college? If you give up now, the opportunity will be worthless to you because you cannot take advantage of it. Too many people blame their bad luck or God for their misery, while they should only blame themselves. If they have done the best to help themselves, they would be prepared to take advantage of opportunities when they come along. I don't want my son to be one of those people.

"You have to believe in me too, Son. As long as I live, I will do everything I can to make sure you'll have a chance. Nothing will hurt me more if I sacrifice everything in my life for you and your brothers, then you cannot do anything with your lives because you counted yourselves out a long time ago. Don't do that to me, all right?"

I had never seen my mother so serious before. She must have been very upset to give me such a long lecture. At the same time, my mother had succeeded in convincing me I could never give up. If I did, I would never be worthy of her sacrifice. I nodded and told her I wouldn't think of quitting again.

"Good. That is more like my son. By the way, don't let those kids who taunt you get to you. They don't know any better than you. If anything, they know much less than you. They may laugh at you now, but if you keep your head and continue to study and work hard, you will have the last laugh. You are smarter than most of them, so you don't have to care about what they say."

My mother's lecture jolted me out of my depression. She reminded me of something I'd read and thought I knew, but never put to practice: that I can be my own teacher. I was spoiled for so long with good teachers who could always answer my questions or who taught me things I did not know. Now, I didn't have that luxury anymore. I had to use my own brain and any textbooks I could lay my hands on to teach myself. My mother told me I could do it. She had often told me how my father and my Uncle Tấn taught themselves when they were young. By self-teaching, my father made it to engineering school. My uncle made it to medical school and became a successful army doctor. If my father and uncle could do it, then I had every reason to be able to do it.

From that day, I put all distractions out of my mind. The kids who taunted me didn't matter anymore. Neither did the teachers. I read all textbooks as much as I could whenever I had any free time. When I went up to the mountain to work on our land, I brought my books along to read and did homework during my rest time. In school, I spent break time to catch up on reading.

Many times, other kids tried to get me to join them. To avoid being anti-social, I joined them for a few minutes in bantering, then quietly slipped away to go back to reading. When kids like Phương made fun of my devotion to studying, I simply ignored them or went to the toilet to be left alone. I soon learned if I didn't react to their taunting, the kids would lose interest in me and turn their attention to something else.

Within one month, I finished reading all my lessons and did all the problems in the books for the entire year. Yet, there was still three months left in seventh grade. As my mother predicted, I was able to learn all lessons and do the problems just by reading the books. Whenever I ran into tough lessons I couldn't understand on first reading, I would read the materials over and over again several times. After some time, the pieces and then the whole of the lessons started to make sense. Day by day, my confidence grew as I proved to myself beyond a doubt that I could learn these materials without anyone's guidance.

Most textbooks we used were written by North Vietnamese as the school administrators made sure all materials we read were "politically correct" (i.e., that these books contained no anti–Communist ideas and paid sufficient praise and tribute to the Communist Party). I found math and science books written by North Vietnamese authors to be inferior compared to textbooks written by South Vietnamese authors. These "politically correct" books generally didn't explain the materials well nor covered them in great depth. Now, I understood why my North Vietnamese teachers were so bad.

Despite finishing my coursework for the year, I was still dissatisfied. I realized that my understanding of science subjects, mathematics, physics, and chemistry was still superficial because of the textbooks' poor quality. Knowing many South Vietnamese teachers still kept their old books, I approached them and asked to borrow these books. The teachers were happy to lend me their books. I became their favorite student as they knew how hard I studied.

Soon, I had enough good textbooks to read. I continued my methodical studying habit for the remainder of the year, plowing through all the books and trying to do every problem there was. I didn't find my study to be demanding nor hard on my life. Instead, learning became my escape from the harsh world I lived in.

The results of my hard work soon became evident to everyone. I routinely got the highest score on exams. There was no question asked in class that I could not answer. I became a thorn in the side of the North Vietnamese teachers. I regularly exposed their incompetence by asking questions they could not answer or pointing out their mistakes. In mathematics, physics, and chemistry, I tutored many classmates as they knew I could always solve any problems. In Vietnamese literature and history, I memorized the details of every lesson, poem, or literary passage. Soon, none of my teachers would let me answer their questions unless no one else in the class could.

As I emerged as the best student, many of my classmates started to come to me for help. I soon learned that I was not the only one who wanted to study. Many of my classmates also wanted to learn despite the distractions and indoctrination. Like I was before, they were frustrated because of our teachers' unwillingness or inability to teach. My performance convinced them I could help them to learn. No matter how much time it took, I never refused any friends who came to me for help.

Soon, I had a group of fifteen friends, who banded together to study.

Because I was always willing to help them, a strong camaraderie and mutual respect developed between us. One of the kids, Cường, became protective of me since I helped him so much. Cường was a strong, muscular kid who lived with his widowed mother. Cường's father was an ARVN soldier who died long ago during the Communist Eastern Offensive of 1972. Since he was the only child and his mother was always ill, he became his family's breadwinner. Outside school, Cường spent his time taking care of his sick mother and working as a cyclo driver. He had driven a cyclo since he was ten, as his father's compensation was not even enough to pay for his mother's medicine. Since he often had to fight other cyclo drivers for customers, Cường became a tough kid. He was fourteen, two years older than I was. Yet, he was already a streetwise kid who had been through hundred of fights.

Despite having to fight daily, Cường nevertheless was an honest and good-natured kid. He was also a filial son, who spent all his money taking care of his sick mother. He was not the brightest kid and started school later than other kids. Yet, he studied extremely hard. He performed reasonably well but became frustrated like the rest of us. Not minding that he was older, Cường was the first to come to me for help. For many days, I spent hours after school explaining and helping Cường to do his homework. Despite studying hard, Cường did not have a good foundation in the basics of science. Thus, it was difficult and time consuming for me to guide him. My patience earned his gratitude and appreciation. To repay my help, Cường assigned himself to be my bodyguard.

When other kids like Phương picked on me, Cường would jump in to stop them. Cường even beat up a few kids who were not smart enough to know when to stop. After a while, other rambunctious kids in class knew to leave us alone.

As the year came to a close, I felt much better about myself. Despite my family's continued dire situation, I no longer worried so much about the future. My attitude was that when the dreaded future came, I would deal with it. For now, I knew I had learned some invaluable lessons. I had become my own master by facing up to my problems instead of running away from them. Furthermore, I learned I was not alone in wanting to do what was right. The kids who came to me for help had shown me that they, too, wanted to make the best of their situation despite the adversity we all faced. When all of us were struggling to find our own direction, I walked forward on my own path and suddenly became the reluctant leader of other kids who also didn't want to quit. While many of these kids were not as fortunate as I would be later in life, I would always remember them for their friendship and courage.

# 7

# Cháu Ngoan Bác Hồ
# (Good Children of Uncle Ho)

Like other classes, our sub-branch of the Ho Chi Minh Avant Garde Youth met once a week to conduct several activities. The fun activities included games, camping trips, learning Morse code and other signaling techniques. The torturous activities were characteristic of a Communist organization. We learned and sang "revolutionary" songs at every meeting, spent days to clean up school, and went on labor camps to plant trees or to build dams. The most hated activity was studying Communist ideology in every session. The fun activities kept us interested in attending the weekly meeting, despite our dislike of working and studying ideology.

When my seventh-grade school year ended in June '76, we were told that the Youth not only would continue the meetings in the summer, but also had even more activities planned. We had more free time in the summer, and the Youth intended to take full advantage of it.

On the last day of school, Vân, our handler, told us with a straight face that she looked forward to having a great summer with our class. This summer would be a great opportunity for us to show that we were exemplary students, deserving to be "Cháu Ngoan Bác Hồ" (good children of Uncle Ho).

It was the first time we heard the expression. By now, we all knew by heart Ho was supposed to be treated as a demigod. Yet, none of us knew what "Cháu Ngoan Bác Hồ" was and why we were supposed to be it. When we asked what it means, Vân smoothly replied that "Cháu Ngoan Bác Hồ" was an award given by the Youth to all of its members who had demonstrated outstanding character, achievement, and closely followed the motto "Học tập tốt, Lao động tốt" (Study well, Labor hard). Laying her bait, Vân went on to tell us that it was a very prestigious award, perhaps the most prestigious award any one of us could win. To win it, we had to participate in all activities of the Youth, particularly the public work activities. Then, we must have good knowledge of the party's history, of socialism, and the life of Uncle Ho. At the end of the summer, Vân would nominate those of us whom she thought deserved the award to the Youth Advisory Committee. The committee would examine the record of the nominees and decide who got it.

When I asked what the award was good for, Vân seized the opportunity to turn her pitch up a notch. The award would be a big plus for our academic record, particularly for those of us who didn't have "revolutionary" family background. Having the award could improve our chances of getting admitted to high school. Between two students who had identical test scores and only one could be admitted, the one who had the "Cháu Ngoan Bác Hồ" award would definitely be chosen over the one who didn't.

We looked at each other. Vân just told us a new version of the "học tài thi lý lịch" (study with talents, take exam with background) story. She knew as well as we did that none of us had "revolutionary background." If she was telling the truth, this "Cháu Ngoan Bác Hồ" award could improve our chances. We didn't know how much faith to put into this vague promise, but at least it offered us a ray of hope.

Vân went on to tell us about the party plenum to be held at the end of the year. The plenum, the third in the party's 46-year history, was "a momentous event in our country's history." It would set the course for our country's economic development and "guide Vietnam quickly, boldly, and firmly on the road to socialism."

We all looked at each other again, wondering what the Communist Party Third Plenum had to do with us. For months, we had heard the propaganda and hoopla on the plenum which was scheduled for December 1976 in Hanoi. Vân was not telling us anything we didn't know.

"What do they do at the party plenum? What does it have to do with us?" Chiêm asked impatiently. The questions were another mistake. They set Vân off on a long monologue about Vietnam's progress toward socialism. "The party plenum was the occasion for our country's leaders to get together to develop the strategies to take Vietnam to socialism firmly and quickly. Out of the plenum, we will see two five-year plans spanning the next ten years. These five-year plans will be the key to take our country from devastation and poverty to being an advanced, prosperous, and strong socialist nation. The party plenum has a lot to do with each of us. Our country is devastated from our twenty-year war to liberate South Vietnam from the American Imperialists and their South Vietnamese lackeys. Now, we have the monumental task of rebuilding our country and bringing prosperity to every citizen of Vietnam, the goal for which so much blood of our people has been spilled. To do this would require the energy and dedication of every Vietnamese, old and young alike. As the elite organization for Vietnam's children, the Youth will mobilize its members to make a strong contribution to the goal of building socialism in our country, following the lead and direction of the party. We will have the honor and the responsibility to make our contribution."

Vân stopped briefly to catch her breath from her monologue, then continued. "Our country is suffering shortages in many raw materials such as paper, steel, or plastics. When the American imperialists fled in 1975, they destroyed many factories or rendered them inoperable. We do not have enough spare parts to repair many of the machines and equipment. We also cannot afford to buy the raw materials from other nations. To solve this raw materials shortage, the Youth will launch the Kế Hoạch Nhỏ (Small Plan) program this summer. The launching of the plan will also be a salutation to the third party plenum. It is a symbol of the Youth's dedication and commitment to following the party's lead."

We were all confused. Ms. Vân was on a roll with her propaganda dissertation again. Yet, she still hadn't told us what the "Kế Hoạch Nhỏ" program was. What were we supposed to do with this plan? Unable to contain my impatience, I raised my hand to ask, "What is the "Kế Hoạch Nhỏ" program? What do we have to do with it?"

"The 'Kế Hoạch Nhỏ' program is a plan to collect and recycle the materials our country needs right now," Vân replied. "These materials are paper, steel, and plastic. Each branch of the Youth in every city will be given a quota of materials to collect. Once you have collected sufficient quantity of these materials, they will be transported to recycling factories. The recycling factories will turn them into raw materials for use in our industries. With the work and dedication of every member of the Youth, we can contribute to the rebuilding for our country by collecting and recycling used materials. To make the program work, we need everyone to contribute. If each member can collect a few kilograms of paper, or steel, iron, or plastics, imagine how much the millions of Youth members can get."

Thái interrupted Vân's monologue to ask how we would find the materials. Shrugging, Vân told us that with our "ingenuity" it would not be that hard. We could start by collecting the papers and plastic at home. Trash landfills would be good places to look, too.

We remained silent, trying to digest what the Youth advisor was telling us. Vân didn't wait for long before concluding the meeting. Our enrollment in the scavenging army of the Socialist Republic of Vietnam had just started.

On the ride home, Thái and I thrashed around the topic of the "Cháu Ngoan Bác Hồ" award. With visions of being able to get into high school and college in my head, I thought it might be worth it to win the award. We knew Vân was only a messenger, telling us what the party told her. The only question remaining was whether we could trust this vague promise that the award would count for something. The Communist Party had lied and deceived our people for so long. If they lied to us again, we wouldn't be surprised.

Yet, we slowly agreed that it might not be bad to win the award. We already spent a fair amount of time for the Youth's activities. Working a little harder was not going to cost us much except for our time in the summer. We already studied too hard not to try to do everything we could to get into high school. It was a long shot, but, but it was the only shot we got.

I was concerned what our classmates would think of us if we went for the award. Laughing, Thái told me the award was nothing more than a title. The award didn't mean we wanted to be a "model" young Communist. It only meant we wanted to do everything we could to improve our chances. Even Diệu and Vân were reciting the party propaganda and exhorting us to behave like good young Communists because they wanted to have a job. They just tried to survive like everyone else in this country. They may be kissing the Commie's ass, but at least they had power over us. As for the rest of the kids, why should we care? Those who knew us knew even if Ho Chi Minh were to come back to life and beg us to join his party, we wouldn't. The rest were just pathetic losers and hypocrites. They had given up and they were jealous of anyone who still didn't want to quit. We didn't have to justify our actions to every hypocrite out there.

Thái's reassurance made me feel much better. As long as we were not stealing, cheating, or stepping over other people, we didn't have to worry about what others thought. Our attention then turned to planning how we would find the scrap paper, steel or plastics to meet our quota. Again, Thái had a ready answer. He knew just about every trash dump, landfill, and junkyard there was in Vũng Tàu, having dug for anything he could scavenge and sell. If I was not afraid of filthy, stinky trash fields, we wouldn't have any problem meeting our quota.

On the following Saturday, Vân told us the collection quota for our sub-branch: 100 kilograms of paper and one ton of iron or steel. Any plastics we could collect would be a bonus. Since there were thirty-two kids in our sub-branch, each would have to collect 3 kilograms of paper and over 30 kilograms of iron. The quota per head didn't seem unreasonable until we realized that we had to compete with thousands of other kids in the city who had the same quota to fill. In addition, we had to compete with hundreds of other people who scavenged trash dumps for a living.

Despite the seemingly high quota for our sub-branch, no one raised any objections. Many kids didn't care about the award since they considered it to be nothing more than bait. If they didn't fill their quota, no one would or could do anything to them anyway. Those of us who wanted to win the award didn't care to object either. We figured we only had to compete against other kids in our sub-branch and school. As long as we did better than most of them, we were golden. Meeting the quota wasn't our concern. Doing better than other kids was the main goal.

For the whole summer, Thái and I scavenged for paper and iron at every trash dump and junkyard in Vũng Tàu. Thái wasn't exaggerating when he said he knew all the dump sites in the city. While I worked on the land to help my mother, Thái did other menial jobs, including scavenging trash, to help his mother.

Thái's background was similar to mine. His parents were also North Vietnamese who fled to the South in 1954, when the Communists took control of the North. Thái's father was a captain in the Army of the Republic of Vietnam (ARVN), specializing in electronics equipment and communication. In December 1974, his father was sent to the United States for further training, and was stranded in America when South Vietnam fell. Back in Vietnam, Thái's family was living in an army barrack in Saigon. After South Vietnam collapsed, Thái's family was kicked out of the barrack. Thus, just like my family, his family had to find a new place to live.

Fortunately, Thái's paternal grandmother owned a house in Vũng Tàu and took his family in. Thái's family was also lucky enough to bring most of their valuables out of the barrack. For the first few months, they lived by gradually selling off their valuables. Thái's mother, who didn't work before the fall of South Vietnam, now had to find some way to make money and support the family. She realized that her family could not live by selling off their valuables forever. She ended up doing many different odd jobs, including smuggling food products between Saigon, Vũng Tàu, and the western provinces of South Vietnam.

Thái's mother barely made enough money to buy food for the family. Thus, Thái and his siblings had to find other ways to help out their mother. Thái tried several different ways of making money. First, he spent months scavenging every trash site in Vũng Tàu, trying to find anything he could clean up and resell. That was how he knew the locations of these sites. However, he couldn't make much since there was stiff competition from hundreds of other kids doing the same thing to help out their families. Besides, it was getting much harder to find anything that could be reused. As the economic conditions became harsher, people no longer threw away anything that still could be used. When tools or appliances broke down and could not be fixed, people would strip them down to sell as parts.

Giving up on scavenging the trash dumps, Thái turned to scavenging fishing boats. Every afternoon, he went to the beach, waiting for fishing boats to return from the sea. When the boats came ashore, he got on board to help the fishermen pack and wash their catches. In return for his service, the fishermen allowed Thái to collect small fish they couldn't sell for good prices in the market. The work was easier than scavenging the trash dumps, and Thái had fish to bring home to feed his family every day.

After a while, Thái figured that scavenging the fishing boats wasn't enough. He bought a thermal container and used it to peddle ice cream sticks to North Vietnamese Army (NVA) soldiers. This venture turned out to be a huge success. Thái quit scavenging fishing boats to switch to peddling ice cream sticks. It turned out many NVA soldiers had an insatiable appetite for ice cream. Some soldiers might buy and eat as many as fifty ice cream sticks a day. Thái theorized that these soldiers must have gone on a sweet binge to make up for their years of deprivation, living and fighting in the jungles. Whatever the reason might be, Thái was happy for his booming and profitable business. Since the soldiers didn't have very much money to pay for the ice cream, they resorted to bartering. The soldiers stole parts of appliances and machinery in their barracks, uniforms, or military food rations, and traded these products with Thái for ice cream sticks. Thái in turn sold this contraband on the black market for huge profits. By trading ice cream sticks for contraband, he made enough to help out his mother, and still had money left over to reward himself with a guitar.

Because of our diligence, we were able to collect more paper and scrap metal than any other kids in our school. Most of the paper we collected was carton boxes. There was little newspaper or writing paper we could find anywhere, as there were many other people who scavenged the same papers to sell in the market. The shortage of finer papers didn't bother us, as the Ho Chi Minh Youth only asked the kids to collect paper but didn't specify what types of paper it preferred. Carton boxes were much easier for us to find and weighed much more than other types of paper. Thus, we easily exceeded our quota.

Our enthusiastic participation in the "Kế Hoạch Nhỏ" program caused both of us to run into trouble with our families. Our mothers chided us many times for doing what they called "Ăn cơm nhà, vác ngà voi" (meaning: We eat the rice of the family, but go out and do other people's work). They wanted us to spend more time working to help out our families. Despite our explanation that we were working to better our chances of getting into high school, our mothers still thought we were foolish to believe the Communists' empty promises. They thought the Youth was just using the nebulous "Cháu Ngoan Bác Hồ" award to get naïve kids like us to do its dirty work. The award would not improve our chances in any way. Further, they thought we were stupid to frequent dump sites, as these areas could be very dangerous.

Our mothers' admonitions got us to work harder at home, but didn't stop us from scavenging. Being young and stubborn, we thought our mothers were too cautious and suspicious of the Communist government. They didn't know we had other reasons for participating actively in the program. We enjoyed the excitement of treasure hunting. We were kids, and we still loved to play. Going out with friends to scavenge was a form of play for us. It was not until a year later we realized that our mothers had more wisdom than we gave them credit for.

Besides scavenging, we also participated actively in other activities of the Youth: camping and doing public work projects such as building dams, planting trees, or cleaning up streets. Throughout the summer, we also represented our sub-branch in numerous "Đố Vui Để Học" (trivia pursuit) competitions against other Youth sub-branches in our school and others. By the end of the summer, I had become the undisputed "Đố Vui Để Học" champion in our school.

I read and memorized every book about the Communist Party and Ho Chi Minh, and all of the "revolutionary" literature that was given to me. Despite how well I had learned these materials, I knew most of these "facts" were fabricated or distorted. To keep myself interested in the propagandistic materials, I constantly tried to sort out in my mind which of these "facts" were true and which were slanted or fabricated. The constant exercise of "cataloguing" information gradually helped me to become a critical reader. Surprisingly, I found myself liking many of the "revolutionary" literary works. Stripping away the ever-present propaganda and praises for the party and Ho Chi Minh, I frequently found in these works the simple, patriotic ideals that had driven so many of my countrymen, both North and South Vietnamese, to fight and die: the desire to win our country's independence, freedom from foreign domination, and the yearning for peace. I also realized these simple ideals were manipulated and colored by all sides in the war to suit their purposes. Tired of the intense indoctrination I had received, I automatically blocked out the propaganda and just simply enjoyed the beautiful verses that eloquently described the simple dream of my people.

Thái and I easily won the "Cháu Ngoan Bác Hồ" award at the end of the summer. However, we learned a bitter lesson in the process. Many other kids also won the award despite not working as hard as we did. While we were glad to win, we started to come down to earth and realize our mothers might be more right than we thought. Other kids got it because their family backgrounds were much less "anti-revolutionary" than ours. Furthermore, the number given out was so many that the award lost its significance. Two out of three kids in every sub-branch won the award. Almost everyone was a "Cháu Ngoan Bác Hồ." Thus, the award would not be much of a point of distinction to better our chances of getting into high school.

The realization of our own naïveté taught us an important lesson. We just relearned for ourselves what our parents had learned long ago: be wary of any promises made by a Communist. Because we did not listen to our mothers, we expended a great deal of energy and time to learn the lesson for ourselves. While we often chided ourselves for our own stupidity, we also knew the lesson we had learned would stay with us for a long, long time.

The "Kế Hoạch Nhỏ" program continued from the summer of 1976 to through the school year 76-77. Learning our lessons, Thái and I didn't participate as much as we did in the summer. However, we still frequented the trash dumps occasionally when pressed to meet our collection quota.

One day my mother asked me if I still went to the trash dump after she returned from a trip to Saigon. Though uncomfortable, I told my mother that I still occasionally did. It was one of the few things about which I didn't listen to her as I should have.

Shaking her head, my mother told me to stop scavenging immediately. I might just get killed collecting that junk for the Commies. When she was in Saigon, Uncle Tin told her about the tragedy of a kid in his neighborhood. The kid was about my age, and also a member of the Youth. Like me, he went to trash dumps to collect paper and scrap metal for the Youth. One day, he stepped on a mine or a grenade in one of these trash dumps and was blown to pieces. The Youth leaders then proclaimed the kid to be a "hero" and encouraged other kids to follow this kid's example to continue giving five hundred percent dedication to the Youth and all of its stupid, misguided programs. The kid's family was left with a dead child, all the expenses for his funeral, and an empty "hero" title. What a good deal for a dead son, bloody child murderers!

My mother's story shocked me and sent a chill down to my spine. My mother was right. Because of our youthful enthusiasm and excitement, Thái and I were oblivious to the signs of danger we'd seen when scavenging. We had occasionally seen rifles, guns, and bullets at the trash dumps. We even discussed where they came from and concluded these weapons must have been tossed there by ARVN soldiers when South Vietnam fell a year ago. Yet, the thought that if the soldiers had tossed their guns and ammunition there then they could also have left explosives as well never crossed our minds. My mother's story made me realize how lucky we were. We had yet to step on any mines or grenades, but I certainly did not want to push my luck any further.

Thinking about it made me sweat all over. I wiped the sweat off my brow and asked my mother why we never heard of the incident. Of course the Youth leaders would keep the story under close wraps, my mother shrugged. If they let it out, the kids would be scared and stop collecting junk for them. Then their program wouldn't be successful and they wouldn't meet their quota. If they couldn't meet their quota, they wouldn't get admitted to their precious Communist Party. Of course, they wouldn't care if the kids stepped on a mine and got blown to pieces. Their mothers cared!

My mother's story ended my days of scavenging for the Youth. Before leaving to start another day of selling in the Vũng Tàu market, my mother left me with the message that I had failed to heed before: "Don't ever do anything more for those Commies than you have to! You won't get anywhere with them."

# 8

# The New Kids in School

My eighth-grade year started out the same way my seventh-grade year ended: plenty of political indoctrination, uninspired teachers, and more pranks pulled by increasingly disillusioned and restless kids. Then, we had two new students from North Vietnam.

When the two North Vietnamese, Nam and Tuấn, showed up the first day, we didn't know what to make of their presence. Both were sons of North Vietnamese Communist Party cadres who moved south to take up administrative posts.

By 1976, the Communist Party had dropped all pretenses about the National Liberation Front and the Provisional Revolutionary Government. These two organizations, mentioned so frequently during the Vietnam War as representing the Vietnamese people in the fight against the Americans and the South Vietnamese government, were now distant memories. Members of these organizations were retired, sent to re-education camps, or given ceremonial posts. To bring South Vietnam under the central control of the Communist Party, the government sent North Vietnamese Party cadres south to take up all powerful administrative posts. Nam's and Tuấn's fathers were part of this corps of cadres sent to the South.

My classmates received the North Vietnamese with extreme suspicion and caution. In the first few days, nobody talked to them. Nam and Tuấn didn't even talk to each other. They could sense the hostility from every other kid toward them. They didn't like the hostility but also didn't want to exacerbate it. Thus, just keeping to themselves was their best defense for the moment.

For our part, we gathered in groups and speculated why they were here. Cường, the cyclo driver, blurted out that these kids were sent to spy on us. Chiêm and Cải had the same apprehension. Since their fathers were party cadres, Chiêm reasoned, these North Vietnamese kids must be hard-core Communists. Since the Communists never trusted the southerners, these kids were sent in to keep a close eye on us. We had to watch what we said when the North Vietnamese were around.

Only Thái and I gave the northern kids the benefit of the doubt. Since all other classes had at least two or three students from North Vietnam, Thái countered, if the two kids in our class were spies, then all other North Vietnamese kids were spies, too. What kind of intelligence could these spies gather on a bunch of impoverished school kids?

For my part, I found it hard to believe that these two shy North Vietnamese could be spies sent to observe us. Looking like fish out of water, they appeared as scared of us as we were of them. If they were spies, then they must have been trained to do so since nine or ten. It was just a little beyond my imagination.

Thái and I couldn't convince our friends to be less paranoid. Not being like us, the North Vietnamese would report to Diệu if they saw us pull the pranks or sing rebellious songs again. If Thái and I wanted to befriend the northern kids, Chiêm shrugged, we did so at our own risk. There was no way he or the other kids would touch those Commies. Despite not being as suspicious as my friends, I still had a nagging fear in the back of my mind that these kids from North Vietnam, unlike us, would be willing to inform on their classmates.

Most of my classmates also came to the same conclusion. The fear of being told on kept us from singing songs with revised, rebellious lyrics for the first two weeks. The peace, however, was soon shattered when some of the kids finally decided to defy even the presence of the two North Vietnamese "spies."

By the second week of school, we got used to seeing the North Vietnamese. No southern kids had spoken to either one yet. However, we no longer gave them as many hostile and suspicious stares as we did in the first two weeks.

My classmates became restless as we had not yet pulled any pranks since school began. Finally, some kids decided to push their luck. They wanted to test if the North Vietnamese students were really "spies" sent to observe us. Through the underground circulation in class, they passed out sheets with revised lyrics for two songs, "Vietnam Train" and "Last Night I Dreamed of Uncle Ho," to everyone except the North Vietnamese. The sheets also tell everyone the plan to sing these songs the next day.

The next day of class started out innocently enough. We began by singing the original lyrics of the song "Last Night I Dreamed of Uncle Ho":

Đêm qua em mơ gặp Bác Hồ
Râu bác dài tóc Bác bạc phơ
Em sung sướng em hôn má Bác
Bác mỉm cười Bác bảo em ngoan
Bác mỉm cười Bác bảo em ngoan.

(Last night I dreamed of Uncle Ho
His beard is long, his hair is so white
I'm so glad, I kissed his cheek
Uncle Ho smiled and told me I'm a good kid
Uncle Ho smiled and told me I'm a good kid.)

Learning from a year of experience, we knew Diệu would respond very quickly if he heard us singing songs with revised, rebellious lyrics. To maintain the element of surprise, we switched to the next song, "Vietnam Train," without changing the lyrics yet:

Năm xưa anh phá núi, em mở đường
Trên đỉnh Trường Sơn đồi núi chập chùng
Năm nay cũng những bàn tay
Lấp hố bom xây cuộc sống tự hào
Nào bao cô gái tự hào
Nào những chàng trai,
Tuổi thanh niên sức như Phù Đổng
Cháu con của Bác Hồ
Đi lập đường tàu thống nhất quê hương
Bạn hỡi đã bao ngày bao đêm gian lao
Lòng sung sướng bồi hồi
Đường tàu ta nối Nam vào Bắc
Tàu Việt Nam, đi nối tình quê hương
Bạn hỡi tất cả vì tương lai mai sau
Vì quê mẹ đẹp giàu
Đường tàu ta nối Nam vào Bắc
Tàu Việt Nam, nối lại đất anh hùng.

(Year ago, I blasted the mountain, you opened the road,
On the vast Truong Son mountain range.
This year, with these same hands,
We covered the bomb craters, and build our new, proud lives.

Hail to all the proud young women,
Hail to all the proud young men,
In their youthful age, with the strength of Phù Đổng*
Children of Uncle Ho,
Who are going to build the rail tracks to unite our country.
My friend, so many days and nights of hard work we spent
We felt so happy and honored.
Our train will connect North and South.
The Vietnam train is going to connect the love of our country.
My friends, we'll do everything for our future.
For a beautiful, prosperous mother land.
Our train will connect North and South.
The Vietnam train is going to reconnect this heroic land.

*Phù Đổng is a legendary Vietnamese hero, who grew from a dumb three-year-old to become a heaven-sent warrior. He defeated the invasion of Vietnam by the Chinese in the first century A.D., then flew up to heaven afterwards.

Nam and Tuấn, the North Vietnamese students, knew these songs well and were singing them along with us. They had no idea what would happen next. Then, suddenly, all other kids started singing the song "Last Night I Dreamed of Uncle Ho" again with the revised lyrics:

Đêm qua em mơ gặp Bác Hồ
Ngồi một mình Bác khóc hu hu
Em thắc mắc em sang hỏi Bác
Bác trả lời "Địa ngục không cơm"
Bác trả lời "Bụng bác đói meo."

(Last night I dreamed of Uncle Ho
Sitting alone, Uncle Ho was crying
I was so curious, I asked him why
Uncle Ho answered: "There is no rice in hell"
Uncle Ho answered: "I am hungry too.")

Sitting in the last row, I, Thái, and Chiêm joined other kids in screaming at the top of our lungs. We were singing and watching closely the reaction of Nam and Tuấn, who sat in the first row. The arrangement for these two boys to sit in the front row was not a coincidence. On the first day of class, everyone tried to get a seat behind Nam and Tuấn. As a result, they were forced to sit in the front row. Everyone wanted to make it as difficult as possible for them to observe his actions, if indeed they turned out to be Communist spies.

We could tell that Nam and Tuấn were horrified when they heard us singing the revised lyrics. They instinctively turned around to see who were singing. What they saw was sixty hostile pairs of eyes staring at them and sixty mouths roaring loudly. Intimidated, they immediately turned back and kept quiet.

Finishing the song "Last Night I Dreamed of Uncle Ho," we immediately switched to singing a revised "Vietnam Train":

Năm xưa anh bán cá, em bán gạo
Ngồi kế cạnh nhau ở chợ Vũng Tàu
Năm nay ta dắt dìu nhau
Bán hết ruộng nương, đi tìm đường vượt biên
Cùng nhau ra biển, chạy dài
Chạy khỏi Việt Nam
Tìm tự do ở phương trời thẳm
Kiếm cơm ăn áo mặc
Kiếm một cuộc đời hạnh phúc yên vui
Bạn hỡi đã lâu rồi chiến tranh điêu linh
Người dân được những gì
Một Việt Nam nát tan nghèo đói
Người Việt Nam thiếu áo mặc cơm ăn
Bạn hỡi trông đợi gì tương lai mai sau
Một quê mẹ đẹp giàu
Một ước mơ không bao giờ đến
Một ngày mai, không thấy ánh mặt trời.

(Year ago, I sold fish, you sold rice,
Sitting next to each other in the Vũng Tàu market.
This year, we lead each other,
Selling all our properties, finding a way to escape.
Together, we run to the sea to escape,
Escape from Vietnam,
To find freedom in the distant horizon.
To find food to eat and clothes to wear.
To find a peaceful and happy life.
My friend, so many years of war have passed
What did the Vietnamese people get?
A devastated Vietnam, mired in poverty,
And the Vietnamese people, desperately lacking food and clothes.

My friend, what can we expect of our future?
A beautiful, prosperous motherland?
A dream that will never come.
A tomorrow without the sun's light.)

By the time we finished singing "Vietnam Train," Diệu was running into our class. He was really angry. The relatively quiet past weeks of school had given him some reason to believe our class had curbed its "anti-revolutionary" attitude. The incident today obviously had shattered that belief. However, this time he had some hope to catch the elusive culprits in our class with the help of the North Vietnamese.

As usual, Diệu started out by asking the kids who sat in the front row and back row if they knew who started the singing. As usual, all South Vietnamese kids denied any knowledge of singing the "rebellious" lyrics or who started it. Then, Diệu turned to Nam and asked if he knew who started the prank and who participated in it.

All eyes stared at Nam in anticipation. All the kids were really nervous now. We had no idea how Nam was going to answer Diệu's question. Whatever his answer was and whomever he was going to point to, Diệu was more likely to believe him than the words of anyone else in the class. Even Nam was feeling the tension in the room. He looked around and again saw the sixty blank stares focusing on him.

"No, no, sir. I...I didn't sing those lyrics," he stuttered. "I..I... had no idea what they were singing. I never heard songs like that before. I sat in the front row so I didn't see the rest of the class. I didn't know who started it and who sang it, sir. I thought the whole class was doing it."

Diệu asked Nam again 'If you don't know who started it, can you point to me who was singing it the loudest here?"

"No, I don't know," Nam shook his head. "Everyone was loud."

Frustrated, Diệu turned to Tuấn and asked the same questions. Like Nam, Tuấn was feeling the tension in the room. Nervous, he kept his head down and gave the same answer: He didn't know who started it and who sang the loudest.

Diệu was getting really upset. His ace in the hole, the North Vietnamese, didn't respond as he wanted. He looked at them and raised his voice. "I thought you two were supposed to be model, good children of Uncle Ho. As such, you have to maintain vigilance against 'anti-revolutionary' attitudes in your classmates. If they are not enlightened, your job is to help them achieve better political understanding. If you can't do that, you can tell me or other teachers so that we could help them. Now, not only couldn't you influence any of them, you are covering up for them so that they would do it again in the future. Is this the behavior of 'Cháu Ngoan Bác Hồ' (Good Children of Uncle Ho)?"

Nam and Tuấn looked at each other and at Diệu again, not knowing what to say. Finally, Nam mustered enough courage to say that they were telling him the truth. Sitting in the front row, they couldn't possibly see who did it in the back. All they knew was that it appeared everyone was doing it.

Shaking his head angrily, Diệu ordered the northern kids to pack up their books and moved to the back row. From now on, Diệu said, he expected the northern kids to keep an eye on "anti-revolutionary elements" in our class and prevent today's incident from happening again.

Nam and Tuấn looked at each other again, clearly uncomfortable of being assigned to the unenviable task of policing the other sixty kids who had yet to show any sign of friendliness toward them. They didn't know what to say. Reluctantly, they picked up their books and did as they were told. Chiêm and Cải had to exchange places with Nam and Tuấn. Suddenly, Thái and I found ourselves sitting next to the two North Vietnamese. Thái and I winked at each other, signaling to ourselves we had to watch what we said now.

In his now-familiar self-important way, Diệu passed out his punishment. All the kids, with the exception of the North Vietnamese, were to kneel for four hours until class ended. Hường, our class head, stood up to protest vehemently. It wasn't fair. Why were Nam and Tuấn excluded from the punishment? How could Diệu assume that all of us did it, but not these two? How come the innocents among us were punished, too? Was it because the northerners were deemed to be more trustworthy than us southerners?

Sitting in the back row, Thái and I gave each other a big thumbs-up, signaling our satisfaction with Hường's question. His willingness to speak out for us was a big reason why he was elected class head again this year. He knew how to use his "revolutionary" background to his advantage. He knew he could always challenge Diệu without fearing retribution.

Diệu's face reddened at Hường's sharp question, but he quickly recovered. "Nonsense," Diệu shouted. Nam and Tuấn were new and couldn't possibly be a party to these "anti-revolutionary" acts. The rest of us had pulled these tricks a hundred times and were stubborn mules to cover for each other. As for the northern kids, if they couldn't point out the culprits the next time we pulled this prank again, they would be punished along with the class.

Finishing his tirade, Diệu turned to exit from the class. As Diệu walked past the front row, he couldn't see Chiêm taking out a pen and flicking it at his back, leaving several blotches of ink on the previously clean white shirt. Chiêm did it so quickly and quietly that Diệu didn't know his shirt was ruined. We all saw what happened and tried hard to kept quiet. Once Diệu had gone, the kids broke out in uproarious laughter. Chiêm had taken revenge for us. Better yet, Diệu wouldn't even know how the ink got on his shirt. His words had come back to bite him soon enough. Even he didn't keep a good-enough "vigilance" against the "anti-revolutionary" devils of our class.

As we knelt on our chairs, we winked at each other happily. We expected this punishment as soon as Diệu walked in. Hường gave it a valiant try, but we all knew it wouldn't be enough. Hường's purpose for protesting Diệu's decision was not to stop the punishment, but to further infuriate him.

Until noon, we knelt on the floor while going through the four classes in the day. This change was a big improvement from last year, when the teachers were not allowed to teach our class while we were being punished. The change was a result of Diệu's realization of the futility of his punishment. Then he was hearing more bitter complaints from the students' parents. Ever a pragmatic person, Diệu stopped suspending our class or making us miss lectures to keep his "bad guy" reputation from growing any further.

For the rest of the day, Thái and I kept quiet. We didn't speak a word to each other or to the two North Vietnamese kids who sat next to us. I kept thinking back to Diệu's "interrogation" of these kids. My fear that they were "Communist spies" sent to observe us was now fading fast. They saw all of us who were singing the "rebellious songs," yet they didn't finger anyone. Even if they told on the wrong person, their words would have had more credibility than the words from any one of us. They had every reason to find a scapegoat for Diệu since they hadn't received a friendly word from anyone. Yet, they didn't. Instead, they appeared extremely uncomfortable when asked to finger the culprits. Maybe they were not as bad as we thought after all.

When the last class ended, I turned to the North Vietnamese and thanked them for what they did today.

Nam was startled. He stared at me before replying, "You are the first to say anything to me. What do you thank me for? I didn't do anything for you."

"I am not thanking you for anything you did for me," I shook my head. "I thank you for not fingering anybody to Diệu. You could easily do that, but you didn't. If you named anybody, he would be kicked out of school permanently. I am glad you didn't do it."

"Why did you even thank us for that?" Tuấn spoke for the first time. "We were telling him the truth. All of you were singing and we saw it. He was looking for a few persons, not the whole class. We don't have any reason to point out any one of you, and not the whole class. It wouldn't be fair."

Tuấn's words touched off a nerve in my head. I never thought I would hear the word "fair" in its true sense from a "Commie" like Tuấn or Nam. Was I wrong in my prejudice against them simply because they were northerners? For the first time, I thought there was some evidence that my perception of "Commie" might not be all correct. Deep in my own thoughts, I didn't respond to Tuấn. Standing next to me, Thái jumped in "Hey, let's go. Why don't we go get our bikes and talk at the same time, eh?"

The northerners quickly agreed. I was thankful for Thái's quick thinking. Leaving the class reduced the chance of other kids seeing us talking to these northern kids. My classmates were still very suspicious of the "Commie" kids. If they saw us talking to Nam and Tuấn for long, they would conclude that we were trying to kiss ass with the northerners. It would be so easy for them to put the hat of "traitors" or "wind sniffers" on us, regardless of what the truth might be. I was not afraid of what kind of hats they might put on my head, but there was no reason to tick them off unless we couldn't avoid it.

Walking to our bicycles, Thái said, "Hey, for whatever reason you did it, we are thankful. You guys are not as bad as we thought."

"Bad! What do you think we are?" Nam gave Thái a puzzled look. "Why do you think we are bad? What have we done? Jeez, if anything, I thought that all of you are bad. No one except you two ever says anything to us. Everybody looks like they want to beat us up or have our heads for dinner. Why?"

Realizing his mistake, Thái backpedaled, "No, I am sorry. I didn't mean to say 'bad.' I meant you guys are not as different from us as we thought. Hey, the guys don't talk to you because they don't know what to make of you. We don't know what to make of you either. You look different from us. Your clothes look funny. Your accent sounds funny. And your fathers are party members. We don't know how you think. Hey, if any of the guys say anything to you, who knows if you may turn around and use it against them later."

Nam and Tuấn looked at each other's clothes: white short sleeve shirt, black pants, and rubber sandals. They gave us a blank, uncomprehending look.

"What is so funny about our clothes and our accent?" Nam asked. "Everyone in the North wears the same clothes we do. Our accent is not funny. I thought your accent is funny."

"Hey, that is exactly the point," I said. "Your clothes look funny because all of you northern people wear the same clothes. You all look alike. You even walk alike. Don't you northerners have any sense of individuality?"

"What is so funny about wearing the same clothes?" Tuấn responded. "We all wear the same clothes because we got them from the same government stores. Why don't you think that your clothes are funny? Look at you. None of you dressed alike. Even the two of you don't even wear clean clothes to school."

"Hey, let's not argue any more, OK?" Thái raised his voice. "We want to thank you, not to get into an argument with you over our differences. We can save that for another day. We'll talk to you guys later."

With that last statement, Thái and I rode off. Before we did, Nam said, "Thanks for talking to us. Oh, would you tell other guys to please not sing those songs any more. We don't want to accuse anybody, but we do not have any choice the next time you do it. Don't put us in a tough spot."

"We'll tell them," Thái and I responded in unison.

Our classmates got the message. They stopped singing the outrageously modified songs but found other ways to frustrate school administrators. There were days that despite all the exhortations from Vân, none of the kids would sing, claiming throat problems. There were days when they sang loudly, yelling at the top of their lungs and emphasizing words in the lyrics that coincided with the parents' names of any kids in class. These pranks bothered Diệu much less since they were not exactly "anti-revolutionary." Still, the pranks caused him and Vân just as much headache. They could not justify punishing our class harshly any more. Thus, they watched helplessly as the students in our class did not become any more "politically enlightened."

With the exception of cursory greetings, Thái and I did not speak again to the North Vietnamese for two weeks. Other classmates had also become less hostile and even occasionally said hello to them. Yet, none approached Nam and Tuấn to start a conversation.

We still did not know how to talk to them without getting ourselves into an argument. While our suspicion that they were "Communist spies" had lessened dramatically, we still were not sure if we could trust them. While Nam and Tuấn appeared to be polite kids and probably could make good friends for us to have, our differences were too great. For the moment, we did not know how to deal with them. Besides, I had too much work to do. I couldn't afford to care about them.

Nam and Tuấn appeared to be the exceptions to the many North Vietnamese kids who came to our school. Talking to other kids in classes 8A2 and 8A1, we found out they did not have as good of an impression of their northern classmates as we had of ours. The students in 8A2 and 8A1 were not anywhere near as hostile toward the northern students as we were. As a result, they treated their North Vietnamese classmates much better than we treated Nam and Tuấn. They didn't have as much suspicion that these kids were "Communist spies." Yet, after a short period of interaction, many kids in 8A1 and 8A2, with the exception of a few who liked to ingratiate themselves with the northerners, refused to be anywhere close to these North Vietnamese students. They told us the North Vietnamese were rude and ignorant idiots. The North Vietnamese students often bragged about themselves and pretended to know things they had no idea of. They also spoke incessantly about the party and paid lip service to Communism. After a while, it was easy for others to see through their ignorance. When the initial curiosity about the North Vietnamese wore off, other kids didn't find it worth their time to get near them.

What I heard made me much less interested in talking to Nam and again. Ignoring the North Vietnamese, I continued to focus on teaching myself. I didn't know then my focus on studying soon got the North Vietnamese students interested in me.

Nam and Tuấn kept their word. Despite seeing and knowing who pulled the numerous pranks in our class, they kept quiet. They did not make any attempts to talk to others, but tried to start a conversation with Thái and I again several times. To avoid talking to them, we always came up with some excuse to run or return to our work, putting them off to another time.

Finally, Nam cornered me one day as I was packing my books to go home. "Would you have a minute to talk?" Nam asked.

His question caught me by surprise. *What does this guy want to talk about?* Not wanting to get into another confrontational discussion, I resorted to my usual delaying tactics: I had to go home to take care of my brothers. Could he catch me tomorrow?

"No, no," Nam said quickly. "Look. I know you don't want to talk to me so you are just trying to blow me off again. When other guys come to you for help, you have all the time in the world. For us, you don't even have a minute to talk. Do you hate us that much? Look, I don't want to get into a political argument with you. I just wonder if you have some time to help Tuấn and me with the chemistry homework?"

*Ah! So that was why he wanted to talk to me.* I was pleased that even these northern boys eventually came to me for help. I was not surprised they had difficulty with chemistry. Ms. Mai, the chemistry teacher, was also a transplanted North Vietnamese teacher. Like most North Vietnamese teachers in our school, she was not competent. Her lectures were boring and incomprehensible. My classmates just slept through her lectures and came to me to ask for help afterward. I couldn't get anything out of her lectures, but more than make up for it by studying on my own. I even embarrassed Ms. Mai several times by asking questions that she had no answer for or pointing out mistakes in her logic. Unlike Ms. Chiên in seventh grade, Ms. Mai was a better person. She didn't try to intimidate me or tell me to shut up. Rather, she tried hard to fill in the gaps in her knowledge. Despite trying hard, she still had a long way to go to become a good teacher.

After a while, I stopped trying to embarrass Ms. Mai. Poor Nam and Tuấn, meanwhile, listened hard to her lectures, trying to get some understanding. I often thought they needed a lot of luck. Watching them in class for the past few weeks, I knew they were diligent, but not particularly bright students. To understand anything from Ms. Mai's teaching, they must be at least as intelligent as Einstein.

"If you are having trouble, why don't you ask Ms. Mai for help?" I asked. "Why me? She is the teacher. I am just another student like you. I don't know any better than you do. Ms. Mai should be very willing to help you guys since she is also from the North, isn't she?"

"Come on," Tuấn pleaded. "You don't want to help us, do you? Look, we've come to Ms. Mai for help, but we couldn't understand her explanation. We are not that dumb. We know you probably know and can explain the subject better than her. You are the best student in this class. All the other guys came to you for help, and you were willing to spend as much time with them as needed. Why can't you spend some time to help us, unless you discriminate against us?"

*Damn! They got me!* Realizing that I couldn't blow them off that easily this time, I reluctantly nodded "All right! All right! I'll help you. Shit. I hate it when anyone pulls that 'prejudice' crap on me like that. Okay, so which of the problems you want me to help with?"

The northern kids were happy I finally agreed to help them. They took full advantage to ask questions about all the problems we had for the past weeks. The few minutes I promised them turned into two full hours. I didn't realize how much time had passed until I finished explaining.

"Shit. I am already two hours late," I swore. "My brothers are probably crying for their lunch right now. My mother is going to kill me. Look, I've got to go."

"Thanks for helping us, Trình," Nam said. "I am sorry we made you late. You don't hate us, do you?"

Nam's question suddenly touched off a raw nerve in my head. I stared back at them before responding, "Do you really want to hear the true answer from me?"

"Sure," Nam and Tuấn looked at each other.

"If you want to hear the true answer from me, you have to swear that you will never tell this to anyone else, or use it to attack me in the political class."

"Okay! 'We swear we will never tell your answer to anyone nor use it to criticize you in the political class," Nam repeated faithfully.

"Shit, that is not a serious swear," I shook my head. "I can't trust a swear like that. That's too easy."

"How do you want us to swear?" Nam gave me a puzzled look.

"You have to say this: 'We swear to God that we'll never tell what Trình says to anyone else, nor use it to criticize him in the political class. If we do, we'll be hit by lightning and go straight to hell, never to be reincarnated. If we survive the lightning, we can never have kids and our faces will be so ugly that even lepers would run away from us.' Now that is a serious swear."

"Okay! We swear," the North Vietnamese kids nodded their heads after a moment of hesitation.

"Say it. Say the whole thing. If you don't, how can I trust that you really swear seriously?"

"Okay! Okay! We swear that we will never tell your answer to anyone, nor will we use it to criticize you in the political class. If we do, we'll be struck by lightning and go straight to hell, never to be reincarnated. If we survive the lightning, we can never have babies and our faces will be so ugly that even lepers would run away from us. Okay! We have sworn, now can you tell us?"

"Not bad, not bad at all," I nodded my head with satisfaction. "Okay, you want to know if Thái and I hate you or not, right? Well, the true answer is we don't hate you, but we can't like you either."

"Why?" Tuấn asked.

"Why? We can't like you because we can't like you, that's why. We can't like you because we can't like your liberation and all the things that you and your northern people bring to the South."

"What do you mean?" Nam pressed. "The liberation frees the South Vietnamese people from the chains of the South Vietnamese lackey government and their American imperialist allies. It unites our country under one free and independent Vietnam. Why do you hate the liberation? What do the northern people bring to the South that you hate?"

Unable to contain myself anymore, I let out a long outburst. "Shit!

Do you really believe all that propaganda bullshit? See, that's the difference between you and us. You really believe it was true, that you people from the North fought all these years to free us from the Americans. You believe it, and you force it on us. We don't believe it a bit. Do you really think that the liberation freed us from the Americans? Hell, no. What it really did was to change who has the power and money in this country. People like your fathers and families now have the power and the money, because you are the victors. People like my father now are in re-education camps and our families lost all of our properties and wealth to you, because we are the losers. I'm sure that you guys know the saying "Được làm vua, thua làm giặc" (If you win, you become king. If you lose, you become the bandits). It was just that simple.

"Shit! Do you really think that you northern people bring freedom and independence to us? Do you really think we are freer than we were before? Do you really think you give us more opportunities under a 'unified and independent Vietnam' than we could ever dream of before? Bullshit! If we are freer than before, why do we have to watch everything we say, fearing that we can accidentally utter something that may land us in the re-education camps. If you give us more opportunities than we had before, then why are people like you virtually guaranteed to get into high school and college, while it would be a cold day in hell if I ever make it to college? Tell me, is that what you mean by giving us more opportunities, that I would have the opportunity to be a coolie even if I don't want to? Shit, if your liberation did not happen, the only thing that could stop me from getting to college or do what I want to do is me. With your liberation, I'll be lucky if I survive until twelfth grade, let alone get to college."

Nam and Tuấn were taken aback by my tirade. They were silent for a long time before Tuấn finally asked, "What do you mean it would be a cold day in hell if you ever get to high school or college? No one ever says you couldn't get into high school. You will take the same exam as we do, won't you? Aren't you the best student in this class? If you can't pass the exam, then who can? I don't understand."

"Shit, you guys are really in the dark, aren't you?" I shook my head. "Or are you pretending to be ignorant? It would be tough for me to get to high school not because I can't pass the exam, but because my father is a "Ngụy Quân" (Illegitimate Army) officer who is rotting in a re-education camp. You won't have any problem getting to high school or even college, not because you are particularly good, but because your fathers are party members. Who are the people who make the rules in this country now? People like your fathers make the rules, and people like us pay the consequences. If you don't believe it, why don't you go home and ask your fathers? That's enough. I've got to run now or my brothers will eat card-board for lunch."

I turned to gather my books. Tuấn and Nam stepped back and watched me, not uttering a word. As I walked out of class, I looked back at them and left my parting words: "Hey, you better remember what you swore today. If you ever mention what I said today to anyone, the light-ning and hell will wait for you somewhere."

I didn't know what effects my outburst had on Nam and Tuấn, but they never got into a political discussion with Thái or me again. They took care to steer any conversation we had away from political subjects. At the same time, they continued to come to me for help with other subjects. The swearing probably kept them from telling anyone what I said, for I never got called in for questioning by the school administrators.

While I no longer refused to help with homework nor avoided talk-ing to them, I still did not put any efforts into building a friendship with Nam and Tuấn. I never told them anything else about my family, nor asked about theirs. The differences between us were too great, and the distrust I had for anyone from the North was too much. In a different time and under different circumstances, I might have become best friends with these two shy, hard-working kids from North Vietnam. Yet, the fresh, new scars of the war's aftermath, inflicted upon my family by the new government, were too painful for me to overlook. These scars accentuated the deep sus-picion and resentment of Communism and anyone associated with it that was passed down to me from my parents' generation. For many years after I had gotten out of Vietnam, I occasionally wondered if it would have been better if I had made an attempt to get to know these kids. Perhaps the efforts would have reduced a tiny bit of the hatred and suspicion that lin-gered on in our country for so many years after the war had officially ended. Or, perhaps, it would have gotten me a spot somewhere in the numerous re-education camps of Vietnam.

# 9

# The Growing Pains

Three months into my eighth-grade year, the kids in my class found out I lived only a few houses away from Trang. They started doing what I feared most: making up gossip about our non-existent relationship.

Last year, I was able to stay off of my classmates' radar screen. Thái was the only boy who knew Trang was my neighbor. Fortunately, Thái kept quiet about what he knew. Thus, I was left alone for a whole year.

Knowing how my classmates loved to gossip, I did not approach nor talk to Trang for the whole year. I didn't want any distractions to disrupt my concentration on studying. Additionally, I was afraid that these rumors would eventually reach my mother, and she would ask me about them. I would not know what to say to my mother. At thirteen, I was a shy and private kid. I kept much of my thoughts and ideas to myself. Even to my mother and my best friends, I did not share my thoughts and emotions.

Despite all my cautions, my classmates finally found out. When they did, I watched helplessly as they started to make up and circulate the gossip. Their discovery was accidental, sparked by the intense rivalry between my class, 8A3, and Trang's class, 8A2.

By the beginning of my eighth-grade year, my reputation as the best student in my class was undisputed. At the same time, Trang established herself as the best student in her class. Suddenly, we found ourselves the academic representatives of our respective classes. The students used us as the indicator as to how good their class was. Suddenly, Trang and I became the weapons for our classmates in their rivalry for bragging rights.

Despite being wild, the kids in my class thought of themselves as the brightest students in the school. They were not shy about expressing their beliefs to students in other classes. Students in class 8A2 were most often on the receiving end of the outrageous brags of my classmates, as classes 8A2 and 8A3 were situated next to each other.

My classmates justified their beliefs by showing how well the best students in our class, particularly me, were doing compared to the best students of other classes. Naturally, the students in other classes disagreed. They in turn touted the achievement of their best classmates. In the ensuing rivalry, Trang and I suddenly found ourselves to be the subjects of scrutiny by the kids in our classes. They were too anxious to claim their bragging rights.

Once I became the subject of their attention, it was not long before my classmates discovered that I lived near Trang. The fact that my family was abjectly poor and Thu Trang's family was well off also did not escape their attention. My classmates were delighted. They had all the ingredients to make up an imaginary, but melodramatic and true-to-the-Vietnamese-tradition love story: a poor, bright young boy in love with a beautiful, rich girl. Outrageous gossip was soon fabricated and propagated. Soon, I found most kids in my class and class 8A2 always mentioning my name and Trang's in the same breath. It didn't matter there was no real substance to the story. What mattered was the kids had someone new and some interesting stories to gossip about.

As the gossip spread, there was nothing I could say to stop it. In the first month, the distraction from gossip was too strong for me to ignore. When I walked by class 8A2, the girls in that class taunted me about Trang. As they could easily find out scores for everyone, daily my classmates compared my scores with Trang's to keep the artificial rivalry interesting. The continued scrutiny and gossip frustrated me. I tried to deny it and stop the comparison, but to no avail. After a while, I gave up and stopped paying attention to what other kids were saying about me. I had had enough. The distraction had disrupted my studying. While I still was ahead of all my classmates, I had not studied well in a month.

After much frustration, it finally dawned on me that the more I protested and denied their made-up stories, the more the kids enjoyed their gossiping. With this realization came my best defense. I acted as if I was dumb and deaf. While the students continued to gossip, they and their gossips no longer bothered me as they did before.

Fortunately, my mother never heard about the gossiping and Trang never said anything derogatory about me. I thought the gossip was bothering her just as much as they bothered me. I did not know how she was dealing with it.

Ironically, the gossip caused Trang to notice me more than before. When I carried water from the well across the street to my house or came home from working on the land at night, I had to walk past her family's factory. Many times, I found her standing at the factory gate and staring at me from head to toe. Embarrassed of my appearance and poverty, I always kept my head down when walking past her house. At those times, I often wished this curious girl would stop staring at me. *What was she doing? Was it her way of getting back at me for all the gossiping spreading in school? Did she find my dirty and haggard appearance amusing? Did she think I was nothing more than a toad wishing to become something more than what it was?* More than ever, I was conscious of my poverty and the self pity that went along with it.

While I never got rid of the embarrassment, I grew accustomed to the gossip and learned how to tune it out quickly. Yet, when I thought I had overcome this bothersome distraction, other boys would not let me forget it. One day, Phương, the boy who insulted me last year, approached me and asked "Hey, how is your 'người đẹp' (beauty) Trang doing, eh?"

Phương caught me when I was solving a tough geometry problem before class started. I pretended not to hear him and continued to concentrate on the problem. Impatiently, Phương slapped my shoulder and raised his voice. "Hey, deaf man! Didn't you hear me? I asked how is your 'người đẹp' Trang doing?"

"Why do you ask me?" I glared at Phương. "She is not my 'người đẹp.' I do not know anything about her. I don't even know her. Now, would you get out of my face?"

"Ah hah! So you are still denying it, eh?" Phương nodded with satisfaction. "What a pity? Every guy in this school knew about you and Trang. What a wonderful couple, a match made in heaven, eh? So why do you keep denying it? Who would believe you? Besides, she is not bad at all, you know! Shit, man, I would kill to have a girl like that. Beautiful. Intelligent. Rich. What more do you want, eh, Bookworm?"

I wondered where Phương was heading with his taunt. I had never liked Phương and always stayed as far away from him as I could. Despite knowing I disliked him, Phương continued to bother me. Phương was a pathetic student. Because he never spent much time studying, he consistently got the worst grades in class. Since he sat right in front of me, he often turned around and begged to copy my answers whenever we had exams. I always refused to let Phương copy my answers. To get back at me, Phương took any chances he had to bother or taunt me. The gossip provided him with the perfect ammunition for his taunts. He tried it several times before, but I easily brushed him off by turning to talk about homework with other students. This time, Phương was not about to let me ignore him. I sensed he was setting me up for something.

"Look, all I want is some peace and quiet to solve my problem, all right!" I grunted. "Now, would you leave me alone?"

"Uh-uh! You can't get rid of me that easily, Bookworm," Phương shook his head. "Hey, you say that all you want is some peace and quiet, right? So you don't want Trang, right? Does that mean that it is okay for me to go and ask her out? You won't object to it, right?"

"Hey, if you want to ask her out, why don't you go and ask her? Why do you ask me? I don't know her and don't own her. You made all this bull-shit up and now you want to convince me that it's true. Get real!"

"Hey, hey. Don't get excited there, Bookworm," Phương laughed. "I am just giving you fair warning that I am going after Trang, that's all. I thought it's nice to let the owner know before I pick off the fruits of his tree. So don't get mad if you see me and Trang going out on a date, eh?"

So, that was it. The bastard was trying to make me jealous and mad. He was trying to hit me where he thought it would hurt. I laughed sarcastically. "Hey, if you want to go after her, be my guest. I hope she doesn't get constipated at the sight of a pathetic idiot like you."

Phương's face reddened. My insulting comment had obviously stung him badly. Yet, he quickly snapped back, "Hey, you better take your words back or else I am going to kick your ass so bad you have to beg for mercy. I am not a pathetic idiot, but you are a pathetic loser. Look at yourself. Do you know what you look like? You look like a dirty, homeless beggar with an attitude problem. You are as dark as an African savage. Your clothes are as stinky as a rag. And I can't believe you think you are such hot shit."

He paused to catch a breath. Before I could utter a response, he continued, "Hey, you may be telling the truth after all. Shit, the more I look at you, the less I believe there could be anything between you and Trang. Yeah, she must be out of her mind if she even ever thought of speaking to you. How could such a girl ever think of talking to a stinky toad like you?"

I laughed when Phương threatened to beat me up. Because of his constant smoking and lack of exercise, Phương was a weak, pale-looking boy. By contrast, I was a dark, thin, but strong kid because of my constant hard work and physical labor. I might not win in fist fights against other bigger, tougher kids, but I certainly could deal with Phương.

Phương probably realized his threat was useless. Thus, he quickly changed from threatening to insulting me. By belittling my appearance and my poverty, he had finally hit my weak spot. Dressing decently was the only area in which Phương was better than me. His family still had money from the days when they operated bars and brothels. Thus, Phương could still afford to wear good, clean clothes. He always came to class dressing in jeans and an unbuttoned white shirt, trying to appear like a cool playboy.

By contrast, I wore the same ragged shirt and pants for weeks. Phương had always had a grudge against me, as I made no secret of my disdain for his showiness and his stupidity. Now, he tried to even the score by attacking my ragged appearance. I wasn't about to take his insults lying down. I stood up, folded my arms, and challenged Phương. "So what are you going to do to make me take my words back, eh? I want to see how the tough Phương 'sì ke' (marijuana Phương) is going to kick my ass. Or maybe he is going to accidentally kick his own ass instead. And what does the stuff about Trang has to do with me? Yeah, she may not speak to me because I don't look and smell all that good. But if she is intelligent, she would know I have some gray matter between my ears. As for you, pathetic idiot, hell probably is going to freeze over before she speaks to you. Why don't you take a look at yourself in the mirror before saying things about other people? Do you know what you look like? A gutless, brainless pimp, that's what. You probably could only say a few words before she figured out you had shit between your ears."

By this time, many students had gathered around us as they sensed a fight was about to break out. Some of Phương's friends had gathered behind him and urged him to beat me up. Hưng, Phương's closest friend and another druggie, stepped up to Phương and asked, "Come on Phương. You are not going to take that from him, are you? Show him what you've got, man. You've got to put him in his place."

Phương looked around, seeing all the kids clamoring for a fight, and looked at me again. I could tell he was nervous since he wasn't sure that he could beat me up. He had gotten himself in a tough spot. He didn't want to fight but he couldn't retreat in front of the surrounding boys. They would never let him forget it.

Gathering all his strength, Phương lunged and threw a blow at my face. I instinctively raised my right foot to kick him, aiming for his groin. My foot reached the target before Phương's blow got to my face. Phương bent back in pain, clutching his groin. All the kids let out a long sigh of disappointment that the fight was over so quickly. Fired up by the cheering and the unexpectedly easy knockout, I taunted Phương. "Hey, playboy! Did you have enough? If you want to beat me up, I suggest that you go and have kids before trying. Otherwise, you may never be able to have kids."

My taunts unexpectedly got Phương very angry. Already humiliated, he could not take my taunts much longer. He took out his sharp writing pen to use as a knife and turned to ask Hưng, his friend "Come on, you got to help me kill this asshole. You can't let him do this to me."

Hưng nodded, took out his sharp pen, and stepped forward to join Phương in attacking me. Now, I suddenly found myself in a dangerous position. I could deal with Phương in a fair, bare hands fight, but I had no chance against both of them, particularly when they had their menacing sharp pens. I instinctively reached for my pen to defend myself, when Cường, the cyclo driver, stepped in front of me.

"Step back, you pathetic cowards before I wring both of your necks off," Cường shouted at Hưng and Phương. "This is supposed to be a fair fight, man to man, between Trình and Phương. You want to turn it into a two on one? As long as I am standing here, if any of you try to gang up on Trình, I am going cut your dick off. Phương, if you still want to fight, then drop your pen and step up to fight like a man. If you don't want to fight anymore, then just bug off. If you try anything funny, you better guard your dick closely or else I am going to cut it off."

Hưng and Phương hesitated and looked at each other. With Cường stepping in, the balance tilted to my favor. The boys in class knew better than to engage Cường in any fight. Though Cường was slightly shorter than me, he was muscular and a veteran of numerous street fights. He was no stranger to fighting with knife, sticks, crowbars, or chains. Though he never confirmed it, my classmates rumored that he practiced martial arts regularly. By contrast, Hưng and Phương were wimpy-looking boys who probably never got into a real fight before. Though Phương was still very angry, he knew better than to make a bigger fool out of himself by pissing Cường off. Slowly, he and Hưng put their pens away.

"Okay, okay! It's cool, Cường," Phương raised his arms up in a gesture of peace. "Because of you, we are going to let Bookworm get away with it today. But next time, I am not going to take that shit from him."

Cường folded his arms, smiled, and did not respond to Phương. Other boys, seeing Hưng's and Phương's cowardice, loudly booed them. Some taunted Phương to engage me in a bare-hand fight again. Phương pretended not to hear them and started to walk away. After taking a few steps, he turned to fire his last words at me. "Hey, Bookworm! Don't cry like a baby and go home to tell your mother when you see me going out with your 'người đẹp' (beauty) Trang!"

"Good luck!" I quickly retorted, not willing to let Phương get away with his taunts. "Don't forget to bring along enough towels to wipe off the rotten tomatoes and eggs she is going to throw in your face."

Phương had walked far away enough not to hear my last taunt. Other kids who still stood around laughed heartily at my sarcasm.

"Hey, thanks for stepping in for me," I turned to Cường. "Those two bastards probably would have me for breakfast if you didn't intervene."

"No problem," Cường smiled cheerfully. "You have helped me more than enough. There is no need for you to thank me. Do you care to hear some advice from me?"

"Sure, what is it?"

"If I were you, I wouldn't taunt Phương after I have beaten him," Cường said. "Everyone saw that you've won, you don't have to taunt him. He didn't want to fight you any more. Let him have a way out. Don't try to corner a dog. It will bite you. Phương may be wimpy, but he could still hurt you. You saw that for yourself, didn't you?"

I realized Cường was right. I was too excited, hot-blooded to stop when I was ahead. By taunting Phương, I nearly got myself hurt badly if Cường had not been there.

"Sure, thanks for your advice," I nodded. "But you also humiliated them as much as, if not more than, I did. You told them to bug off or else you are going to cut their dicks off. Why can you do that and I can't, eh?"

"I can because I always watch my back," Cường shook his head. "Watching my back becomes an instinct for me. You can't because you are not used to watching your own back yet. Remember cowards don't hit you in the front. They hit you in the back, but they get you just the same."

The bells for the first period rang loudly, cutting off our conversation. For the rest of the day, I kept thinking about what Cường said. I quietly thanked God for friends like Cường and the lessons they taught me. Despite being short and stocky, which other people often took to be signs of brutishness or stupidity, Cường was a sharp and streetwise kid. He had taught me a very valuable lesson: don't perpetuate hatred or anger by taunting an opponent that I already defeated. By taunting Phương, I just brought myself problems that I could easily have avoided. Before, Phương did not exactly hate me. He just found enjoyment in hassling me. Now, I had caused Phương to hate me with a passion, for I had humiliated him in front of everyone.

Suddenly, I realized I had not done what my father asked me to do when I was faced with insults from other people. My father asked me "not to lower" myself to the level of my tormentors. He asked me to respond to their insults not with fists, arguments, or insults, but by showing that they were wrong about me. Yet, the first time I was really insulted, I forced Phương into a fight he did not wish to have and made him into an enemy by humiliating him. *Had I become as bad a person as he?* If Cường had not pointed out my stupidity, I probably would have reveled in my "victory" today. Instead, Cường's advice made me remember what my father taught me before he left. More than ever, I realized how hard it was to do the things he taught. I still had a lot of growing to do before I could become the man my father wanted me to be.

A few weeks after my fight, I came to class one day to find my classmates surrounding Chiêm, who was talking excitedly. Curious, I put away my books and joined the group to find out what was going on. I heard a boy asking Chiêm, "Are you sure he is dead? He was in class on Friday last week."

"I know he is dead," Chiêm nodded his head gravely. "His house is only a block away from mine. I walk by his house every day. I knew he was in a coma since two days ago. Yesterday, when I stopped by to visit his family, they just took his body back from the hospital. He is dead. I saw him."

"What are you talking about?" I asked Chiêm. "Who is dead?"

"Công Sún is dead, Bookworm! "Chiêm looked at me sadly. "He was climbing the plum tree in his back yard to pick plums when a branch broke. He fell and his head hit the ground hard. His family rushed him to the hospital, but they couldn't do anything to save him. He was in a coma since the fall until he died. The doctor said there was a blood clot in his head, but they don't have any equipment or medicine to treat him. Shit, they just left him lying in a bed until he was dead. His family said he died early morning yesterday, and they took his body home. I just visited his family and saw him. Man, Công is dead!"

Chiêm's voice trailed off to a sob. Like other boys, I was stunned to hear the news. I saw Công just three days ago, yet now he was dead. How could that be? Could a kid so young like Công have died so easily? Aren't children like us supposed to live for a long, long time before we have to worry about dying?

Yet, Chiêm left no doubts that Công was really dead. I could still see Công's mischievous grins when he spread the "mắt mèo" on the teacher's chair, anticipating the havoc that the devilish filaments would wreak on the unlucky teacher who was about to sit on it. Công was not a good student. If anything, he was the craziest boy in class. Yet, I sensed that his devious actions probably stemmed from frustration and anger with the changes brought about by the new government. To his friends, Công was always loyal and honest. He was one of the boys who came to me asking for help with homework. Yet, now he was gone forever. The news was too fresh and devastating for me to accept that one of my friends had left this life.

Chiêm's sadness gradually turned to anger as he continued to tell the

boys details about Công's death. The doctor in the hospital said they did
not have medicine or equipment to treat him. All they did was to put him
in a bed, cover him with a blanket, and try to spoonfeed him porridge.
Could we believe that they didn't have anything to treat a dying kid? They
didn't have anything for him because he was a poor kid and his father was
a former policeman for the South government. If Công was a Commie
cadre or the son of one, they would definitely try much harder to save him.
This was the Communist heaven shit they always tried to brainwash us
about. It was not any different from the evils of the capitalist or monar-
chy they always exhorted us to topple. If you were a poor kid at the bottom of society, you were still treated like dirt. The only difference now was
the rulers were our comrade Communist cadres and their families.

I left the crowd and Chiêm's monologue to return to my chair. I did not
feel the same anger as Chiêm did, just an overwhelming feeling of sadness.

Two days later, my classmates and I attended Công's funeral. We followed the mourning procession and walked the two miles from his home
to the cemetery. Hường and Chiêm were among the four people carrying
Công's coffin. The sky was cloudy and the air was humid. When we were
halfway to the cemetery, the rain started to fall heavily. Despite the rain,
we marched on silently.

The usually loud and crazy boys of class 8A3 were uncharacteristi-
cally quiet today. We all had come to Công's house to visit his family and
to see him one last time. Now, on the way to the cemetery, every boy was
lost in his own thoughts. Công's death reminded us of how fragile our life
was. We all heard his family telling us the story of how little the hospital
staff could or would do to save Công. The precious little medicine the hospital still had left was reserved to treat VIPs, high-ranking Communist
Party cadres and their families. The poor, common citizens like us would
at best get a bandage or an antibiotic shot. What happened to Công could
happen to us. I shuddered to think that I might be seriously injured someday and have to go to the hospital for treatment. It might be better to stay
home and accept my fate.

After Công's coffin was lowered into the grave, we each grabbed a
piece of the freshly dug earth and threw it on the coffin. We stood still in
the pouring rain to pay respect to our departed friend one last time. I quietly prayed that Công would find his peace in heaven. Perhaps Công was
the lucky one among all of us. He had left his frustration, angers, and a
hard life behind, while we still had to wake up to face a dark, ominous
future tomorrow.

# 10

# The New Economic Zone

In December 1976, the much-hyped Communist Party Third Plenum took place. As members of the Ho Chi Minh Avant Garde Youth, we were exhorted by our handlers to work as hard as we could to celebrate and show our appreciation for this "momentous event." We were told the third party plenum would pull our country out of poverty and put it on the right track to achieve a "socialist" paradise.

We knew little of what happened in the plenum except for what the school administrators and advisors told us. What I remembered was the third party plenum approved the two five-year economic plans with all kinds of grandiose industrial and agricultural targets. The plenum also reaffirmed Vietnam's "commitment" to socialism. For kids like us, the grandiose political jargon meant little. We'd heard them daily and tuned them out quickly. At the same time, we had yet to understand what the five year plans and commitment to socialism would mean to our families.

During the Vietnam War, the destruction of the countryside and the concentration of wealth in the cities had caused the huge migration of people to urban areas. Cities like Saigon were overpopulated while many villages in the countryside were abandoned. For years after the war, unemployment in the cities kept rising, as there was no more foreign aid. Meanwhile, many areas in the countryside remained abandoned. To meet the targets it set for the five-year economic plans, the Communist Party decided to forcibly move large numbers of people from the cities to these abandoned areas. These mostly uninhabitable areas were euphemistically called "Vùng Kinh Tế Mới" (the New Economic Zones or NEZs).

While the goal of redistributing the population to less-populated areas to increase agricultural production appeared to be logical, the execution of this policy was crude and brutal. The policy became another means for the Communist Party to tighten its control over the South Vietnamese. Soon after the party plenum was over, bands of "Công An" (security agents) started to target families they wanted to move to the NEZs. The targeted families were those the government did not consider to have "legitimate" means of earning a living. What "legitimate" really meant was up to the local security agents to interpret.

The doomed families were given a few weeks to gather all their belongings. Then, they were forcibly put on buses and shipped off to the New Economic Zones. The New Economic Zones were usually rough, swampy, and desolated areas, which had no electricity and little potable water. While they were given nothing to build or to farm with, these families were told to build their own dwellings and farm the land to feed themselves. After many years living in the city, these people were told they now had to earn an "honest" living with their own hands.

At first, the government focused its effort on redistributing the population to the largest city in South Vietnam, Saigon. Most families that were sent to these areas were families of former government officials and military officers of South Vietnam, who were now spending their time in re-education camps. After these families were sent away, their homes in the city were confiscated and became the property of the government.

People sent to the New Economic Zones quickly ran into all kinds of problems. As city dwellers, they were not used to working on the land and had a hard time learning how to farm. Many people quickly contracted diseases such as malaria or jungle fever. After the food supplies they brought along had run out, many families simply packed their belongings and returned to Saigon. Since their homes had already been confiscated, these people became homeless and lived on the side streets of Saigon. Sooner or later, these people were rounded up by the security forces and sent back to the New Economic Zones. Yet, people returned to the city from these zones faster than the security forces could send them there.

The returnees from the New Economic Zones told horror stories to other people who were yet to be sent. Soon, the words "Vùng Kinh Tế Mới" (New Economic Zones) became synonymous with "living hell." As a result, South Vietnamese city dwellers tried many different ways to avoid being sent to these areas, including planning escape from Vietnam.

While the government's move to relocate people to the New Economic Zones had yet to reach Vũng Tàu in early 1977, people here were already well aware. The many horror stories associated with these areas were already widespread. Thus, like city dwellers elsewhere, planning to avoid the New Economic Zones became the top priority for people here.

In February 1977, I lost a few more friends. Some quit school and moved with their families to countryside villages where their parents were born. Other kids quietly disappeared from class for a while before we discovered they had escaped from Vietnam. Chính, the vice head of our class, did not show up for school in late January. We did not notice his absence for a week, until one of the boys rode his bike by Chính's home and noticed that it was boarded up by the local People's Committee. Only then did we learn that Chính's family had escaped from Vietnam. We never knew where Chính's family had gone to make the escape and whether they made it safely to a country of asylum.

Phương, my nemesis, also disappeared from class in late February. After the third day of his absence, we speculated that he, too, had escaped from Vietnam. When Thái came by Phương's home to check it out, our suspicion was confirmed. Phương's house was also boarded up by the local security agents.

However, we soon learned Phương's family did not make it past the coast guard patrol. When Thái and I rode across a military camp one day, we saw Phương and many other people working in a rice field under the watchful eyes of soldiers. We immediately understood what it meant. Phương and these people were arrested by security agents or the coast guard when they made their escape. Now, they were put to labor in the rice field as part of the punishment for their escape. Phương and his family were eventually released from the labor camp, but he never went back to class.

The news about the New Economic Zone caused my mother more worry and stress. Other than farming a piece of mountain land, our family didn't have a means of earning a living that would be considered "legitimate" by the Communist government. If anything, my mother's trading activities in the open market were considered illegal. My mother constantly feared if the policy of sending people to the New Economic Zones reached Vũng Tàu, our family would be among those first to be sent. Yet, there was nothing we could do to avoid it. My mother could not find any other "legitimate" means of employment. Thus, we continued with our daily existence with another hovering, dark cloud.

Fortunately, until the day I escaped from Vietnam, neither our family nor any families we knew were sent to the New Economic Zones. While we were not sent to the NEZs, we had to participate in an increasing number of public work projects. The People's Committee required each family to put in several days a month to work on public projects such as building dams or dikes or planting trees. People who went to work on these projects had to provide for their own transportation, food, and medicine. The projects became another tax on the already very meager resources of poor people like our family.

Almost no one was exempted from the obligation to participate in these projects. Since my mother could not afford to miss any day selling, I always represented my family in these projects. Then, our school also had public work projects every student had to participate in. These projects were similar or identical to the projects of the city wards. Thus, I ended up spending a week every month to work for the "people." Besides the exhausting physical labors, these projects further strained my family's means of subsistence. More than once, I had a fever for weeks from working in dam-building projects in the rain for days, making myself a big burden on my mother's already-strained shoulders.

In 1977, we endured two more currency changes. Under the Communist government's inept management of the economy and undisciplined printing of money, hyperinflation, ranging in thousands of percent, was the norm. The sight of people carrying bags full of money just to buy rice was common. The government's solution for inflation was simply to change the cash currency. In the "brilliant and correct" minds of the party members, the best solution was to change old money for new. Vietnamese dutifully lined up at banks to exchange their old one hundred thousand "dong" for a new one thousand dong bill. Of course, this paper money game did not stop inflation, and within a few months of the first change, the government ordered another currency change to make it look as if the money supply in the country did not increase.

The frequent currency changes also served another purpose: the government's continued quest to destroy the "tư bản mại sản" (capitalist) class. While the first currency change had hurt millions of people, the Communist government still was not satisfied it had completely eliminated the capitalists. To ensure the power of the "capitalists" would be reduced to the point where they no longer posed a significant threat, the Communist government continued its many tactics to strip them of their wealth.

After the first currency change, most well-off people had learned their lesson. They converted a major part of their wealth into gold or other hard assets. Thus, the later currency changes were not as successful in taking away people's wealth. Additionally, many corrupt officials were willing to divulge to people that a currency change was coming for a fee. Thus, while these events were supposed to be secret, people already learned about them months ahead.

With the increased number of work projects that we had to participate in, the disappearance of my classmates as their families escaped from Vietnam, and the frequent currency changes, the second half of my eightgrade year passed by quickly. The constant distractions made it impossible for the kids to concentrate and study. Thus, I was grateful when school finally came to an end in June. I was also anxious to see what would happen to the ninth graders in our school. At the end of this year, it was their turn to take the entrance examination to get into high school.

In the last week of school, the girls in our neighboring classes started passing out their "lưu bút" (yearbook) for their friends to sign. These yearbooks often were nothing more than a notebook, with hand-drawn pictures and decorations.

One day, Liên, a girl in 8A2, stopped me and gave me Trang's yearbook to sign. Being reticent, Trang had asked her friend to give the book to me.

The invitation caught me by surprise. I didn't know what to do. I did not know the girls in the neighboring class well at all, and none of them ever asked me to sign their yearbooks. Now, Liên, whom I did not know at all, was asking me to sign Trang's yearbook. Was this a trick set up by some devious students so that they would have more materials to fuel the wicked gossip that already ran amok?

Since Phương disappeared, my classmates did not talk about Trang and me as much anymore. I was so glad for it. Now, I had no reason to let anybody fan the gossip again. I was about to refuse Liên's request, when I saw Trang looking at me intently from inside class 8A2. I realized then it was not a trick. It was a first attempt from Trang to communicate with me. For two years, we had always pretended to ignore the other's existence. If I refused now, I might never have a chance to communicate with her again.

Reluctantly, I took the yearbook and asked Liên, "What am I supposed to write? I never wrote in a yearbook for anyone before."

"Hey, it's your job to figure it out," Liên smiled mischievously. "Just make sure you return it to me by break time."

I walked to my seat and opened the yearbook. Its pages were decorated with many hand-drawn pictures of flowers and cute animals. There were many passages written by her friends, wishing her a great summer. I found a blank page but couldn't think of anything to write. While I was still twirling my pen, Thái walked in and sat down next to me. Seeing the yearbook, Thái's eyes lit up like he had found a secret treasure. Somehow, he immediately knew it was Trang's yearbook.

Like a cat pouncing on a mouse, Thái peppered me with questions. "Was I finally bold enough to talk to her?" "Did she come to me?" "Were we going somewhere?" It took several minutes for me to get the message through to my closest friend that there was nothing more than what he saw, Trang asking me to write in her yearbook. Then, Thái turned his attention to advising me what to write. "Write something flowery and flattering, like her eyes were as bright as the morning light or something," Thái suggested. Only when I relented and agreed to consider his suggestion that Thái smiled happily and left. After thinking for awhile, I finally wrote down a short passage:

> Dear Trang,
>     Though we never have talked, I thought we always knew a little bit about each other. I am flattered you've asked me to write in your yearbook. I do not know what to say, except to wish you a wonderful summer. I hope we will have opportunities to talk and to get to know each other better in the future.
>     I do not know what the future holds for me or whether I will be back to school for next year. If I don't, then this may be the first and last time I write to you. In that case, I thought I would leave you with my favorite lines from the wonderful literary piece *Bình Ngô Đại Cáo* by Nguyễn Trãi:
>
>> Nhật nguyệt hối rồi lại minh
>> Càn Khôn bĩ rồi lại thái.
>> (The sun and the moon were dark,
>>     but became bright again.
>> The universe was drowned in sorrow,
>>     but would be filled with happiness again.)

I wrote the passage down on a piece of paper and was about to write it into the yearbook when Thái returned. Grabbing the piece of paper out of my hand, Thái read it then shook his head vigorously. Laughing, he derided me for writing something so nerdy and idiosyncratic. "What does the couplet 'Nhật nguyệt hối rồi lại minh, Càn Khôn bĩ rồi lại thái' have to do in here?" Thái asked. Why couldn't I write something simple and sweet so the girl could understand?

Unruffled, I shrugged off Thái's criticism. Maybe it wasn't anything romantic, but the writing reflected me, I responded. There was nothing between us anyway, other than probably a budding friendship. I would rather write something honest than some flattering, flaky words I didn't mean. Throwing up his hands in mock exasperation, Thái lamented that my writing might be the end instead of the beginning of something beautiful.

I smiled nonchalantly and proceeded to write the passage in the yearbook. As planned, I gave the yearbook back to Trang through Liên during break time. I did not know what Trang thought when she read the passage. Neither of us had a chance to talk to each other before the school year ended. I was still too shy to approach her whenever anybody else was around.

Like the previous summer, my 1977 summer was filled with work. Unlike the previous summer, I did not bust my butt to collect paper and scrap metals for the Youth. Learning from our experience of last year, Thái and I were determined to do the least possible to get by with our involvement in the Youth. We even plotted a strategy on how to do the least possible and still be able to win the nebulous "Cháu Ngoan Bác Hồ" (Good Children of Uncle Ho) award.

We'd figured out after one year that paying lip service to the party and Uncle Ho and the appearance of dedication were better rewarded than actual hard work. Thus, we directed our energy to different tasks this summer. We shouted the Youth's slogans and sang its songs louder, faster, more readily than last year. We stayed later after meetings to help the advisors with their tasks. And we readily volunteered and committed to whatever preposterous goals the advisors set for our group. When the commitments weren't delivered, we always found excuses to blame on unforeseen circumstances or the non-co-operation of other people (but never on any specific individuals). After a while, we noticed an interesting behavior pattern from the advisors: just the simple promise to try harder next time was enough to satisfy them. So much for their "high standards" and dedication to the causes of the party and Uncle Ho.

Our strategy paid off. At the end of the summer, Thái and I got the award of "Cháu Ngoan Bác Hồ" for the second year. However, just like last year, too many kids were given the award. The only difference is that there were more kids who didn't do anything and still got the award this year versus last. By now, we really understood the way things worked. This award would not make a difference on whether we would get admitted to high school. It was simply one of those cheap, meaningless rewards the Communist Party and its puppet organizations gave out to exhort people and children to contribute and dedicate to whatever plans or goals the party set. By now, we understood that our parents' admonition to beware of the Communists' promises wasn't an exaggeration.

# 11

# The Choices We Made

My ninth-grade year started out with a more somber mood than last year. For most of my classmates, this might be the last year they ever attended school. With "anti-revolutionary" family backgrounds and rebellious behaviors for the past two years, the boys didn't believe they had a chance for further education.

Without further schooling, a hard future awaited us. Some of us would have to find whatever work we could get to support our families. For some less lucky, the People's Army of Vietnam was waiting for our conscription. Neither of these options appealed to the boys. Many believed when this school year was over, their lives would cease to have any more joy. Thus, they were determined to have as much fun as possible now.

The new school year brought me closer to the dreaded future that, following my mother's advice, I had put out of my mind in the past year. No matter how I tried to push it away, the nagging fear that my life would be going nowhere after this year stayed foremost on my mind since day one of school.

Despite the fear, I continued to teach myself all subjects. In the summer, I had borrowed the textbooks for the next school year from my teachers and studied them thoroughly. By the first week of school, I had finished reading and doing homework for half the school year. At the rate I was going, I would finish the curriculum by the fourth month of school.

The new school year also brought some differences. Hường, our class head for the past two years, did not return to school. With Hường and Chính gone, Thái and I were elected to be the new class head and vice head. We didn't mind taking up the task. The job of being the class heads had very simple responsibilities. All we had to do was to check the attendance daily and lead the salutations to the teachers at the beginning of every period.

I was surprised Hường did not return to school. Of all the southern boys in class, Hường was considered to be guaranteed to get into high school and college. With his mother's years of service as a spy, there was no question about his "revolutionary" background. On top of it, he was a good student, despite not studying hard. While he was four to five years older than the other boys in class, he didn't mind mingling with us. On the contrary, he enjoyed having a crowd of curious boys following him and listening to his stories of exploits with prostitutes. Of all the reasons I could think of for him to quit school, the only one that would seem plausible was that his family had escaped from Vietnam. But then, Hường and his mother would be the last people I expected to escape from the country.

Hường's house was only two blocks from where I lived. One afternoon, after coming home from school, I went to visit Hường. I found him lying on a hammock and playing his guitar. He was wearing only his shorts and a pair of sandals. At 18 years old, Hường was a tall and muscular young man. He had a strong, square jaw, with rugged features and bright eyes that always seemed to twinkle with laughter. He was also a pretty good guitar player and singer. When I came in, he was in the middle of playing and singing a love song.

"Hey, Bookworm," he nodded his head toward a little chair. "It's good of you to come. Sit down. What's up with you?"

"Not much," I replied. "I just came back from school. I thought I would stop by to see you before I go up to the mountain."

"Ah, still working hard to feed your family hey! I know. Life is getting harder for everybody."

"Yeah! Life is tough and then we die," I nodded. "And life is not fair. Some people just get it better than others. Anyway, I came to see you because I am curious. Why didn't you return to school this year?"

Hường sat up on the hammock and looked at me with amusement. He ran a hand through his tousled hair, and smirked. "Why didn't I return to school? Well, Bookworm, tell me a good reason why I should return?"

"Why? You've got everything you need to succeed, so why are you not using it? You can sleep between now to the end of the year and you still get admitted to high school. You are doing damn well in class despite just messing around. You are one of the smartest, most talented guys I know. If anybody has an opportunity with his life in this country, it's you. And all you have to do is to show up in class. So why are you not doing it?"

"Bookworm, you know one but don't know two," Hường smirked again. "Do you really believe going through school and getting the diplomas is the way to get ahead these days? You are still too naïve. You act as if you still live in the old days where smart and educated people will get on top. No, no! Education will not get you that far these days. But being in the right organization and doing the right service for the government would."

He paused for effect then continued, "You see, I am eighteen now. My mother is earning peanuts working in the Ward People's Committee. She can't afford to keep me in school forever, and she is getting old. All her years of service to the revolution didn't earn her much, but at least she can get me into the right organizations to earn a living. You see, I got accepted to be a 'Công An Hải Quân' (coastal patrol police). It's a good place to be, since I will draw a salary. Better yet, overtime, I may be able to make more money than just my salary. See, even if I grind my pants on the school bench for the next ten years, I may not get a better job than this. So why waste the time, hey?"

I could scarcely believe my ears. Hường, one of the guys I liked better in class, was joining the "Yellow Dogs" security agents that we all hated so much. It took me a few seconds to recover from my shock.

"Hường, why?" I asked. "I thought you are one of us. I thought you hate those 'Yellow Dogs' as much as anybody."

"Well, that was then, and this is now! You see, I've been doing a lot of thinking this past year. I've got to be practical. I am at the age where I have to start earning good money because my mother is getting old. I can't continue to go to school and work on the land like you. Life is getting tougher and one has to survive. I am not a good merchant, peddling stuff like other people. I tried, and I made peanuts. And guess who is on top of the food chains these days? Unless you are a Communist Party member, you can't do better than being a "Công An." Heck, these guys make better money than just their salary."

"You are telling me you are joining the 'Yellow Dogs' so that you can make money by taking bribes or taking things from other people?" I raised my voice. "You can't be doing that!"

"Hey, it's the way things work now," Hường shrugged. "C'est la vie, boy. I figure it was nice to sing all those wonderful songs that we did last year, making fun of the party and Uncle Ho and all. But I can't do that forever. I got to make a living. I can't fight the party and the system. And if I can't fight them, why not join them. At least, I will be able to live well."

"Are you saying you are willing to sell your soul and conscience just to make a living?"

Unruffled by my question, Hường calmly responded "I don't have a lot of options, Bookworm. And I don't pretend to be righteous either. I am just trying to survive like everybody else. How many choices do you think I have? We are all prisoners of our circumstances. You think I have a lot of opportunities because of my mother's service to the revolution? Hell, we don't have shit. You see us having any electrical appliances in this house? My mother doesn't have much money, and she doesn't make much money either. We are dirt poor, you understand! And we don't have relatives from abroad who send us money like other people. At least you and others can try to escape from this country if you can't take it anymore. We can't escape even if we can't take it any more than you can. My mother doesn't have any money to pay for our passage. Even if she had money, nobody would want to talk to her about escape anyway. See, all those years of service to the revolution means that nobody would dare to touch my mother. They are all afraid she is a spy and will report them to the government. Heck, she is part of the local government. So there goes that option."

"I see," I said mechanically.

"Don't you even try to tell me about morality and conscience! The world has turned upside down for everyone. Everyone is just trying to survive. If you are screwed by the system, then you run to your morality and conscience as your defense. If you have the power to screw, and don't use it, then you will be screwed. The way I look at it, I would rather do the screwing than being screwed by someone else."

"So, you won't hesitate if someday you have to screw your friends? You won't have any qualm about putting me or your friends away if you are required to?"

Hường was silent for a moment. He shook his head wearily. "I hope it never comes to that, Bookworm. I don't think I have the heart to screw my friends. But I have to survive, too! I don't know what I will do if that situation ever arises. Maybe, I just need to take a post away from this town, so that I will not have to face that."

"I see. So, when do you start?"

"I won't start training until next week. Right now, I am just fooling around with my music."

"I've got to go." I got up, not having anything left to say. "I can't honestly say I wish you good luck in what you do, because what you do will hurt other people like us."

"You don't have to, and I don't want you to," Hường shrugged. "Just stay out of trouble, and stay out of my way, so I never have to arrest you."

I left Hường's house to go to the mountain. Anger and sadness overwhelmed my consciousness. I was not angry at Hường. He was as honest and candid to me as he could be. I was angry at the system and the Communist Party for causing the corruption of our souls. For all the defiant acts of rebellion that we did in the past two years, one by one, we were surrendering to the relentless forces that were changing our lives. Those kids who could leave Vietnam had escaped. Those who couldn't, like Hường, turned to join the oppressors. What would happen to all the boys of yesterday when we finally had to make the choices that would determine our survival?

# 12

# A Brief Moment of Glory

A distraction kept me occupied for a few months of my ninth-grade year. We were told that a citywide academic competition would be held in early 1978. Focusing on only two subjects, mathematics and literature, the competition would be the first of its kind since 1975.

The news elicited nothing more than a yawn from my classmates. Their apathy for studying had gone up another level since the year before. I wasn't much more interested than my classmates. Though I suspected I might be selected to compete, I was still smarting from my foolish participation in the "Kế Hoạch Nhỏ" program. For me, awards and recognition, in the new Vietnamese society, were nothing more than empty baits set by a manipulating government for the young and the foolish.

Uninterested as I was, I was still picked to represent my class. The method to select the representatives for the competition was straightforward. The class advisor, the teacher chosen to sponsor a class, chose a representative for each class. Five other students and I, each representing his or her class, formed the team our school fielded for the competition. Though I didn't care much about the competition itself, I was excited and nervous to learn that Trang was selected to represent her class. At last, we wouldn't be able to avoid each other anymore.

For three months, the six chosen students studied an extra hour after school every day under the tutelage of two teachers, Mr. Thuần and Mr. Tuấn. Mr. Thuần, a mathematics teacher, tutored and taught us to solve many problems not included in the normal curriculum. At 50 years old, he was a thin, small man with a quiet, serious demeanor. I had a class with him in eighth grade and had always enjoyed every period he lectured. More than any other teachers, Mr. Thuần had kept the political content (the praising of the party and Uncle Ho or condemnation of the American imperialists) out of his lecture as much as possible. Knowing that I was an eager and motivated student, he often suggested more homework for me to do and spent time with me after school to explain it.

All the students knew our teachers had to integrate the Communist Party doctrine into their lectures because the school administration required them to. The principal, Mr. Vũ Văn Nghiên, was a North Vietnamese Communist Party member. He was appointed to the post two years ago. Since Mr. Nghiên came to our school, the number of "criticism and self-criticism" sessions for the teachers had increased significantly. So was the pressure for all teachers, no matter what subjects they taught, to "enlighten" their students politically via "skillful and appropriate" incorporation of the party doctrine to their lectures.

Since Mr. Thuần did not do much political preaching, he faced a lot of criticism from the school administration. A rumor persisted that Mr. Thuần would be forced to retire after this year, since the school administration was not happy with his "lack of political enlightenment."

Mr. Tuấn, a 40-year-old teacher who taught history and literature, was the opposite of Mr. Thuần. Mr. Tuấn was overzealous in preaching the "greatness" of the party and Uncle Ho. Despite his zeal to conform to the administration's wishes, he was also a knowledgeable and experienced teacher. Strongly disliked by most of my classmates, Mr. Tuấn had gotten more than his fair share of the pranks they pulled.

Both Mr. Thuần and Mr. Tuấn were committed to preparing us as well as they could. Mr. Thuần gave us many difficult algebra and geometry problems to solve. Mr. Tuấn made us wrote many essays critiquing the "revolutionary" literary works we studied for the past year. For the first time in two years, I actually got critical comments on my writing when preparing for the competition.

Studying for the competition also gave me some brief moments of joy. Studying in the same classroom with Trang, I had a chance to observe her from a close distance, rather than being observed by her and feeling self-conscious about my poverty. However, we still did not talk to each other. After the periods were over, we always headed to our bicycles and pedaled home, continuing to pretend not to see nor know the other existed.

The competition came on a day in late January 1978. It was held in a high school in Bến Đình, about two kilometers north from my dwelling. Following the instructions from our teachers, we came to the place at 7 A.M.

When I arrived, I learned that there were fifty students participating in the competition. The proctors divided the participants into three different classrooms. As the students filed into their assigned seats, the administrating teachers read out the rules for the day.

The competition took the whole day. In the morning, we were given four hours to write an essay critiquing a poem written by a Communist poet. After an hour lunch break, we had three hours for a tough math test. Two teachers patrolled each classroom to make sure no participants were cheating.

By a stroke of coincidence, Trang and I were assigned to the same classroom. Worse yet, she sat directly in front of me. This was the closest I ever was to her. The closeness in space and the fact that Trang was looking nicer and neater than usual caused me endless distractions through the day. She was dressed in a clean, crisp, white blouse with long dark pants. Her hair was nicely tied in a bun. She looked sharp but nervous. Though we both came to the place half an hour early, we still had yet to say anything to each other.

When we all were shown our seats, Trang set her book bag down and for a very quick moment, turned around, smiled at me, and said, "Good luck." I was too surprised and could only mutter a lame "Thank you." By then, she already turned forward, listening to the instructions.

The morning session was quiet save for the sounds of the students' pens scratching furiously on paper. I knew the poem we had to critique well, but was having trouble keeping my train of thought straight. I got into spurts of writing a paragraph or two, and then looked up at Trang's back. Then my mind drifted off to thinking how nice it would be to be able to talk to her and be her friend. Before I knew it, I wasted ten, fifteen minutes staring blankly into the air. I had to pinch myself several times just to regain my concentration. Fortunately, the four hours given were enough for me to fill three pages with thoughts and ideas that came in fits and spurts.

When the morning session finished, we filed up to turn our papers in to the teachers. I was hoping that I would have a moment to talk to Trang. I was hoping to ask how she did on the essay and make up for my clumsy response to her "Good luck" wish earlier. However, Trang quickly turned in her paper and headed out to meet with her friend, the girl representing class 9A1. I missed my chance. Feeling drained and disappointed, I scurried to an empty corner of the building to munch on the cold steamed corn and yam my mother made. I didn't feel like talking to anyone at all.

Finishing my lunch, I returned to my seat and stared at the ceiling. I missed Thái and the other boys from my class. Since morning, I hadn't talked to anyone here except for the sudden flash of greeting with Trang. If Thái were here, he would laugh and tell me to forget the competition altogether. *Bookworm,* he would say, *there is no way you can concentrate sitting next to Trang, so why bother? Besides, isn't it better to look at a pretty girl you like than write a meaningless essay about a poem of a long-dead Communist?*

A few minutes before the afternoon test began, Trang and other students came back to the room. This time, she quickly settled into her seat and didn't look at me as she did in the morning. It was just as well. If she did, I probably would stammer and get distracted worse than I did before.

After the teachers passed out the exam, I forced myself to concentrate on working the problems. The thirty algebra and geometry problems on the test were long and difficult. This time, I kept my head stuck to the book. Around the room, the only noises were the scratching sounds of the pens punctuated by the occasional sighs of other students. I knew the sighs well. It was the sign of frustration by students who got stuck on problems they couldn't solve.

An hour into the test, unexpectedly, Trang turned around to me and asked if she could get some ink from me. She had run out of ink.

I was startled. The concentration I had fought so hard to maintain was broken. Yet, remembering my clumsiness this morning, I steadied myself not to look like a fool again. Pushing my ink bottle toward her, I showed her that I had plenty of ink left. She could take as much as she needed. With a short "Thank you," Trang quickly poured some ink from my bottle into hers and turned back to her problems. It took me another five minutes to snap out of my funk and return to the test.

After two and a half years, this was the first time we had spoken to each other in full sentences. I suddenly felt a sense of joy and hopefulness. Maybe she didn't think badly of me after all.

The math test was the toughest I had ever taken. When it was over, I thought for sure I had failed badly. I couldn't solve several problems at the end for there wasn't enough time. However, I found some consolation when I saw other frustrated faces in the room. Maybe I wasn't the worst idiot in this room after all.

After turning her exam, Trang waited for me to turn mine in, then asked, "How did you do?"

I was so happy that she waited and started the conversation first. I took in a long breath before answering, "I don't think I did well at all. I didn't finish all the problems."

"Yes, this exam is too difficult. I didn't do well, either. I got stuck on half of the problems."

I was happy and surprised at her openness. Emboldened, I made an attempt at consolation. "Well, if it is difficult for us then maybe it is also difficult for everybody else. Who knows? We may still have a chance at winning something."

"Maybe you have a chance," Trang shook her head. "I know I don't. At least not on the math."

By this time, other students had already left. We packed our books and started walking to our bicycles. Not knowing what else to say, I tentatively suggested, "Your house is close to mine and it is already dark. If you don't mind, maybe we should ride on the same road home?"

"Sure."

Her ready agreement warmed my heart. After two years of wanting to but never having the guts to talk to her for fear of being looked down on, I finally had the chance to get to know Trang. She wasn't the snobbish rich girl I was afraid she would be. There was much I wanted to talk to her about. At least the ride home would give us some time to talk.

To my dismay, I found my bicycle had a flat tire. I must have ridden over something sharp this morning, causing the tire to have a slow leak. At this late hour, I would not be able to find anyone to patch the tire.

The sky was getting dark and it started to drizzle lightly. Trang had already unlocked her bicycle and wore a raincoat. She walked her bicycle next to me and asked, "Are you ready?"

I felt so disappointed. I was looking forward to riding home and talking to her. Now, with my flat tire, I would have to walk home alone.

"No. My bicycle has a flat tire," I shook my head dejectedly. "I have to walk it home and get it patched tomorrow. It is starting to rain. Why don't you go home first. I'll be okay!"

To my surprise, Trang looked concerned. She thought for a moment then said "I will walk my bicycle home with you. I am not in a hurry. Besides, the rain is light and I have my raincoat with me. Do you have your raincoat?"

"Yes, I do. Thank you."

"No, I have to thank you for helping me out today. If I didn't get the ink from you, I probably would have turned in blank papers."

Under the darkening sky and the light rain, we walked our bicycles home while bundling in our raincoats. Candles lighted up the houses along the road. Smoke from firewood coming up from the many homes along the way reminded me I still had to cook dinner for my family. Yet, I was too happy to be with Trang to think about cooking. We walked along in silence, each not knowing what to ask the other. For me, there were so many things I wanted to ask her. Yet, I could not form my words coherently. Fortunately, Trang broke the silence first. "I see you go up to the mountain every afternoon. What do you do up there?"

"My family has a piece of land up there," I replied. "I go there to work on the land."

"Really? How far is it? What do you do on the land?"

"It is about two kilometers up in the Núi Nhỏ mountain," I said with a tinge of pride. "Well, I plant yam and bananas up there. Sometimes, I dig up tree roots and dry them to use as firewood."

"You use tree roots for firewood? Aren't they smoky and messy to burn?"

"They are not that bad if you dry them thoroughly. Besides, it saves money. We can't afford to buy coal or firewood anyway."

"Isn't working on the land hard?" Trang asked with genuine curiosity.

"Yes, but it is not that bad. I got used to it after a while. The worst part about it is that I am alone up there most of the time. Sometimes, the only companions I have are the little monkeys."

"Are there snakes up there?"

"Yeah. I came across two or three snakes on the road to our land before," I replied, wondering why girls were so afraid of snakes.

"Uh! I am scared of snakes," Trang shook her head. "If I see them, I would freeze. I wouldn't know what to do."

"Why? Snakes are not that bad," I shrugged. "They are harmless. The snakes I see up there are usually small. Sometimes, I see them crossing the dirt trail. All I have to do is let them pass, then go on. They are not out to bite me or anything."

"I don't know. Snakes look so slimy and scary to me! Anyway, I don't want to talk about snakes anymore. You said that there is no one near your land at all?"

"The only thing near my land is a little Buddhist temple," I replied. "There are a few monks who live in there."

"Do you ever go into the temple?" Trang asked.

"A few times after I finish working," I nodded. "I usually go in there to pray to Buddha to protect my father."

"I am sorry," Trang said sincerely. "I heard about your father. Do you know where he is now?"

"Yes. He is in a re-education camp in Long Khánh. He was moved to this camp last year. Before that, they put him in a camp somewhere in the North."

"It must be tough living without your father. I don't know how I would do without my parents."

We were both silent, deep in our own thoughts. My heart was warmed by the sympathetic words from Trang. But I didn't want to continue talking too much about my hard life. I was too proud to want pity from anyone. As Trang was silent, I continued, "My dad writes to me sometimes from the camp. He even made a Chinese Chess set himself and sent it to me."

"Really? Is it nice?"

"It is more beautiful than any chess set you could buy in the market."

"Do you play it often?"

"I do. But only with people I like. I don't want to lose any pieces of this set that my father made for me."

"I see. Are you always a hopeful, optimistic person?" Trang asked suddenly.

"What do you mean?" I was surprised by Trang's question.

"Well, I thought that you are always so optimistic. At least, that's what I gather from what you wrote in my yearbook. Remember, didn't you write that your favorite couplet from *Bình Ngô Đại Cáo* was: 'Nhật nguyệt hối rồi lại minh, Càn Khôn bĩ rồi lại thái (The sun and the moon were dark, but became bright again. The universe was drowned in sorrow, but would be filled with happiness again)'?"

"Oh! I remember. Well, I always have hope because my father taught me to never give up hope. Our family has little. If we don't have hope, then we have nothing, and we would be nothing."

"But what do you hope for?"

"Well, I hope that someday my life will be better than now. I don't know how and where, but if I get a chance to continue learning and do something with my brain, then that will be more than enough."

Trang wiped the rain from her hair, then looked straight in my eyes. "I admire you for your strength and hope. Sometimes, I wish I had the same strength and hope as you do."

"Why?" I didn't expect the statement from Trang at all. "You have so much that I and other people don't. Your family is well off. Your father doesn't have to go to re-education camp. He still runs the ice factory, doesn't he? Why are you so pessimistic?"

"It looks that way to everyone else, doesn't it?" Trang sighed. "Yes, I am a rich girl, who only has to study and play and don't have to worry about anything, right? Maybe that was right before, but it won't last."

"What do you mean?"

"My father spent his whole life to build his business, this ice factory," Trang replied slowly. "That was his hard work for the past 20 years. That was all his money, savings, sweat, blood, and tears he put into it. But he won't have it much longer. My father has managed to keep the factory from being nationalized for two years, but now he can't stop them anymore. The government is going to take over the factory in a few months. It will no longer belong to us."

I was sad by the revelation from Trang. It must have weighed heavily on her mind. So much that she had to share it with me to lighten the burden. But I was not too surprised. The Communist government would eventually get to every one of us, even to a family as well off as hers. I couldn't think of anything else to say, except to ask, "So what will happen to you and your family?"

"Oh, we will have to move out of there," Trang said matter-of-factly. "We have another house in Lý Thường Kiệt Street, so we will move there."

"What will your dad do?" I asked lamely. "What will you do?"

"I don't know. My dad hasn't done anything else except run that ice factory for his whole life. Without it, I don't know what he will do. We are not that bad off, so I will still go to school. What about you?"

"I don't know," I shrugged. "I guess when this year ends, I will know. Whatever happens, I always believe there will be brighter days ahead."

"Yes, I think I have to think like that, too," Trang nodded. "I hope there will be brighter days ahead for me and my family, too."

Not wanting to continue on the depressing topic of the future, I tried to steer the conversation to a different direction. "Did you like the poem we had to write about today?"

"It's all right," she shrugged. "I don't like the revolutionary literature we learned very much. This poem is better than others, but it is still revolutionary literature. There is too much war, killing, and hatred in it for me."

Trang's answer surprised me. Yet, it gave me a better glimpse to understand her.

"So what type of literature do you like?" I asked.

"I like the old, classical Vietnamese literature that we learned before. I also like some American novels I had the chance to read."

"American novels? Where do you get that? Can you really read them? Can you read English that well?"

"No, no," Trang laughed. "My English is not that good. See, my father has always wanted for all of us someday to be able to go abroad and study in America. So, before 1975, he bought a lot of books about America for us to read. He even has several American novels that were translated into Vietnamese. He encourages me, my brother and sister to read them so that we will know something about this big country."

"Really?" I asked. "Do you want to go to America?"

"I don't know. It may be nice to go there. But I don't know how I could live without my family. Besides, does it matter? We can't get out of this country anyway."

"I don't know," I shook my head, not wanting to face the bitter reality. "Maybe if you really want and pray for it, it will happen. I think it will be so nice to go and study in America. My father told me the Americans have lot of schools and their schools are huge. They have more scientists and more scientific knowledge than any other countries. Not like here, where even our biology teacher doesn't know enough to teach us."

"You want to go to America, too?"

"Well, it is only a dream!" I wiped the rain that dripped down on my forehead. "My father told me a lot about this country when he was still around. He wanted me to go there and study to become somebody. But we all have our own fate. Now, my father is in jail, and I am plowing the land to get something to eat. Yes, I will go to America all right, in my next life!"

We were so engrossed in the conversation that we didn't realize we had arrived at our homes. The long distance somehow seemed so short. The rain started to come down harder. We bade good bye to each other, then rushed to our homes.

I went to sleep that night with a light, happy feeling. I didn't think at all about the academic competition. All I could think about was the wonderful conversation I had with Trang. After two years of irrational fear and embarrassment, I finally learned there was a thinking, feeling person with her hopes and fear behind this reserved, beautiful girl. Yes, the scary, uncertain future awaited all of us. But then, all I could do was savor this sweet experience, for it might not come again for a very long time.

I was told by Mr. Tuấn, our literature trainer, that the results of the competition would not be known for at least a week. Each participating school had a teacher represented on the grading committee. The teacher representing our school on this committee was Mr. Tuấn himself.

On the Friday after the competition, Mr. Tuấn asked me to see him in the teacher's lounge. There was no one else in the room except for Mr. Tuấn and me. Motioning for me to sit down in a chair, Mr. Tuấn asked how I felt about my performance in the competition last week.

"I thought it was all right, Teacher," I said. "The essay was not difficult but the math test was. I think I did okay but I don't know if it was good enough to win anything."

"You know I was on the grading committee for this competition," Mr. Tuấn said slowly, emphasizing each word. "Well, we have the results already, and it will be announced next Monday when the school gathers in the morning for the weekly singing of the national anthem. Now, I am going to tell you the results before anyone, but you must promise not to tell it to anyone else."

"Yes."

"Our school did quite well in this competition," the teacher said while watching my face closely. "Our team took three top prizes in the competition. We won first prizes in mathematics and literature, and a second prize in literature as well. This result is much better than we, the faculty, had hoped for."

"You probably wonder why I am telling you this. It is simple, really. You won the first place in mathematics and the second place in literature. Hồng Ngọc of class 9P1 won the first place in literature. You and Hồng Ngọc have really done well for our school, so it is only fair you know ahead of other people. Really, we are very proud of you!"

The news caught me totally unexpected. I was ecstatic. First place in mathematics and second place in literature! My hard work really did pay off. The kids in my class would brag about this achievement for a long time. Yet, I was a little sad Trang didn't win anything.

"Thank you, Teacher," I said slowly, trying to be modest. "I really owe it to you and Teacher Thuần for spending so much time with us."

Mr. Tuấn hesitated for a second, then said, "You are welcome. Well, there is something else I thought you should know."

"What is it, Teacher?" I asked, wondering what this mystery was about.

"I don't know how to put this well, so I won't try. It is something the grading committee wants to keep quiet. I am violating regulations by telling you, but I will tell you anyway. If this competition proves anything, it proves that you are the best student in this school, and for that matter, in the city as well. You should have won first places in both mathematics and literature. Your essay was the best essay. Everyone on the grading committee agreed on it.

"However, the city school administrators were not comfortable seeing you taking first places in both subjects. In fact, they asked if we could regrade your essay so that you would not win a prize in literature. Well, I don't want to go into it further than that, other than at the end, we agreed to a compromise to let you take second place instead of first."

I was shocked! The first shock was learning I did so much better than I imagined I could. First places in both subjects! I could imagine the joy and pride that my mother would have when I shared the news with her. Then the news that the city school administrators wanted to nullify my achievements hit me. I was silent for a minute, trying to digest the meaning of the news, before asking "But why, Teacher? Why do the city school administrators want to take the victory away from me?"

"I debated to myself long and hard before deciding to tell you this," Mr. Tuấn sighed. "I know the students in your class, maybe even you, don't like me. You kids may think I have found the 'enlightenment of socialism' too quickly. I understand. I know what the students' families have gone through. I know it is difficult for you to understand or to accept what I do. I don't really worry about what the students think of me. I am a teacher, and I love what I do, teaching the bright students who someday will do something good for this country. That is what keeps me here, in the school. Bright, wonderful students like you, who work so hard to go somewhere. You kids have something we older people don't have, the energy and the ideal of youth to want to do something good. I want to be there to give you the passion of learning that will keep you going. So what if I have to praise the party and Uncle Ho a little louder? It is a small price to pay. If I don't teach, the principal will find other North Vietnamese teachers for you. Then, it will be worse.

"I tell you this so that you know how proud I am of you. We in the faculty know how hard you work and can only imagine how far you could go if circumstances were different. It was not fair the city school administrators want to take away your victory. Their reason was they didn't want a kid with an 'anti-revolutionary' family background like you to be a hero. It wouldn't fit the image the party is portraying for the 'lackeys' of the American imperialists."

"But, Teacher, how is that different from letting me win first place in mathematics and second place in literature?"

"It doesn't make much sense, does it? Well, your winning those prizes is a compromise. Most of us on the grading committee fought the pressure to take it away from you. The math test is straightforward. The scores are what they are, so there is little they can push us to change it. The essay is subjective, so there are more opportunities for people to poke and challenge our assessments. The administrators don't push it too hard because they are concerned that the teachers would get upset and start telling other people. Then this academic competition to showcase the brilliance of socialist education would really turn into a farce."

I knew Mr. Tuấn was telling me all he could. I also realized my classmates and I might have misjudged him. If he didn't care, he would have never told me this. He might lose his job if anyone ever learned what he was telling me. Gathering my books, I got up and thanked him. He didn't have to tell me to keep it quiet; I promised to and left.

I was deep in thought on the way home. That night, when my mother came home, I shared with her the news of my achievements and how I nearly had all of them taken away. When I was through, my mother hugged me.

"You've really made me proud, Son," she said quietly. "I am not surprised at the results and what the Communists try to do. Count yourself lucky that you still get to win. But no matter what the results of the competition are, you know how well you did, right?"

"No, Mother. I don't know. The tests were tough, and other students may well have done better than I did."

"No, that's not what I meant, Son. The ultimate test is not so much whether you have beaten other competitors, but if you have beaten yourself. If you have given the best you can give or worked the hardest that you physically and mentally could, then you have done well. I know my son would always do that, right?"

"Yes, Mom. But it is still nicer to win!"

"Yes, it is."

On Monday, after all the students had gathered in the schoolyard to sing the national anthem, the principal, Mr. Nghiên, went up to make his weekly speech. As Mr. Tuấn had told me, he announced the results of the academic competition after his long speech exhorting the students to follow Uncle Ho's motto of "Study well, Labor well."

The students of class 9A3 and 9P1 cheered loudly when Mr. Nghiên announced Hong Ngoc and I had won the first prizes in the competition. He called us up before the gathering so that the students had the chance to cheer their new "heroes." As I went up to where Mr. Nghiên was, I cast a glance toward class 9A2. Trang was there, clapping her hands hard. She was also looking straight as me, as all other kids were. I thought I saw a look of admiration, and sadness at the same time, in her eyes.

For the rest of the day, I was congratulated by friends from all classes. Yet, I didn't feel happy. I still remembered what Mr. Tuấn told me last week. I understood the unspoken message Mr. Tuấn was trying to tell me. My glory, if winning this academic competition was it, would be short lived. The city school administrators, all Communist Party members, would get their chance at me, the kid whose father was an officer in the "Ngụy Quân" (the Illegitimate Army) and a "lackey" of the American imperialists. Winning this academic competition had done nothing to change the certainty that I would not be in a Vietnamese high school after this year.

# 13

# The Winds of War

In February 1978, many events happened that brought additional pressures and problems to our already-threatened existence. At this time, many armed skirmishes between Vietnamese and Cambodians happened in the Mekong Delta western provinces. The People's Committee's loudspeakers in our neighborhoods started broadcasting news of innocent Vietnamese living in the border being massacred by Khmer Rouge bandits. Tensions and fear started building as we sensed where this was leading. Vietnam would once again be plunged into war.

As an avid student of Vietnam's history, I knew well of the long-entrenched enmity Cambodians had toward Vietnamese. The implacable hatred was passed down from many generations and was not without good reason.

Since the late 1300s, successive Vietnamese dynasties, starting with the Trần Dynasty, had pushed southward to expand the border. Over a period of 600 years, our ancestors had invaded and annexed countries to the south. The people and cultures of these countries vanished, having been destroyed or assimilated into the Vietnamese people and culture. Many provinces of South Vietnam were land that once belonged to the Cambodians. In fact, large populations of Cambodians still lived in many provinces.

As conquerors, our history textbooks never had anything to say about the atrocities that our forefathers might have committed in their expansionist quests. As the vanquished, the Cambodians passed these stories down through many generations. For many Cambodians, the Vietnamese were the enemies that took the land that rightfully belonged to them. Their hatred for the Vietnamese exhibited itself through brutal massacres committed against Vietnamese living in Cambodia in the 1970s. During the Lon Nol regime, many Vietnamese males living in rural Cambodia were killed, decapitated, and their bodies thrown down the Mekong River. These incidents, known as "cáp duồn" (beheading), became the "boogie man" stories Vietnamese mothers living in the Mekong Delta would tell their children to make them be quiet.

By 1978, the Khmer Rouge regime of Pol Pot was well into its bloody quest of exterminating millions of Cambodians. Their violence didn't stay just within Cambodia. Occasionally, bands of Khmer Rouge guerillas crossed into Vietnam, massacring Vietnamese villagers and soldiers in the western provinces. When the People's Army of Vietnam retaliated, many battles between the Vietnamese Communist troops and the Khmer Rouge, former comrades in the war against the Americans, ensued.

The conflicts turned the Communist Party propaganda machine to high gear. It steadily increased the volume and frequency of its shrill condemnations of the Pol Pot regime. Every day, the neighborhood loudspeakers broadcast condemnations of the Khmer Rouge, and in school, news of the atrocities committed against Vietnamese living near the border flooded in. In this tense atmosphere, patriotic fervor ran high in my school. Even my classmates believed Vietnam should invade Cambodia and remove the Khmer Rouge from power. Invasion, they believed, was the only way to stop the terror inflicted on the Vietnamese living near the border. Many of my friends were also gung ho to teach those "savage Khmer Rouge" a good lesson.

Besides turning up its propaganda machine to arouse nationalistic anger, the Vietnamese government also began mass mobilization for its army. Then, the dark realities of war started to dawn on us. At that time, we were kids turning fourteen or fifteen. It would only be a few short years before we would be drafted.

Having lived through the attack on Vũng Tàu three years before, my classmates and I had no illusions about the glory of war. For most of us, being the sons of the former soldiers of the Ngụy Quân (Illegitimate Army), being drafted into the People's Army of Vietnam was like getting a death sentence. Growing up in the South, we had learned of the reputation of high casualties in the Communist army. We also knew of the Vietnamese Communists' long history of sending boys as young as ten into battles behind the justification of liberation and independence. While the official age for youths to be drafted was eighteen, we might well be drafted long before reaching our eighteenth birthdays.

Youths in our neighborhood began to be drafted and sent to the

Vietnam-Cambodia border. Many stories from these young men started circulating back to our city that further heightened our worst fears. The newly enlisted conscripts were given only a few weeks of basic military training before they were sent to the border. Furthermore, they were separated into "good elements," those who were Communist party members or who were considered to be sympathetic to the party, and "bad elements," those whose families were involved with the South Vietnamese government in the past. The "good element" soldiers were given better weapons and used as reserve troops. The "bad element" soldiers were given inadequate and old weapons and used as point men on patrol or in dangerous assignments. The message could not be any clearer to us. Our lives were most expendable. The army commanders would not hesitate to sacrifice us as they saw fit.

In this atmosphere of agonizing fear and nervous anticipation, my neighborhood received its first casualty of the war. One young man in the neighborhood was drafted two months before. After four weeks of basic military training, his unit was sent to a village at the Vietnam-Cambodia border. His platoon was given the job of guarding the village. One night when the whole platoon slept and the sentry dozed off, the Khmer Rouge guerrillas stealthily came in and killed all of them. After killing the Vietnamese soldiers, the Khmer Rouge went on to decapitate and cut open their torsos, taking all their guts, hearts, and insides out.

When the body of the young man was sent back to his family, the brutal realities of the war became obvious to all of us. During the entire Vietnam War, our city had been well insulated from most of the fighting. I only knew of the war through accounts in the newspapers and televised footage of battles. I had also seen refugees from Central Vietnam who ran for their lives during the Communists' Easter Offensive in 1972. A large number of these refugees lived in temporary shelters in my high school. But I had never known a neighbor's family whose son was killed in such a savage manner. The tragedy shocked me into the realization that it could well be me who would next be killed in an equally gruesome manner.

As I walked by the house of the mourning family, my mind was filled with confusion, fear and desperation. I did not want to die. I did not want to fight for a regime that sent my father to prison, confiscated our property, oppressed and sent us to the brink of elimination. I did not want to kill and hate a people whom I hadn't seen or known before. I did not want to be a part of the instrument the Vietnamese Communists were using to export their brand of Communism to other countries. Yet, it was very clear to me that it didn't matter what I wanted or didn't want; my fate would be determined by the same people who didn't hesitate to sacrifice the lives of millions of Vietnamese youths during the Vietnam War.

The winds of the impending war with Cambodia, while increasing the tensions and fear among all of us, also resulted in more demands on the students. Our school administration, under Mr. Nghiên, the senior Communist Party member, exhorted all students and faculty to increase "vigilance against possible sabotage by our 'enemies,' who would particularly take this opportunity to undermine our progress toward socialism!" We never knew exactly who the "enemies" were and what they looked like. From the teachers' explanation, the "enemies" were anyone who wanted to derail Vietnam's steady, strong march toward the Socialist Paradise. We were told to watch for anyone who ever said anything against the party and Uncle Ho. We were told to look for any suspicious strangers who did not look like they belonged in the area. Even those who damaged or vandalized the "people's property" were the "enemies" we needed to look out for. The "enemies" were all around us and it was our patriotic duty to "smash their anti-revolutionary plots."

I knew that the heightened propaganda aimed to turn the kids into a network of informants. We would become part of the instruments the Communist Party used to keep the populace under control, particularly in the time of coming war. As more young men were sent to the battlefields, we would be the party's eyes and ears watching over dissidents or anyone who ever harbored a thought of rebellion.

Conveniently, the principal also used this opportunity to make us to work on guard duty for free. In March '78, Nghiên began requiring teams of students to guard the school through the night. All the boys in ninth grade were required to stay over and guard the school against vandals and "saboteurs" at night once every two weeks. The girls were exempt from this duty. The guard schedule was administered by Diệu, leader of the "Đoàn Thanh Niên Cộng Sản Hồ Chí Minh" (the Ho Chi Minh Communist Youth League). Each night, there was a team of twelve to fifteen boys sleeping over and watching the school.

My first three shifts of guarding the school were relatively uneventful. We never saw anyone who looked remotely like a "saboteur" near the school. On the night of our shift, we congregated in school at 7 P.M. After roll call, we checked all the classrooms, restrooms, and the teacher's lounge. After 9 P.M., we crowded into the teacher's lounge to talk, play games, or sing. By midnight, we took turn sleeping, always leaving two boys awake to keep vigilance.

The worst thing that happened to us was being woken up to change shifts. The boys of 9A3 class never woke their classmates up gently. As restless, creative kids, we enjoyed playing jokes on each other. The more cruel the method, the more we remembered the lesson to never sleep too soundly while on guard duty. One time, I was deep in REM sleep when a painful, burning sensation in my feet woke me out of my deep slumber. I shot right upward to find pieces of burning paper stuck between my toes. From then on, I always took the first shift of watch to avoid having to be woken up.

On another night, Chiêm was sleeping when the smell of burning hair and smoke overwhelmed his nose. He woke up to find himself stripped of his pants and most of his pubic hair burned away by the two boys from the previous shift. By the next day, the story of Chiêm's burned pubic hair, added with liberal embellishments, was propagated around school by my gleeful classmates. Chiêm didn't dare talk to any girls for months afterward.

On a night of guard duty in early April '78, we had an unexpected guest. Dũng, an alumnus of our school, came to hang out with us. Dũng was an 18-year-old man with a lightly built frame. When we were in seventh grade, he was in the ninth grade. He knew a few boys in my class, as we often played soccer against the boys in the 9th grade classes before. I didn't know much about Dũng, other than that his father, a policeman in the former government of South Vietnam, went to re-education camp for two years. Last I heard of him, I learned that he didn't make it to high school. He probably failed the background test like most of us would. Since then, I had not seen him at all.

There were twelve boys from class 9A3 on guard duty that night. Thái, Chiêm, Thành, and I made up the tamer element of the group. The other eight boys, Tấn, Phú, Phước, Đông, An, Giang, Hiền, and Lâm were some of the craziest kids in our school's history.

Dũng came in with two packs of cigarettes and two packs of beer. He passed the goodies out to all the boys. While Thái and I politely refused the beer and the cigarettes, other boys were more than happy to enjoy them. Dũng came with many things to talk about. Soon, we gathered in the teacher's lounge around Dũng to listen to his stories.

Dũng was a funny and talkative man. He inhaled several deep smokes before telling us his story. We should be thankful that we only had to guard the school, Dũng said. Someday, we might have to be on guard duty on the battlefield front. Then, we would really have the chance to shit in our pants. He should know. He was drafted and sent to the Cambodian border two months ago. After two months, he couldn't take it anymore and deserted the army.

All of us got really interested. Dũng was a deserter and he had been to the border of Cambodia. He would have lot of good stories to tell us. The boys prodded him to tell us what happened. "Why did you desert?" we asked. "Wouldn't the police pick you up from your house right when you show up and send you straight to jail?"

Throwing up his hands in a mock gesture of exasperation, Dũng laughed at our excitement and told us to calm down. He had the whole night to tell us stories. He had been out of school for two years, since he failed the entrance examination to high school. His father was recently released from re-education camp and unemployed. His mother peddled stuff here and there and made some small bucks. Dũng was lucky to find an apprenticeship on a fishing boat. He went to the sea with the crew to fish. His pay was his meal, sleeping space on the boat, and a small share of the fish they caught.

Then the Cambodian conflict happened. The head of the People's Committee in his ward nailed Dũng as one of the first boys to be drafted because his father couldn't cough up enough coffee money. One day, Dũng was a fisherman. The next day, he was a new "poor dumb ass" in the "glorious People's Army of Vietnam."

"It's not that bad to be a new poor dumb ass of the People's Army," one of the boys laughed. "At least, they give you food to eat, don't they?"

"It's bad if you are the dumb ass going through it," Dũng retorted. The new conscripts went through four weeks of military drills, with lots of running and crawling through ditches and barbed wire. As far as shooting went, Dũng got to shoot only a few bullets from his AK rifle in his entire soldier career, and all of it in training. "That would make me a pretty good soldier, hey?" Dũng laughed sarcastically.

"Why couldn't you practice shooting more?" we asked. Dũng replied that the People's Army couldn't afford for new dumb asses like him to waste too many bullets in practice. Didn't we remember our political lessons? The soldiers of the glorious People's Army of Vietnam would always do better in battle than the savage Khmer Rouge — even though we couldn't quite figure out how the trigger worked.

After four weeks, Dũng's unit was sent to the border in Tây Ninh province. The new soldiers were reinforcement to existing units to patrol and protect the Vietnamese against the Khmer Rouge's raids from across the border. For a month, Dũng and his comrades didn't see any Khmer Rouge fighters. Their guard duties were monotonous and boring. One night, Dũng had a night shift from 2 A.M. to 8 A.M. with two other soldiers. The soldiers sat in their own holes, about 20 meters apart. Dũng dozed off for half an hour at 3 A.M. When he woke up, Dũng got scared because it was too quiet. Going over to the other soldiers' posts to see how they were doing, he found both of them dead, their heads cleanly cut off. Some Khmer Rouge sappers crawled into their positions, killed the soldiers, and no one heard a sound. He had no idea why he wasn't killed, too. After that night, Dũng figured he'd better pack his bag and desert from the army fast.

All the boys were shocked. The horror of what Dũng described slowly sunk into our heads. We could all imagine ourselves, young boys who just barely learned how to hold a gun facing silent killers who would come for us in the dead of the night. Dũng took another swig of the beer then continued with his story.

That was the first time the Khmer Rouge sappers came for them. The Vietnamese soldiers were really scared so the camp commanders doubled the guard at night. Nobody dared to sleep on his shift anymore. Then, two weeks later, the unit had a platoon making a routine patrol in the woods outside the camp. One soldier stopped behind to take a piss. He disappeared. The next day, his body was found with all his arms and legs chopped off. Then, Dũng decided he had enough. On his next patrol, he found a bush to throw away his uniform in, changed to civilian clothes and walked all the way from Tây Ninh back home.

"Why didn't your units attack the Khmer Rouge to retaliate?" Thái asked. "If they could attack you, you better pay them back, right?"

"We would, if we knew where their bases were," Dũng shrugged. A war with Cambodia had yet to be declared. To retaliate, the Vietnamese soldiers conducted a few raids across the border. They didn't find any Khmer Rouge guerrillas, but got a few chickens and cows from the Cambodian farmers for their effort.

"Would a war happen soon?" we started asking ourselves. How much longer could Vietnam take this crap from the Khmer Rouge? Puffing his cigarette, Dũng predicted a war would mean nothing but bad news for dumb asses like us. Once we were in Cambodia, it would get even more dangerous. The Khmer Rouge soldiers were the students of the Vietnamese Communists on guerrilla tactics. They might have fewer weapons and men to fight the Vietnamese army. But on their land, they could find a thousand unpleasant ways to send poor boys like us to our ancestors.

Steering away from the depressing topics of war and death, Thái asked Dũng how he avoided arrest by the local security agents. In reply, Dũng told us he had been hiding for the past three weeks at his uncle's house in Bà Rịa. He hadn't gone out in the daytime to avoid being seen by anyone. Last night, he came home at midnight to see his parents. Then, he would leave for the Mekong Delta tomorrow. He came to see us because hiding at home for three weeks without talking to anyone nearly drove him nuts. After tonight, we wouldn't see him again. In the Mekong Delta, he would be working on a fishing boat, and if his luck held out, maybe one day, he could say goodbye to the glorious land of the party and Uncle Ho.

We were excited. Dũng was openly admitting he was about to escape from Vietnam. I wondered if he had had too many beers. At once, we all asked him when he would make the escape. Apparently, Dũng wasn't as drunk as I thought. Laughing, he told us to enjoy the beer instead. He didn't know when and where the escape would take place. Even if he did, he couldn't tell us.

It was close to midnight. We divided into groups for guard duty. Some went to sleep to wait for their shifts. Other boys stayed awake with Dũng smoking and talking about the uncertain future. At half past midnight, when his cigarettes and beer had run out, Dũng said goodbye and took off.

Thái and I took the first shift at guard. While the other boys slept, we reminisced about the good old days when we were little boys who never even had to think about death. When our shift was over at 1 A.M., Hiền and Tấn took over. Tired, Thái and I found a corner in which to lie down and fell asleep soon after.

Normally, the worst thing my classmates would do on a night of guard duty like this was to play jokes on each other, like what they had done to Chiêm. Tonight, the stories Dũng told caused some to think a little harder about their future. Always restless and resentful of what the government had done to their families, the boys' anger and fear were inflamed by the dreaded future they could expect through the stories from Dũng. Unknown to me and my tamer friends, the other eight boys were planning the most spectacular prank they had ever pulled.

When they were sure the four of us were fast asleep, the rowdy boys went to work. Some defecated while others went to the outhouse to collect more human feces. Taking the waste with them, they went to every classroom to spread them under every chair and table. Pictures of Ho Chi Minh in all classrooms also received liberal doses of the human waste. I never knew if this action had satisfied their anger. For sure, one thing did happen. They did carry out, in a symbolic way, their threats of making Uncle Ho eat shit.

We woke up next morning at 6 A.M., gathered our belongings and went home. The four of us who weren't included in the plan knew nothing of what happened when we slept. As class started at 8 A.M., I was in a hurry to get home to freshen up, get my books and came back to school.

When I got back to school a few minutes before eight, I immediately sensed something was wrong. The students who arrived early in other classes were standing outside pinching their noses. The boys of our class, 9A3, were standing outside as well, but with glee in their faces. Some of the girls in the class next to us, 9A2, went to get buckets of water and brooms to clean their classroom. Other girls were giving us, the boys of 9A3, dirty looks.

I asked Lộc, one of my classmates standing outside, what happened. Grinning, Lộc told me to go in the class and find out for myself. When I walked in the classroom, the stinking odor of shit hitting my nose told me the story. Looking up at the framed picture of Ho Chi Minh in the front of the class, I was horrified. Clumps of yellowish, dried feces covered Ho's eyes, ears, nose, mouth, and beard. Thái, my closest friend, came in at the same time. Confused, I turned to ask Thái a stupid question: "Who did this?"

Shaking his head, Thái replied he was about to ask me the same question. Whoever committed this act did it in all other classes as well. He would bet it had to be the boys who were on guard duty with us last night. We were all going to be in serious trouble this time.

Thái's prediction came true soon enough. When the faculty and school administrators arrived and learned of the situation, they decided to cancel all classes for the day and got the students to clean up their classrooms. On everyone's mind, the prime suspects for this odorous crime were the twelve boys from 9A3 on guard duty the previous night. As we cleaned our classroom, we could hear the curses from the boys and girls of the classes next door. More than a few of these curses referred to "the animals of class 9A3."

The principal, Mr. Nghiên, decided to take on the investigation himself. The incident was considered the most serious crime ever committed in our school, not because of the trashing of the classrooms, but because of the most irreverent desecration of Ho Chi Minh's pictures. Nghiên sent for all of us who were on guard duty last night to meet with him one on one. Chiêm was the first one to be sent for. As he went down to the principal's office, we glanced at each other and braced for the worst. Only then did I notice that six out of the eight crazy boys of our group last night had not come to school today.

After fifteen minutes, Chiêm returned. He looked dejected and lifeless, as if all the air had been knocked out of him. Then, it was Thái's turn. As Thái went, we gathered around Chiêm to ask him what happened.

"Shit, Nghiên just kicked me out of school," Chiêm let out a long sigh. Nghiên wouldn't take Chiêm's word that he didn't do nor know who did the deed, either. Chiêm was kicked out for not telling Nghiên anything and the only way he could come back to school was to name those who did it.

After Thái returned, it was my turn. Thái told the boys the same story and packed up his books to go home. As I walked into his office, Nghiên was busily writing on his notepad. Not even looking up, he pointed me to a chair and grunted, "Sit down."

I sat down on the chair and tried to compose myself for the storm that I knew would be coming. When he finally finished writing, Nghiên looked up at me. His hooded eyes searched for every trace of nervous, guilty look on my face for a minute before he spoke. "Look, I've just expelled two of your friends because these boys don't have the sense to be honest with me. You and I are both educated people, so why don't I just get straight to the matter. If you have any sense, don't waste my time with lies. I just have a question for you: Who did it? Who trashed all the pictures of Uncle Ho and all the classrooms?"

"I don't know, Mr. Nghiên," I responded while trying to be as calm as I could. "I just came in this morning and found out at the same time everyone else did."

"If you are insisting on covering for the guilty as your friends did, this meeting will be over very quickly," Nghiên's eyes narrowed. "You were in the group that guarded the school last night. Your job was to protect the school's property against vandals and saboteurs. This crime is clearly an act of sabotage, and you don't know about it? No one but the twelve of you who slept here last night were in a position to commit this crude, heinously disrespectful crime. And you expect me to believe you didn't do it and didn't know who did it?"

"Mr. Nghiên, it's the truth," I pleaded. "Please let me explain. I was in here on duty since 9 o'clock last night. My first shift of watch was between midnight and 1 A.M. From 9 P.M. to 1 in the morning, nothing happened. I even checked all the classrooms before I finished my shift. After my shift, I went to sleep at 1:30 A.M. and didn't wake up until 6 this morning. After that, I went straight home and just came back here. I didn't find out about this until I came in. I really don't know who did it, Mr. Nghiên."

"All right, you wasted enough of my time already," Nghiên frowned. "You didn't tell me anything the other two boys hadn't. I see you boys are really a stubborn, stupid bunch. Well, if you insist on protecting your guilty friends, you will be expelled from this school permanently, starting from today. If you want to be readmitted here, you must tell me the names of the guilty before I find out who they are. Maybe the next few weeks of staying at home will get you to see some light."

"Mr. Nghiên ...," I stammered, trying to make one last plea.

"That's enough," Nghiên shouted. "Go! And get Thành to come down here."

Knowing that it was useless to argue, I stood up and walked back to my classroom. After telling Thành that it was his turn, I gathered my books to go home. On the way out, I caught Trang looking at me from outside her classroom. She was sweeping the water out of her class to the drainage pipe in the balcony. The expression on her face was a mixture of anger, sadness, and disappointment. Knowing I could not answer the question "why" in her eyes, I shook my head and walked away.

I pedaled my bicycle home with legs that felt like they were cast in concrete. So, this was the bitter end to my years in school. I knew I would have little hope anyway of going further beyond this year. But I wanted to stay in school to the very end. Now, fate, or rather, my angry, discontented classmates had forced it to end a lot sooner than I wished. Yet, I knew I could never point my finger at them for Nghiên, even if I knew exactly who did it. The code of honor among us, never tell on your friends, was sacred. I was not about to violate it for two more months of school.

I could not help but laugh at the bitter irony of fate. Just two months before, I was the hero of the school after winning the city academic competition. Now, I was expelled for a crime I didn't commit. How fast did that wheel of fate turn for me! Now, I had at long last come to face the dark, dreaded future.

# 14

# The Last Goodbye

To my surprise, my mother took the news of my expulsion better than I expected. She patiently listened to my explanation from beginning to end. Instead of yelling at me, my mother told me I did the right thing by not pointing a finger at my classmates without actually seeing any of them do it.

But the biggest surprise was hearing my mother saying that this expulsion didn't matter much because fortune would soon be changing for our family. When I asked her what she meant, my mother just told me to be patient. I would understand soon enough. Despite her evasion, I already guessed the implications. Given our family's circumstances, the only thing that made sense to me was that my mother was planning for us to escape from Vietnam.

Ever since April 30, 1975, many people had tried to escape from Vietnam by fishing boats of various sizes. Many successfully reached the shores of freedom. An equal or greater number had perished at sea or run into pirates in the Gulf of Siam. The mass exodus reached an all-time high in 1978, when the Vietnamese Communists intensified their persecutions of the Chinese-Vietnamese.

Though a small minority, the Chinese-Vietnamese possessed most of the country's businesses and economic wealth. Besides racism, the Vietnamese Communists also considered these people as the "evil capitalists." The government conducted several operations to take away the Chinese-Vietnamese's wealth and get rid of them. Many Chinese-Vietnamese businesses were confiscated and nationalized. From 1975 to 1978, the government also conducted three currency changes. While the currency changes affected all Vietnamese, the Chinese-Vietnamese were hit the hardest, as they had the most cash.

However, being savvy merchants, the Chinese-Vietnamese quickly learned to hide and disperse their wealth. They transferred their wealth to gold and American dollars, then hid these gold and dollars underground in the living rooms of their houses or in the back yards.

Realizing that the Chinese-Vietnamese were hiding their wealth, local Communist officials often conducted search-and-seize operations. More than once, I had heard of and seen Communist soldiers suddenly enter the houses of people whom they suspected were hiding money and search everything in their houses. The soldiers came equipped with axes and shovels, and dug up the living rooms and back yards for the "hidden treasures." They took away any money they could find. The government justified this daylight robbery as "taking back the money that the capitalists made on the blood and sweat of the working people." However, people quickly became better at hiding their money. Some hid money in the houses of their less-wealthy relatives. Some found secret spots to bury their loot.

As life was becoming more unbearable, the number of people escaping by boats from Vietnam, many of whom were Chinese-Vietnamese, increased dramatically in 1978. The availability of ports and fishing boats in Vũng Tàu made it a popular place for many escape attempts. To stem the escaping tide, the Vietnamese coast guard increased its patrols and the security forces increased their surveillance on visitors from other cities. Even then, the number of escape attempts from Vũng Tàu continued to rise. Many boat owners and escapees "greased the palms" of the coastal patrols and security agents so that they would turn the other way. Others who didn't or couldn't pay faced a much higher chance of getting caught or killed before their boats made it to international waters.

In March 1978, I saw the casualties of an attempted escape for the first time. A group of Chinese-Vietnamese organized an escape at a beach not too far from our home. Sometimes after they made it out to the sea, the coast guard discovered the escaping boat and started a pursuit. For some reason, the captain of the escaping boat decided to ignore the coast guard's warning to stop. Subsequently, the patrol vessels opened fire on the escaping boat and blew it to pieces. There were no survivors. A few days later, the escapees' bloated bodies were washed ashore on the beach where I went swimming regularly. Out of curiosity, I went to see their bodies. It was a bad idea. The sight of the decomposing corpses gave me nightmares for the next month. It took more than ten trucks to carry the dead bodies to the morgue.

As the vehicles carrying the dead bodies drove past my neighborhood, I realized the grim risks of escape. Even if escapees made it past the coastal patrols, they still had a slim chance of survival at sea. Most fishing boats people escaped in were not seaworthy. Many were built to travel in rivers only. Often, out of greed, boat owners put more people on their boats than they could reasonably accommodate. The extreme crowding made the escapees utterly miserable during the voyages and increased the chance of foundering at sea. Most people who contemplated escaping from Vietnam knew the risks. Yet, if given the chance, few would refuse.

I didn't have to wait long to have my suspicions about my mother's plan were confirmed. A week after my expulsion from school, my mother took my younger brother Trung to Saigon. When she returned, she told me that Trung would stay with my Uncle Tín in Saigon for a while. Another week passed before my mother finally told me she had sent Trung to escape with the families of Uncle Tấn and Aunt Trâm. I only knew they went out to the South China Sea from somewhere in the Mekong Delta.

A month passed before we received a cryptic telegraph from Uncle Tấn telling us that they survived the voyage. Three days out at sea, their boat was rescued by an Australian ship. According to maritime laws, Australia granted resettlements to everyone on the boat. My uncle's and aunt's families and my brother would soon be going to Australia after a stopover in Singapore.

The news relieved my mother visibly. However, it didn't last long. She soon made several long trips out of town and always came back tired and dejected. This time, it didn't take me long to guess she must be working on the next part of her plan to get all members of our family out of Vietnam, one by one. Yet, I didn't have the heart to ask her. My mother had enough worry on her mind. If I knew any part of the plan before I had to, it would cause her unceasing stress. In her eyes, I was still a naïve, trusting little boy. I could unwittingly bring danger to us all, if I were to tell any of my friends.

With no school to attend, I suddenly had a lot of time on my hands. Not that another two months of school would have done me any good. I had finished all the lessons and homework for the year months ago. To fill the morning hours I normally spent in class, I often went to Thái's house to chat. One day, I found him sitting in front of his house, with only his shorts on, reading a Chinese kung fu novel. Seeing me coming in, he put the novel aside, yawned, then greeted me. "Hey, Bookworm. Good to see you! Isn't it fun not having to go to school, hey? "

"Not really," I grunted. "I am bored already."

We sat and chatted for hours. Thái told me that the principal, Nghiên, ended up expelling all twelve boys on guard duty that fateful night. None had yet to come back to him to name the culprits. Yet, Thái had learned something else that could eventually get us back in school. Like me, Thái had noticed the six boys who didn't show up after the night we guarded the school. Like us, they were expelled even though they never sat down to face Nghiên. They had never showed up to even make a case. Getting suspicious, Thái went to their homes to investigate. He found that the families of two boys were gone for a few days, and their relatives from Saigon came to stay at their homes. It was a clear sign their families went somewhere to escape. The relatives were there to take the belongings left behind.

Another boy, Giang, wasn't at home when Thái came. Giang's mother told Thái that he went to work with his uncle on a trading business. Giang was not going back to school. The only boy Thái found at home was Lâm. Still laughing over the event, Lâm admitted he and the other boys committed the deed. Lâm wasn't going back to school since it just wasted his time. He was still cracked up over their desecration of Uncle Ho's portraits. He had never felt happier in his life. Like other boys, Lâm had a plan. Like Dũng, he found work on a fishing boat. He would be out at sea most of the time. It sounded like Lâm was waiting to escape as well.

I slowly felt the resentment swelling in my chest. Lâm and other boys who trashed the school had their way out. Only innocent, dumb fools like Thái and me got kicked out of school with nowhere to go

Flashing his easy smile, Thái told me not to worry. He had a plan to get us readmitted to school. Nghiên, our cantankerous principal, had said we could come back to school if we named the culprits. Since we knew some of the boys had left town, probably never to come back, we just had to wait for a week or two. Then, we would come in and tell him we had spent several days busting our asses to investigate the crime. As a result, we found his "criminals," the boys who disappeared. We were innocent and thus, would be allowed back in school.

I was skeptical that the plan would work. Nghiên had the reputation as a cunning, suspicious bastard. He wasn't going to take the bait easily. Thái wasn't the least bit concerned. There was no way Nghiên would know his "criminals" had fled town. Nghiên wouldn't even lift his lazy ass to go to these boys' homes to check them out, Thái said. At worst, Nghiên might ask the "Yellow Dogs" to pay the boys a visit. Then, we would tell Nghiên we never knew of it. What was Nghiên going to do? Insist that we lie to him. Even if the desecration of Ho's pictures hadn't happened, he always assumed we lied to him anyway. But, he didn't have proof. So, if he insisted that we continue to remain expelled despite having come to tell him what he needed, we would tell the whole town what a vindictive, lying asshole he was. Old Nghiên would let us back in. He was an asshole, but also a smart politician. He would let us back in.

Thái's confidence was infectious. We had nothing to lose, he insisted. We didn't need to be in school for the rest of year, since we finished our lessons long ago. As for next year, who knew whether any of us could really get into tenth grade. The best we could do now was to refine our plan, figuring out what we would say if we were to come in and see old Nghiên again.

The talk helped to clear my head. Thái was more right than he realized. Getting readmitted to school wasn't important. My chances of continuing on with schooling next year were low to start with. Soon, it would be irrelevant anyway if my mother was successful with her plan. Yet, deep down, I knew I still wanted to be let back to school, just so I could tell Trang I didn't do this crazy thing. If not, how could I tell her?

I never had the chance to carry out the plan Thái suggested. Two weeks later, my mother was allowed to visit and take supplies to my father in the re-education camp. This visit was her third in three years. Unlike previous visits, my mother took me along this time. I didn't know at the time, but events would unfold quickly to change my life forever after the visit.

During the past year, my father was moved around to at least three different camps. Six months ago, he had been moved to a camp in Long Khánh, a province eighty kilometers from Vũng Tàu. Like previous visits, my mother spent a large part of her savings to buy dried foods and supplies for my father. Laden with stuff, my mother and I went on a rough three-hour bus ride to the camp.

It was the first time I went into a re-education camp. On the outside, it looked like an army base, fully protected by barbed-wire fences and watchtowers. I was told that land mines were placed at the perimeter of the camp, both to fortify it and to prevent inmates from escaping. The camp was built at the edge of a jungle, a few hundred meters from the main road. To get to the camp, we walked and carried our bags of supplies across an open field. By the time we arrived, there were hundreds of other women ˺ children, each carrying heavy bags of food and supplies, waiting anx-
˹y at the camp's gate for their turn to meet their husbands or fathers.
fter two hours of waiting, we were allowed inside the gate. The
˹ place with my father was a small straw hut, furnished with a

bamboo table and two rotting wooden benches. Two soldiers, their guns at the ready, stood guard at the front and back of the hut. Ten minutes after we went in, my father came. I tried hard to hold back my tears. It was the first time I had seen my father in three years. Now with my own eyes, I finally saw what the "People Army" had done to him. The hard labor, continuous mental torture, and the lack of food had made him lose considerable weight. While my mother did not weep aloud, tears silently streamed down her face. Though my father's face was pale and his frame had thinned considerably, I could still see the defiance in his eyes.

He smiled weakly and put his hand on my mother's shoulder to calm her down. In a low voice, he said, "Don't cry. Aren't you happy to see me?"

"Yes, I am," my mother replied while drying her tears. "But you should have taken better care of yourself."

My father smiled, turned and waived me to sit next to him. "Come here, Son. Are you tired from the trip?"

"No, father," I shook my head vigorously, though I was bone tired.

"Good. Your mother wrote and said that you did very well in school. You won that academic competition two months ago. You made me very proud, son."

"Yes, Father," I said nervously, hoping my mother did not tell him about my expulsion from school as well. "I was just lucky."

Fortunately, my father changed his topic. "Your mother also told me that you've been good in taking care of your brothers and helping her. That's my son. Then, I don't have to remind you how important it is for you to help your mother. By the way, did you like the Chinese chess set I made for you?"

"Yes, it is so beautiful, Father. How did you make the chess set?"

"Oh, we have some very skillful artists in this camp. They made all the tools to make the pieces. All I did was to cast the pieces and carve the characters."

"I love the set, Father. No other boy in town has a Chinese chess set as beautiful as mine. How are you doing in here? You look so skinny!"

"For a prisoner, I am doing quite well, Son," my father replied with a wink. "There isn't a lot of food in the camp, so I learn to appreciate food a lot better. Come here, I want to show you this."

I rose and joined my father at the window of the hut. Pointing to the trees around the camp that we could see, he asked, "Do you notice anything unusual with those trees?"

"No," I shook my head. I looked hard and still couldn't find anything unusual about the trees. "They looked normal to me."

"If you look closely, you would notice that the low hanging branches of those trees are stripped bare of their leaves," my father smiled. "Look at those banana trees over there. See if they have any leaves left?"

"No, Father. What happened to them?"

"Well, we have over a thousand prisoners in this camp, and no toilet paper. At first, there were newspapers to use, but they ran out fast. Then, it was the banana leaves' turn. They ran out even faster. Now, there are no leaves left on any of the low branches of these trees. If you want to go to the toilet, you have to go deep into the woods to find some toilet leaves now."

My father stopped for a moment and gave me a wink. "Do you know what this story means, son?" he asked.

"No, Father," I replied, feeling a little confused.

"Well, Son, this is a glimpse of the 'Socialist Paradise' future of our country," my father said quietly. "Don't forget what it means."

"Yes, Father," I nodded with a grim smile. I understood the point my father was making. All the propaganda and empty promises made by the Communist government couldn't change the reality. My father had no illusions about their capability, or lack of it, to bring prosperity to Vietnam. He told the story so that I would never have that illusion either.

Nodding with satisfaction, my father walked back to the bamboo table. In a low voice, he asked my mother "Have all the arrangements been made?"

"Yes," my mother nodded. "He will go to Saigon in two weeks to visit brother Tín's family and other relatives. Then, later, he will take the train to the North to visit his grandpa."

Following my parents' conversation, I was suddenly confused. I knew they were talking about some plans for me, but they didn't seem to make any sense. My paternal grandfather died many years ago. While my father still had his sisters living in North Vietnam, he had lost contact with them since 1954. In addition, my mother never told me about this trip to North Vietnam. So what was it that my parents were talking about?

Unable to contain my curiosity any further, I interrupted my mother "Mother, how am I going to see grandpa in the North?"

My mother put a finger to her lips to tell me to be quiet. She stopped me just in time before I blurted out the next sentence, "Isn't Grandpa dead for forty years now?"

My father nodded to me to keep my silence, then said to my mother, "Go on."

"He will be going with his cousins, Hằng and Bình, the daughter and son of Uncle Lê," my mother replied. "They would take good care of him. He will be okay!"

"That's good," my father nodded. "That's all we could ask for. Beyond that, it really is just up to God."

Suddenly, I realized what my parents were talking about. I just remembered I had heard the expression "going to North Vietnam" before. It was one of many slang expressions used by many southerners to mean "escape from the country." My mother was going to send me to escape from Vietnam with my cousins Hằng and Bình two weeks from now. That's why she was taking me to visit my father this time. This trip was not simply just to visit my father. It was for me to say the last goodbye to him. The realization made me dumbstruck and scared. I opened my mouth to say something, but could not utter a word.

Looking at my face, my father knew I understood. "It looks like you understand what we are talking about," he said in a low voice. "Can my son keep a secret?"

"Yes, father."

"Good. Soon you will embark on a dangerous journey. You will go to an uncertain destination, alone. We won't be there with you. You will have to face the dangers by yourself. Are you scared?"

"Yes, I am," I said, not trying to hide the fear that was written all over my face.

"It's OK to be afraid, son," my father nodded. "But you can't let it paralyze you. At some point, you have to be brave and strong. I have all the faith in you. Do you still remember what I told you three years ago before I left?"

"Yes, Father." I looked up proudly at my father. "You told me to use my head and think for myself. You told me not to fight with people who may look down on us. Instead, work and study really hard, so that someday I will rise above others. And I should stop being selfish, and do all I can to help mother and my brothers."

"Good," my father nodded approvingly. "It looks like you have learned most, if not all, that I could teach you. Remember, don't ever forget your responsibility to your family, relatives and this country. Don't forget all the sacrifices your mother has made for you all these years. I just pray that Buddha will protect you. May Buddha protect us all."

"I will never forget, Father," I nodded vigorously.

"Can you make me two very important promises?"

"Yes, Father."

"Promise me you will never forget who you are and where you come from, no matter where you end up," my father said softly. The intense look he gave me left no doubt how seriously he meant them.

"I promise, Father," I nodded quietly.

"Promise me that one day, you will return here, even if just once," my father asked again. "Come back and do what you can for your family, and people who are not as fortunate as you. Will you do that?"

"Yes, Father, I will. I will. I will not fail you."

"For the journey ahead, as dangerous as it is, you have to go," my father continued. "You have to find life in death. You have to be braver and stronger than you have ever been. There is no future for you in this country. You can't stay here."

While my father spoke, I silently nodded my head to let him know I understood. Outwardly, I maintained my control and stayed calm. Inside, I was utterly confused and afraid. I had seen people die from escaping. I was certain I would be making my escape with my cousins on a fishing boat not unlike those in Vũng Tàu. I had heard many other people talk about the chances of survival at sea in one of these boats. The most optimistic estimate for the chance of survival was fifty-fifty. Even if the boat didn't founder at sea, the escapees still had a high risk of running into the Thai pirates in the Gulf of Siam. I had heard many stories of the killings, plundering, and raping committed by these Thai fishermen turned pirates against defenseless refugees at sea. They were as cruel and brutal as any pirates that ever lived. Running into the Thai pirates at sea was not unlike meeting death itself.

Even if I were to survive and reach a country of asylum safely, what would happen to my family? Would my mother get into trouble with the local authorities? Sooner or later, they would find out that my brother Trung and I had escaped. Who would help my mother to take care of my two younger brothers when I was gone? Would I ever get to see my father, mother, and brothers again? What would happen to me in a strange land, among strange people whose language I didn't speak?

The uncertainties, the inherent dangers, and the thought of losing my family forever were swirling in my head. Despite my misgivings, I knew I had no other choice. It was not cheap to get a spot on an escaping boat. My mother had mentioned several times the fortune boat owners were demanding from potential escapees. The average price per person was five or six taels of gold (the equivalent of about $3,000 or $4,000 at the time). I didn't know how my mother managed to pay for me. I estimated her lifetime savings would not be worth more than two taels of gold. Did my mother use all her money to pay for me?

I fought to hold back my tears. My mother had sacrificed her entire life for the family. All these years, she had worked so hard to keep us fed and support my father in jail. In the three years since 1975, I had not seen a smile on her face. She hadn't eaten anything good, bought anything for herself, nor even had a good night's sleep. Since the beginning of 1978, she kept having nightmares that one of my brothers or I would be drafted and then get killed on the battlefield of Cambodia. She also was constantly worried about my father's fate. Every day, she faced the constant harassment of the local authorities and the task of evading the hated security agents at the market. Now, she used her savings to get me out of Vietnam, so that I could live and have a better life. Her love and sacrifices for all of us were unbounded. The strength and will power that kept her going were incomprehensible to me.

For all that she had done, I could not let my mother down. Even if I had to go into what appeared to be certain death, I still could not refuse. If I stayed, I might be able to help her a bit, but I would also be a big burden on her shoulders. Besides, I could not bear the thought of doing anything that might make my mother unhappy. She had suffered more than enough. If there was anything I could do to bring a smile to her face, I would have done it. I was never able to do so. Now, I could not refuse to escape and make her feel worse.

"Your mother and I always worry that you are still too young and too naïve," my father continued. "There are many unscrupulous people out there. If they can't use or manipulate you, then they will find ways to pick on or abuse you. Remember what I told you about rising above your oppressors, Son. The more they cause you to be angry and hateful, the more you have to try not to be like them. Don't ever give in to hate."

"I won't be like them, Father," I said, trying to muster some convincingness.

"You don't have to prove it to me, Son," my father said gently. "In the days ahead, you have to prove it to yourself that you have the courage and strength to rise above all adversities. You realize we may not be with you for a long time, maybe never again. I want you to always remember who you are, where you come from, and walk your own path. Have the courage to take the long, hard road. Remember that only your heart and your head can tell you what is the right thing to do."

"Yes, Father," I replied weakly, holding back the tears that were waiting to pour out. "I will never forget."

My father nodded with satisfaction, then turned back to my mother. "How are you holding up out there?" he asked.

"It's not easy, but I manage," my mother replied, her eyes conveying more of the hardships she faced than the words. "My sister in France sent some money last month to help, and my father helped a little, too. So it's all right. How are you holding up in this place?"

"It's not the most luxurious military barrack I've lived in, but I'll survive," my father smiled. "I am doing better here than some of my colleagues. Many don't have anyone to visit and bring them supplies. A few had passed away."

I stopped listening to my parents. I was too immersed in my own thoughts. Now I had come to face a new future. It was more exciting, but also infinitely more dangerous and lonely than the one I thought I would face.

A few minutes later, my parents' conversation was interrupted by the soldiers, who came in to tell us that our time was up. It was hard to say goodbye. Both my father and I realized it might be the last time we ever saw each other. Yet, there was nothing we could do about it. From now on, everything was up to God.

My father stood at the hut and watched us depart. Even after we had exited from the gate and were a long way from the camp, he still stood there. Though he never said it, I knew his heart must be breaking apart, knowing he might never see me or my brothers again. If I were to succeed in my escape, then it would become my brothers' turn. The family my parents had loved and sacrificed so much for to keep together would soon be breaking apart, with each of the children heading straight into dangers to find hope and a better future elsewhere.

I kept looking back, trying to photograph his image into my memory. For the rest of my life, I would never forget the image of my father, a gaunt, lonely prisoner in black pajama uniform, standing at the barbed-wire fences and peering at the world beyond. I knew that no prison could chain the spirit in him.

# 15

# The Tango with Death

After the visit, my mother told me the necessary details about the escape. She made me memorize the addresses of my relatives who were already living in Western countries. Once I made it safely to an asylum, I would know how to contact them to get help.

She also made me memorize a Buddhist prayer to Quan Thế Âm Bồ Tát (the Merciful Buddha) that was supposed to bring us Buddha's protection. Whenever I ran into dangers or desperate situations, I should pray for and have faith in Buddha's protection. It was the only shred of hope we had.

Two weeks later, my mother took me to Saigon to visit my maternal grandparents and other relatives. My escape would take place in a week, on May 19, 1978. The planners had chosen this date, the supposed birthday of Ho Chi Minh, for security considerations. Their assumption was that the celebrations around this national holiday would cause the security agents to be less watchful for escapees.

Though Vũng Tàu was a coastal city where many escapes took place, I would not be making my escape from here. Somehow, my mother got me a place on a fishing boat in Cần Thơ, a city in the Mekong Delta. Though my mother never told me, I suspected she negotiated a deal with the boat owner. In exchange for giving her a space, the boat owner got potential clients my mother referred to him.

The last night before leaving Saigon, I spent time with my grandmother. It was a difficult and emotional time. My 75-year-old maternal grandmother, who was half deaf, kept telling me that once I reached an asylum country, I must immediately write home to let everyone know that we're alive. She made me promise that no matter where I might be in the future, I got to go back to Vietnam someday so that she could see me before she died. I promised her I would. I never was able to fulfill my promise. My grandmother died in 1986, long before I could have gone back.

My mother told me to study hard and make something out of myself if I were to survive the voyage. Like my father, she admonished me not to forget where I came from and my responsibilities to the family. My mother reminded me that my own worth would come from within, from what I would achieve and do for others, not from how I would look nor what I would have. To walk my own path, I should never copy other people's thoughtless and extravagant behaviors.

Though she tried hard, my mother couldn't keep from crying. She knew full well the dangers that lay ahead. She knew this could be the last time she saw me, whether I made it safely to another country or died at sea. She also worried that in the uncertain future, how could I, a weak and helpless boy of fourteen, deal with a tough, unkind world alone.

I couldn't help but join my mother in crying. I felt more confused and afraid than ever. Yet, I knew that I could not turn back. In my head, the words of my father kept echoing: "You will have to find life in death. You will have to be braver and stronger than you have ever been. There is no future for you in this country. You can't stay here. As dangerous as it is, you have to go."

I repeated these words again and again to build up my courage. After a sleepless night and a last tearful goodbye with my mother and grandmother, I went on a bus with my cousins' family and headed toward Cần Thơ. Before I got on the bus, my mother took out and gave me a U.S. quarter. She told me to use it only in emergency. It took her a long time to save and buy this American coin. Therefore, I should not spend it carelessly.

My cousin Hằng, a 30-year-old widow, became the mother hen for our family's escaping party. Besides me, she also brought along her younger brother Bình, and her two children. Her son, Thái Dương, and daughter, Tú Quỳnh, were only three and one year old, respectively. My cousin Hằng knew full well the risk. Yet, she felt she had no other choice if her kids were to have a better future. They had to escape from Vietnam. They would either make it alive together or die together.

## Getting on Board

We arrived in Cần Thơ at noon on May 18, 1978. Upon arrival, we immediately checked into a tiny, dingy hotel. For the rest of the day, we holed up inside the tiny hotel room. My cousin Hằng went out once to buy food. She was afraid that since we were not local people, it would be easy to attract the suspicion of the local security agents.

Before leaving Saigon, we were told that a contact would come to our hotel room at night to take us to the boat. It was best to stay out of sight until then.

At 9 P.M., the contact came. A tall, thin man wearing black pajamas, the contact told us we would go in several small groups. That way, we avoided raising suspicion from the local people and the security agents. Bình and I would go first. Later, he would return for my cousin Hằng and her children.

We carried our luggage and followed the man. The three of us boarded a puny cyclo, while the skinny driver huffed and puffed heavily to get the heavy load to move. The sight, if anybody else were to see, was comical. However, we were too nervous to think it was funny. We were sure to raise the suspicion of any security agents if they were to see us. Fortunately, the cyclo driver managed to take us to near the river bank without any incident. After paying the driver, we made our way toward the river. We had not spoken a word to each other since leaving the hotel.

The night was hot and humid. The area was desolate, with no one in sight. Feeling extremely nervous, I looked around for sight of any security agents, ready to run for my life at the first sign of trouble.

So far, things had gone smoothly. Yet, I thought the best-laid plan still could go sour at any time. I had heard stories of people getting caught as they boarded their boats because their careless behaviors aroused the suspicion of other people and security agents. My mother told me many times if things were to go bad, I had to elude capture and make my way back home. If I couldn't, I might end up in prison for a long time. Now, for the first time in my life, I knew how it felt to be prey.

Fortunately, there were no traps waiting for us. After one last check, the contact signaled us to follow him down the bank into the river.

I found myself suddenly knee-deep in mud. The suction force of mud pulled the sandals right off of my feet. Wading through the mud barefooted, I saw a small sampan make its way toward us. A man stood on the sampan and used a long stick to push on the river bottom, propelling the boat toward us. One by one, we climbed on board and the sampan silently moved outward.

Five minutes later, the sampan docked next to a fishing boat. About fifteen meters in length and four meters in height, the boat was cloaked in total darkness. It didn't look any different from the other fishing boats around it. The strong smells of fish and mud made me feel sick and nauseated. Slowly, we followed our guide and climbed on board. Two men were standing and smoking on the deck. They motioned to us to move quickly inside. Fumbling through the darkness, we crossed the deck into the engine room, where another man showed us where to stow our luggage. We were told to find a place to lie down and keep quiet. The conversation was carried out in whispers, as if everyone was afraid what was said might be heard by the people on the neighboring boats or the omnipresent ears of the security agents.

It took me several minutes to adjust to the darkness inside and familiarize myself with the boat's layout. The interior was divided into two main parts, an engine compartment at one end and a huge cavity that took up the remaining space. There were railings along the sides of the cavity. This cavity was the storage room for the fishermen's catch. It became the sleeping place for the escapees on the coming days.

Feeling nervous and excited, I lay down in the cavity and listened attentively to all the noises. We were the first escapees to come on board. Beside me and my cousin Bình, there were two other crewmen smoking on deck. Our guide had gone back to shore. Besides the whispered conversation of the two crewmen, the only other noise was the sound of water crashing against the hull. I kept wondering how long it would take for the security agents to notice the unusual activities going on here. How could these people take more escapees on board without arousing suspicion? If the security agents were to get on board and inspect, we would be caught for sure.

An hour later, more people started to come on board. They quietly settled into the boat's cavity and found places to lie down. At first, it was quiet since most of the people who came early were adults. However, from 11 P.M. on, many children came on board. The cavity became much more crowded. The children couldn't keep as quiet as the adults. The strange atmosphere inside the boat, the crowded conditions, and the unpleasant smells of the river and human sweat made the kids uncomfortable. Many kids started to cry. Even though parents tried hard to calm their children down, the boat became very noisy. I was more afraid than ever. The kids' crying would attract attention for sure. It was only a matter of time before security agents would come on board to catch us.

The crewmen became anxious at the kids' crying. As well as anyone, they realized the crying would attract unwanted attention and jeopardize the escape. They told the parents to keep their children quiet. Families that couldn't stop their kids' crying may be taken back to shore. Many arguments ensued after the crewmen made their threats, making the situation even worse. Fortunately, after a while, the kids calmed down and silence gradually returned.

My cousin Hằng and her children didn't come on board until well past midnight. As she made her way in the dark to the cavity, she fell and sprained her ankle. We helped her lie down in an already very crowded place. Bình and I helped to place our nephew and niece next to their mother.

After a few minutes, my nephew couldn't stand the smells and the cramped, uncomfortable position any more. He started to cry uncontrollably. His crying threw everyone into a state of panic again. No matter what his mother tried to do, he couldn't calm down.

One of the escapees, a man in his early forties, threatened to throw my nephew overboard if he wouldn't stop crying. Though she could hardly move, my cousin Hằng became so enraged she dared the man to walk over her dead body. If the man were to touch her son, she would make sure that everyone on the boat rotted in prison.

Fortunately, other people stepped in to calm them down. The man walked away, mumbling curses. Hằng went back to comforting her son. Soon, my nephew fell asleep. As the crying stopped, we all breathed lightly again.

By 2 A.M., everyone had come on board. Bodies lay everywhere in the deep cavity. I had to bend my legs to keep them from being in someone's body or face. In the dark, I counted the people I could see and thought there must be at least fifty people. This boat was probably never meant to take on more than six. Later, I found out I was not too far off. Including the crew, the final tally was sixty human beings on this decrepit floating tub.

The nervous and uncomfortable night slowly passed. As the first rays of sunlight passed through, I got my first clear look at my fellow escapees. The cavity was packed solid with bodies, like a sardine can. There were fifteen kids. My niece Tú Quỳnh, at one year old, was the youngest.

The oldest escapee was a 70-year-old woman, who came on board with her nephew's family. She was weak and could hardly move. Her nephew was so busy taking care of his wife and kid he hardly paid attention to his aunt. I wondered why this old lady bothered to risk her life escaping.

I could see the anxiety and nervousness on each face. Until the boat got moving, the security agents could come on board at any time. It seemed like an eternity.

By this time, my legs were so numb from the bending I couldn't take it any longer. I climbed up to the engine room. A mechanic, two crewmen, the boat owner's son, and the captain were there. They warned me to keep my head down and be quiet, but didn't force me to go back to the cramped cabin.

Half an hour later, the mechanic started the engine and the boat moved away from the river bank. Everyone let out a sigh of relief. The night's silence was quickly replaced with the loud noise of the engine and the cacophonous conversations in the cavity. I decided to stay in the engine room, even though its floor was very dirty. At least there was room up here to stretch my legs and some fresh air to breath.

When the boat got to the middle of the river, the captain idled the engine and held the vessel in place. Several crewmen lowered big buckets into the river to fetch water and poured it into two empty gasoline barrels. The mechanic, a tall, greasy-faced man in his late thirties, told me they were getting drinking water for the journey.

Hearing the mechanic, I was shocked. I never drank water that wasn't boiled before. Yet, here, the crewmen were getting unboiled water from the Mekong River for the voyage. Curious, I came up to the dock to see for myself. I never forgot the sight. On both banks of the river, people were washing clothes and kids were urinating and defecating. The river water itself was red with dirt and alluvial sediment. The sights didn't seem to bother the crewmen at all. They didn't bother to even clean the storage barrels before pouring the water in.

The crewmen's nonchalant attitude shocked me more than the dirty Mekong River water. I could see rusting metal particles inside and outside the barrels. Though standing from afar, I could still smell gasoline from these containers. Unable to contain my curiosity anymore, I asked the crewmen why they didn't clean the barrels.

A skinny, smelly crewman immediately told me to shut up and get back inside. Sullenly, I retreated back to a corner in the engine room. The water in the gasoline barrels, with all its mixture of rust, gasoline, sediment, dirt, soap, detergent, and human waste, was what we had to drink for the next several days. Every time I drank it, I took a deep breath, closed my eyes and pinched my nose, then gulped it down quickly. Even so, the terrible taste of the water still lingered in my mouth for several minutes afterward. Even today, I still can't believe the thoughtlessness of the people who organized the escape.

Half an hour later, the boat started again. Two men from the deck, one muscular and the other bald, came inside the boat. The bald man called for attention then said, "We are on our way. This boat is going down the Mekong River and out to the South China Sea, near Côn Sơn by 5 or 6 this afternoon. We are well stocked with food and fuel. Once out in the South China Sea, we will head straight south for Western Malaysia. With luck, we should make it there in three days."

My cousin Bình had climbed up to the engine room and sat beside

me. Whispering, I asked him who the man was. Bình told me that he was
Mr. Đang, the boat owner. My cousin Hằng knew him from Saigon. A former schoolteacher, Mr. Đang somehow had the money to buy the boat half
a year ago then organized the escape.

Above, Mr. Đang turned to the muscular man and continued. "I'd like
to introduce you all to Mr. Dần. Mr. Dần will navigate this boat to Malaysia
for us. Mr. Dần is a former captain in the South Vietnamese Navy. I have
all the confidence in Mr. Dần's ability to bring us safely to freedom."

The captain nodded to everyone. A few people clapped their hands.
After the brief introduction, both men left and returned to the deck.

I poked my head out the window of the engine room to look at the
river and the town, trying to remember the last image of Vietnam. The
sun was coming up. It was going to be another hot day in the Mekong
Delta. The river bank at 8 A.M. was already bustling with activity. There
was a certain peacefulness and charm to the city of Cần Thơ on this early
morning. Yet, I thought to myself, the peacefulness in this town, like any
other cities in Vietnam, hid many untold stories of tragedy and suffering.

The last thing I saw was a large, white statue of Ho Chi Minh standing at the Ninh Kiều pier. Ho's statue waved its hands and stared down at
the Mekong River. Today was May 19, 1978, a national holiday celebrat-
ing Ho's birth. If he was alive, Ho would be 88 or 89 years old. Though
he was long dead, what he had done had determined the fate not only of
millions of Vietnamese alive but also of generations yet unborn. Well, we
were a few of millions who risked our lives to escape the fate that he had
imposed. Looking at his statue, I mumbled, "Uncle Ho, if you are there,
goodbye to you, too. I won't be missing you."

There was not much to do except sit tight and wait until nightfall.
We were not out to international waters yet, and the coast guards could
still stop us at any time. As long as we were still inside Vietnam's waters,
we had a great chance of getting arrested.

I looked around the cabin to familiarize myself with the faces of the
people on board. People were quiet and kept to themselves. There was a
family of six, where the kids kept calling their parents "maman" or "papa,"
and interjected their conversation with bits and pieces of French. I thought
it was strange. Who were these people? Why couldn't they speak normal
Vietnamese? In another corner, there sat a couple who were plumper than
the rest of the passengers. The man was fat and swarthy. He wore a tur-
ban on his head and a sarong instead of regular pants. Later, I learned the
man was an Indian-Vietnamese named Ali. He happened to be the only
passenger who spoke English fluently.

To the left and facing me and my cousins sat the family of the man

who had threatened to throw my nephew overboard last night. The man
was with his wife and his two sons. He was well-built and probably in his
mid-forties. He had an air of arrogance about him. Later, I learned that
his name was Thành and he was a martial art instructor. I didn't know
how good his martial art was, but he was always quick to threaten to beat
someone up

People lay still and kept quiet. It was as if they were afraid their conversations could be heard by security agents above the deafening roar of
the boat engine.

After an hour of cramming my legs, I climbed up to the engine room
again to stretch my body. The engine room was situated at the stern. On
each side, there was a small square window. The windows were big enough
that I could sit on them and look outside.

The boat engine was a big block, placed in a deep cavity at the middle of the engine room At the bottom, the engine block was connected to
the rudder that turned and propelled the boat forward. I poked my head
in the cavity and looked at the engine block with fascination. It was a big,
black thing covered with grease, little pumps and wires. The mechanic,
sitting on the other side of the engine room with only his shorts on, saw
the look on my face and laughed. "Kid, you know anything about engines?"

"No. Do you?"

"Of course I do. I am the chief mechanic on this boat. If this damn
thing breaks down, I'll fix it."

"Really? Do you have the tools for it?"

"Well, you never know if you have all the tools or even if you have
the right tools on a journey like this, kid," the mechanics shrugged. "This
engine looks simple enough, so it shouldn't have too many problems. At
least, you should pray that it will not have any problems I can't fix, son,
because if it does, then we are all screwed."

As the mechanic spoke, I took a closer look at him. He looked to be
in his late thirties. He was tall and lanky. Parts of his face, arms, and legs
were covered with black grease. He sported a little beard that wasn't well
trimmed. His hair was long and unkempt. Yet, his face was pleasant and
his mouth had a perpetual grin to it. He was the friendliest person on the
boat so far. I decided that I liked him and wanted to get on his good side.

"My name is Trình. What's yours?" I asked.

"The name is Sơn, kid."

"Do you always work on boat engines?"

"No, kid," Sơn lighted a cigarette and let out a puff. "I am a real
mechanic. I made my living fixing cars before 1975. Since 1975, there were
not many cars for me to fix, so I turned to fixing motorbikes. Mr. Đang,

the boat owner, brought me on board three months ago, because he didn't have anyone who knows what to do with this engine. So here I am, kid, the only expert about engines on this floating tub."

"Do you know if the engine is powerful enough to get us to Malaysia?" I asked, braving the cigarette smoke coming from Sơn. "The boat seemed to be going so slow, even in the river."

"This engine has four blocks of power, kid," Sơn nodded. "It should be enough."

"What is a block?"

"Well, it is sort of a measure of how strong an engine is, like horse-power or something," Sơn said. "The bigger the number, the more powerful it is. This boat is big, so it needs four blocks of power or more to propel it."

"But is it strong enough to take us across the sea?" I pressed.

"It should be, kid. If we could, we always want bigger engines. But hey, there aren't many big boat engines left around. You see, most boats with engines that powerful left the country already. Even if you have it, installing an engine with more power than four blocks on a boat like this would cause all kinds of suspicions and problems from the police when we are in port. Heck, those 'Yellow Dogs' would have fun coming up here every day harassing Mr. Đang for coffee money."

Sơn took another puff, then poked at my rib cage. "Don't worry, kid. I know of boats with only two-block engines that have made it across the sea. So we will be okay."

I went to the window on the left side of the engine room and peered outside. We had gotten to a wider part of the Mekong River, where the banks were much farther apart. There weren't many boats and people in this area. Just outside, the exhaust pipe in the rear of the window spewed heavy black smoke into the air. The wind blew the smoke to the front. As I stuck my head out, I caught a whiff full of smoke in my face. I quickly ducked back inside, coughing in spurts.

"Keep your head inside, kid," Mr. Sơn chuckled. "If you want some fresh air, wait for another three or four hours, then you can go on the deck. By that time, it should be dark, and we should be out in the sea."

I nodded, and laid down on the greasy floor of the engine room, using my arms as pillow for my head. I thought about my mother and younger brothers in Vũng Tàu. My mother probably was back to Vũng Tàu today, selling her stuff in the market like usual. How sad and how much pain she must feel not knowing whether I would make it alive or perish at sea for one, two or even three months! My brothers would ask why their oldest brother was missing, and my mother wouldn't tell them for at least two to three weeks. By then, even if she didn't tell them, they would have figured it out. They, too, had known of too many of their friends who had escaped.

My thoughts wandered idly to Thái, then Trang. Maybe I would never see them again in this lifetime. I hadn't given Thái any clues that I was about to escape. I had kept my promise to my mother not to leak a word to anyone, not even to my closest friend, about the journey with no return. It wouldn't take Thái long to figure out that something had happened with me. I had told him I was going to Saigon for two weeks to visit my relatives. I thought I saw a suspicious look on his face, but he didn't press me much further then. Within two weeks at most, he would come to my house to look for me. If he didn't find me then, he would know, regardless of what my mother told him.

I regretted never having the chance to talk to Trang again after the long walk home in the rain three months ago. It was the first and the last time we ever spoke to each other. I never had the chance to explain to her that I didn't know of nor took part in the prank of spreading feces all over her classroom. Well, it really didn't matter now. In a few days, I would either be dead or make it alive to another country. Either way, we probably would never see the other again.

Time slowly passed. By nightfall, I was very hungry, but there was nothing to eat. Sometime after noon, I found some oranges the boat owner had hidden in a compartment when I came down to visit my cousin Hằng. I ate some myself, and peeled some for my cousins, nephew, and niece. The boat owner would soon find out his secret cache of fruits was depleted. He might be upset but would not know who had eaten them, for I had used my body and my shirt to shield other people from seeing me eating the oranges. It was the first time I had stolen anything in my life, but I didn't feel too guilty. Mr. Đang had said the boat was well stocked with food and people would be fed. No one had fed us since the morning. I rationalized I was merely taking Mr. Đang's words at face value.

At about 6 P.M., a woman cooked a big pot of rice and some food, and distributed some to everyone. It was the first and last full meal anyone would get for the rest of the journey. The rice smelled of gasoline because it was cooked with the water in the cursed, rusty barrels. Nevertheless, I was too hungry to be picky. I swallowed everything and still was not full. Everyone ate quickly, as if they also realized this might be their last full meal. Feeling tired and still hungry, I retreated to a corner of the engine room and tried to get some rest. In a few minutes I fell asleep.

At midnight, the cold, piercing wind rudely woke me up. I was wearing shorts and a short-sleeve shirt because it was very hot and humid during the day. After taking a few minutes to adjust my eyes to the darkness, I saw the mechanic sitting across from me, smoking his cigarette. I asked him if he knew where we were. Son told me that we were at sea, but still in Vietnamese waters. In another hour or two, we would get to international waters. Then, we would not have to worry about the coast guards anymore. I climbed down to the cabin to get my pants and jacket. Soon, I had my entire wardrobe on: a shirt, a jacket, pants, and shorts. Still, the clothes weren't enough to protect me from the pricking wind.

I had to take great care to not step or fall over anyone in the cavity. The air was very humid and filled with the strange, combined smells of human sweat, fish, and the food someone had vomited. My cousin and her children were sleeping. I was surprised to see the kids sound asleep. They had been crying all day because of the uncomfortable environment and strange people. My nephew also suffered from a severe case of seasickness. He had vomited everything he ate earlier in the day. I got my clothes quickly and climbed back up to the engine room, avoiding waking them up. I was getting very nauseated. It was a lot warmer in the cavity than in the engine room, but there was no way I could stay in there for another minute. I would rather brave the cold than inhale the cavity's air for the rest of the night.

We made it to international waters without any incident. I was told by the mechanic, who had been informed by the captain, that we were out of Vietnamese waters at about 1 A.M. I breathed a sigh of relief. We had passed the first danger, being stopped or shot at by the coast guards.

I didn't know how the captain knew or whether he was just guessing. He only had a compass and a map of Vietnam's coastline. The sky was pitch black and as far as I could see there was water all around us. Even if he had traveled this part of the sea for all his life, how could the captain tell where we were in this vast expanse of water? I thought he was just guessing as much as anyone else.

The sea was calm, but its vastness inspired awe in me. I strained my eyes to look in all directions, but could see nothing. If the weather turned bad, and if we were all to die in this sea, nobody in the world would ever know. Suddenly, I realized just how insignificant our lives were. The sun would still rise tomorrow and the earth would still turn. And the disappearance from the earth of the sixty wretched human beings on this flimsy boat would not change anything at all.

I tried to put all the scary thoughts out of my mind and slept again. I had a very uneasy sleep. In my dream, I was still at home, chopping wood on the mountain in the midst of a torrential rain...

I woke up early the next morning. The day was hot and the sea was still calm. I came out to the deck to take a look at the sea. A crewman sat in a small cabin on top of the boat, holding the steering wheel. The mechanic was already up, smoking his cigarette. The captain was in the engine room, still sleeping soundly. He must have been very tired, since I woke up several times during the night, and saw him sitting at the window of the engine room, staring out at the sea. Some people in the main cabin had already woken up, but were lying still in place. No one was in a hurry to do anything.

I asked Son where we were. With an assured air of authority, the mechanic told me we were about six hours south of the southernmost point of Vietnam. With luck, we would make it to Malaysia in two and a half days. I looked around. There was nothing in the sea except for our boat. It was as if our boat and all the miserable human beings in it were the only things that existed in the world. The more I looked out at the vast, empty sea, the more I became scared. I tried hard to suppress my fear and thought of more positive things.

For the whole day, I didn't have much to do except lounge around the deck. A few times, I came down to the cavity to play with my nephew and niece. My cousin's ankle was swollen now. She lay in the same place for the whole day, while her children crawled around and cried.

The woman who cooked the day before cooked some more rice again. However, the boat was rocking much harder now because of the waves. The boat's rocking motion made it much harder to cook. Suddenly realizing that there was not so much gasoline or firewood to cook with (the boat owner didn't have the foresight to stock up on these items), the woman ended up cooking only two pots of rice for the sixty persons on the boat. As the rice had to be rationed, each person could get only a handful. Not only that, it was only half cooked. I took my share and gobbled it in less than a minute. A few people who were smart enough to bring some foods along with them ate at the envy of the others. They didn't offer to share their food with anyone else. They ate sparingly. When they finished eating, they wrapped up the food and kept it right next to their bodies, as if they were afraid that other people might steal the food from them. I suddenly realized these people expected the worst on this journey and these morsels of food might just mean the difference between life and death to them.

By nightfall, my hunger intensified to the point where all I could think about was food. However, there was nothing to eat. The woman who had cooked for the past two days, Ms. Tuyết, said that she could cook only once a day. There was not that much rice anyway. Therefore, we must eat sparingly in case the journey lasted more than a few days. If we ate too much now, we might die of hunger later if something went wrong.

As the sun went down in the west, the wind got stronger and colder. Dark clouds started to gather in the eastern horizon. The waves also became more violent. I went up to the deck to see how the ocean was outside. What I saw scared me. The ocean was no longer calm. The waves, while still relatively small, formed in the distance with white foam on top of them. As the waves hit the boat, they tossed it up and down in the ocean like a little toy. Not having the stomach to watch any further, I went inside and prayed to Buddha for protection.

Mr. Dần, the captain, was getting very worried. He turned the steering wheel over to another crewman, and came inside. The people sitting or lying in the cavity were already getting agitated and nervous from the stronger-than-expected rocking of the boat. Dần straightened himself and announced "Attention, please!"

At his call, the noise level rose for a while before slowly dying down. Mr. Dần patiently waited until he could be heard again then continued, "It's not good news but I need to tell everyone what is going to happen so you can prepare. You can already guess the weather is getting worse. From what I can see in the sky and the wind, I think the ocean is going to get a lot rougher in another few hours. We probably are going to be in the area of a small storm here."

When the captain mentioned the word "storm," the noise from the whisperings and sighs rose again. Dần waved people to quiet down before continuing. "The crew and I will stay up all night and try our best to steer this boat out of the storm. As for you, you will need to tie up your belongings neatly so that they won't fly around, injuring other people when we get into rough seas. No one should go on deck, other than the crew. If you fall into the ocean at night, there is no one who can save you."

When Dần stopped, almost everyone fell into a state of panic. Ali, the Indian-Vietnamese man, asked, "Captain, do you know how strong the storm is and how long it will last?"

"No, I don't. We don't have any radio. Even if we did, we couldn't hear anything out here. My guess is that it won't last more than a few hours. That's all. Please rest and tuck your things away."

With that parting statement, Dần returned to the steering cabin. The noise level rose several decibels as people started talking about the impending disaster. I could hear much chanting and praying to God, Jesus, and Buddha for protection, to help us pass this storm alive. It was difficult for me to believe this small boat would be able to withstand any kind of storm. It was also obvious to everyone else on the boat. The scene in the cabin was a mixture of a comedy and a drama. Some people lay still and stared at the ceiling. A family was sitting together, praying to Jesus, while a woman next to them was chanting incantations from a Buddhist prayer book. The cacophony of prayers and chanting created an eerie, foreboding feeling of disaster.

I was exhausted, hungry and very thirsty. Even the drinking water, contaminated with gasoline and God knows what else, was rationed. I only got a small cup of that cursed water for the whole day. I curled up in a corner of the engine room and found a piece of foam to plug my ears. I tried to lull myself to sleep by silently praying to Buddha. Slowly, overcome by exhaustion, I fell into a tired and uncomfortable slumber.

A painful feeling in my head rudely woke me up. It took me a minute to realize what had happened. The boat was rocking violently, careening from side to side. In my sleep, the rolling motion of the boat slid my body toward the wall of the engine room and knocked my head right into it. A small bump swelled up as the testimony to the collision. However, I was too overcome by fear to even remember the pain.

We were right in the middle of the storm. It was raining heavily. Occasionally, there were deafening sounds of thunder in the distance. Outside, waves several feet high kept coming toward the boat, lifting it up then throwing it right down. It felt like a rough roller coaster ride, except we didn't have any seat belts to keep us in place. If the boat didn't get over any of these deadly waves, then we were lost. The winds were blowing violently, bringing the rain water inside the boat. Then, water was coming into the engine room through the windows every time the boat descended into a trough. Before I realized what had happened, a torrent of sea water splashed all over me. The engine room, already slippery, became even more so now that it was wet.

Everyone in the boat was awake. The children were crying like crazy, while their parents were not in much better shape. Many people huddled together again and prayed to their gods. Nobody needed any explanation to know what we were in. The cacophonous music of terror and fear was paralyzing.

I grabbed hold of the wall of the engine room and slowly made my way toward the window. I wanted to look outside to see how bad it was. I lost my hold a few times and slid right back to where I started, crashing against the corner of the engine room. However, I didn't feel the pain. Eventually, I succeeded in reaching the window. To avoid getting sucked out into the sea by the violent winds, I locked my feet securely against a crevice and used both hands to grab the railings of the window.

The sky was pitch black, and the sea was raging with towering waves. The raindrops struck against my face and body, leaving stinging, painful feelings. The boat was turning from side to side in such violent motions that I thought sometimes it was at a 45-degree angle with the surface of the water. Sticking my head out of the window, there were instances I thought my face was just inches away from the sea's surface. The mechanic, who locked his arms and feet to a corner of the engine room to keep himself from sliding, yelled at me to get away from the window. He thought I was crazy to even get near it. If I lost my hold and fell into the water, then there was nobody or anything that could save me from certain death. After a minute, I had seen enough. Slowly, I crawled back to the corner where the mechanic was, while hooking tightly to some holds with my hands and feet.

Hanging on to the holds for my dear life, I yelled at the top of my lungs to be heard above the roar of the winds. "Mr. Son, when did the storm start?"

"It turned rough five minutes ago, kid," the mechanic grimaced and yelled back. "You better start praying to whatever god you worship. Even if the damn waves don't bury us at some point, they can still break the hull of the boat into pieces."

"How?"

"Kid, you know how much force there is when these waves crash against the boat? Just give them time. They will pull all the nails and glues out of this tub. Then we will really be lost."

"How long can the boat hold out?"

"Three to five hours max, kid."

The rocking motion of the boat became more violent. As the boat came up to a very high wave then descended into a deep trough, one of the two water barrels flew from the engine room to the deck, then crashed through the railings and fell into the sea. As it rolled through, the barrel was just inches away from crushing my feet. It was an act of God that the barrel didn't roll the other way and fall into the main cavity at the bow. If it had, many people would have been killed or seriously injured.

Slowly, I fought to gather my composure. I shook my head several times to shake myself out of this numbing terror. I had no doubt we all were about to meet our maker very shortly. I closed my eyes and silently prayed to God to give me a quick and painless death if the boat were to founder. Dying by drowning is a painful and slow death. Just the thought of it made me shudder with fear. I prayed to God to protect my father, my mother and my brothers who were still in Vietnam. They would never know where and how I died.

Suddenly, all the memories of my short fourteen years of existence, like a movie, started playing in my mind. I remembered again all those wonderful days before the Communists took over South Vietnam. In those days, I was a pampered child, who had nothing to worry about except for studying and playing. I saw footage of the war on TV and read about it in newspapers and magazines my father brought home, but I never had a feel for it. It was as if the war was happening somewhere else and to somebody else. I never thought that the tragedies of war would happen to me or to my family.

Life held so much promise for me then. I grew up in those days, dreaming to someday become a great general who would end the war and bring peace to my people. My father, on the contrary, had hoped I wouldn't have to become a soldier like him. He had so much hope and expectations for me. He expected me to become the best student in my high school. He had hoped that when I got to the age to go to college, I would be able to win some scholarships to study abroad.

But all of our hopes and dreams, like the hopes and dreams of millions other Vietnamese, were shattered with the fall of South Vietnam. The three very tough years I lived under Communism had taught me the invaluable lessons of patience, humility, and perseverance. I had never lost hope for a better future. Those three years also made me a much older person than the fourteen-years-old boy I was. Now, all of my hopes, dreams, and lessons that I learned were about to be buried with me in the dark, cold waters of the South China Sea.

Suddenly, I felt an uncontrollable anger at the injustices of God. Why did misfortunes and tragedies keep befalling people like us, who had never done anything to hurt anyone? How could those hated Communists go on to kill and oppress millions of Vietnamese with impunity and nothing seemed to ever happen to them?

Slowly, I tried to shake myself from the feelings of self-pity, anger, and fear. I tried to remember the last words my father told me before we parted: "You should never give up hope! As long as your heart still beats and your eyes still see, no matter how bad the situation is, you still have a chance to win and survive. If you give up hope, you won't even see the chance if it is there." I repeated these words again and again in an effort to psych myself up and convince myself that this was not yet the end. Gradually, I felt better. I locked myself firmly in a corner of the engine room and closed my eyes to get some rest.

Outside, the storm raged on. While the waves didn't take the boat to the bottom of the sea, the constant pounding on the boat started to take its toll. An hour after the storm started, there was a leak on the bottom of the engine cabin, and water started to flood in. The water pump was broken shortly after, and the water level steadily rose. The crewmen weren't able to seal the leak since they didn't have anything to seal it with. Instead, they tore up their shirts and tried to plug the hole with the fabric. If nothing else was done, the boat would sink in about an hour. There was only one solution to the problem: use a pail to manually scoop and throw the water out of the window in the engine room.

After sizing up the situation, the captain quickly put together a plan. He requested all the men on the boat to take turns and work in teams of two to throw the water out. The crewmen, the captain, the boat owner and three other men who took turns steering the boat were exempt from this labor.

At fourteen, I was considered to be a man. Sơn told me I, too, had to do my part if I wanted to live. All the men on the boat were immediately organized into teams of two to start scooping and throwing the water out. Together, six teams were organized. There were four or five other men, including Ali, the Indian-Vietnamese, who claimed they were too sick and weak to do their part. I had serious doubt whether these men were really too sick to work. These same selfish laggards continued to use the excuse to avoid doing the work for the rest of the journey, even while other men were already exhausted from the labor.

Each team was to work for one hour, then rest for five hours before starting again. My team, a middle-aged teacher and I, would be working on the second shift. My cousin Bình was in another team that worked the fourth shift.

I was very tired, thirsty, hungry and feeling dazed from seasickness and the storm. Weak and small as I was, I wasn't excluded from the labor. I didn't bother to argue with these men. I didn't want to be thought of as lazy or a liar. I also wanted to live. If I refused to work and everyone else did the same thing, we would surely die. Even though I didn't believe we had much of a chance for survival, I didn't want to give up hope.

I stayed in my corner and tried to rest, preparing for the long hard labor that was to come. After the first team had finished, my partner, Mr. Tiểu, and I took their place. I sat on the window of the engine room, hooking both of my legs securely into some holds to prevent myself from falling into the ocean. Even then, it was a precarious position. The wind was howling angrily. Many times, I thought the wind nearly sucked me out of the boat. Tiểu stood down in the engine cabin, scooped the water with a pail, then handed it to me. I then poured the water out to the ocean then handed the pail back to him. His position was much more secure than mine, but his share of the work was much more tiring. Tiểu was a big, severe looking man. Looking down at the engine cabin, I could see that the man was up to his thigh in water.

I was soaked from head to toe from the rain and the splashing waves. After 15 minutes, I felt as if my arms were about to fall off from my body. I also had never felt so cold in my life. The relentless wind kept beating against my soaked body, and the chill penetrated to every nerve in my body that was still sensitive. The hunger and thirst suddenly became insignificant compared to the painful tiredness and the hellish cold. Many times, I thought I was about to collapse. It was with the greatest will that I managed to keep my eyes open and refused to faint. I didn't say anything nor complain to anyone. Mr. Tiểu was not in much better shape than I. He was also soaked and extremely tired. As for the people in the main cabin, they were submerged in water up to their necks. There were no dry places in the boat.

The exhaust pipe was placed not too far from the window, and the smoke coming out of the pipe was blown straight to my face. I tried to keep my head away from the smoke. Nevertheless, within half an hour, my face, head, and neck were blackened. With the waves tossing it sideways, the boat lurched violently from side to side. Many times, I thought my face was just inches from touching the surface of the water. The will to live kept me from giving up. If I were to close my eyes for a few seconds or relax my holds a little bit, I surely would have fallen into the sea and never be seen again.

By the time we finished our shift, I felt as if every muscle and nerve in my body were screaming out in pain. I slowly crawled back to my corner in the engine room and passed out.

I didn't regain consciousness until my partner, Tiểu, came and woke me up. Five hours had passed since I passed out, and it was now our turn again. I was still very tired and sleepy but the rest break was over. I took a few minutes to stretch my aching and abused body. It was going to be another brutal hour of hard work.

I suddenly realized the boat was no longer shaking as violently as before. The rain had stopped and the sun was shining outside. I couldn't believe it! God was merciful after all! The storm was over and we were still alive. I had completely lost all consciousness for the past five hours. Had the boat foundered last night, I would have been an ignorant ghost.

The sudden realization brought a renewed source of strength to my tired muscles. I climbed back to the window and began the mechanical task of taking the bucketful of water and throwing it out the window again. The ocean was calm now. The towering waves of the previous night were no longer there. It was as if the storm last night had never existed or it was just a product of my imagination.

Yet, something was not right. The boat engine was not roaring as it did yesterday. The boat was dead in the water, not going anywhere.

The mechanic was perching on the other window, directly across from me, smoking his cigarettes. He looked cheerful. Taking one puff of his cigarette, he asked me, "How are you holding up there, kid?"

"Not too good!" I shook my head vigorously in an attempt to get some sympathy. "My arms ache all over. I hope my back holds out, too."

Tiểu was standing knee deep in the water in the engine compartment. While bending to scoop and hoisting the water bucket to me, he chimed in, "Try standing down here and do my job and see which is more painful. At least you are young. This work is murder on the back of an old man like me."

"You are right, Mr. Tiểu," the mechanic shrugged. "But we all have to do this, or we die. I still have to fix this damn engine and keep it running, and I am not exempt from this work either."

"Yeah, yeah!" Tiểu grunted. "Is it me, or is the water coming in here faster now?"

"You are not imagining it," Sơn nodded. "The leak on the bottom is getting bigger after all the battering this boat took last night. I tried to plug the hole with some cloth and tape, but it didn't help all that much."

"When did the storm stop?" I asked.

"Just about an hour ago, kid. I can't believe you slept so well through all that rocking and bumping."

"I thank the merciful Buddha for saving us."

"Keep praying to Buddha, kid. Our trouble is not over yet. See, we survived the storm, but we are still in very bad shape. The hull took a lot of beating from the waves last night. If the sea gets rough one more time, this tub can easily break apart. Not only that, the rudder is broken. Don't you notice that we are stopped dead in the water right now?"

"Yes, I was going to ask you why. So, what are we going to do?"

"You are going to keep throwing the water out to keep this tub floating, kid." Sơn wiped some of the smoke dust and grease from his face. "There are two men swimming under the boat right now to replace the broken rudder. When they are done, then I'll start this engine to get us going again."

"Yes, I am, I am," I nodded. "How long before they finish?"

"They've been at it for half an hour, kid," the mechanic bobbed his head in mock exasperation. "They'd better be done soon. Then, it will take me another hour to get this baby going again."

"Did anyone get hurt last night?" I asked.

"Now, that is a real miracle." Sơn puffed on his newly lighted cigarette. "Mr. Dẫn was up in the steering cabin the whole night, trying to keep the boat going with the waves to lessen the impact against the sides. He nearly got blown out to the ocean. Well, we are lucky he didn't. But we are not that lucky, kid. All his navigational tools, the map, the compass, even the chair in the steering cabin are now somewhere on the bottom of the ocean. Heck, even Dẫn has no idea where we are right now."

I shut up and tried to absorb what Sơn's words meant. The storm last night must have blown us off course, and even the captain had no idea where we were. In addition, our water supply was reduced from two barrels to one. While we escaped death last night, our situation now was still desperate: we were lost at sea with little food and water left in a disabled boat.

My optimism evaporated. Nevertheless, I still felt better than last night. My clothes began to dry as the sun came up. I no longer felt the penetrating cold of the wind. While working steadily, I silently prayed to Buddha to save us from death again.

Looking out the window, I could see nothing except for water. It was as if our boat was the only thing floating in the South China Sea. The meager energy I recovered from my five hours' slumber quickly dissipated. I hadn't eaten or drunk anything for the past eighteen hours. My throat was burning with thirst and I could hear my stomach growling incessantly. At my request, Sơn got me a small cup of the gasoline-laced water. He now became the jealous guardian of the water barrel, which became the key to our survival for the rest of the journey. I quickly gulped down the precious cup. The water still tasted terrible, but at least it relieved the burning sensation in my mouth. Tired, thirsty, hungry, and afraid as I was, I still managed to maintain a stoic expression. The three hard years of living under Communism had taught me the virtue of silence: it saved energy, and it hid my vulnerability. Besides, it was useless to complain to anyone anyway. Everyone was facing the same thirst, hunger and danger.

When we were relieved of our shift, I was ready to collapse again. I staggered to my corner and lay down for half an hour. I couldn't sleep again because the sun was coming up. It was getting hot.

By now, the crewmen had successfully replaced the rudder. Mr. Sơn tinkered with the engine for another few minutes, then the boat was moving again. Since no one had any idea where we were, the captain decided to move southward, using the position of the sun as an indicator of direction. He estimated that we probably were blown northeast last night, so if we moved in the southwest direction, we should be able to reach Malaysia in four or five days. As soon as I heard his projection, my heart sank at the thought of staying on this decrepit boat for such a long period. Even if the sea wouldn't get rough again, I was not sure if my aching body could withstand the agonizing labor, thirst and hunger for another day.

After an hour of rest, the soreness and pains in my muscles subsided somewhat. With a little bit of energy returning, my pessimism slowly retreated. I kept talking quietly to myself that I should be glad that I was still alive and not injured. If God didn't let me die in the terrible storm last night, maybe he wouldn't let me die. Maybe this was just another test of God to see how much I could take. To me, survival now became a duel between me and a supernatural power. So far, I had won because I was still alive.

After mumbling for fifteen minutes to psych myself up, I walked outside to the deck. A section of the railing had been demolished by the flying water barrel last night. The surface of the sea was so calm, I had trouble believing that a violent storm just passed by us three hours ago.

I breathed in deeply, enjoying the fresh air and the cool, soothing breeze. My spirit was given a boost when I saw Ms. Tuyết start to cook some rice. At least within an hour I would have something to eat.

Suddenly, I saw something white on the horizon floating toward our boat. I called out to the captain and other people on the deck to see if they could tell what it was. Sơn went to the main cabin to get binoculars. By the time he found it, the thing was getting close to our boat already and we could make out what it was.

I felt a chill in my spine. The floating thing was a woman's corpse dressed in white. From her clothes, I had no doubt she was Vietnamese, and a boat escapee just like us. She must have been drowned for a few days, for her body was bloated up to twice the size of a normal person. Her skin was turning a ghastly gray color. The appearance of the corpse was so horrible I thought I was about to vomit. I couldn't stand the sight any longer and quickly went back inside. The sight of the corpse haunted me for the rest of the journey. I sat down, closed my eyes, and quietly prayed to Buddha to save us from the fate that had befallen this unfortunate woman. It was such a terrible sight that every time I thought about it, it brought a cold shiver all over my body.

I was snapped out of my funk by a call from my cousin Hằng to come and help her. When I came down to the cavity, my cousin asked me to get water for her kids. She and everyone else in the cavity were lying submerged in water up to their necks. My nephew and niece were crying loudly. I had to beg Mr. Chiên, the new guardian of the precious remaining water barrel, for two cups of the cursed liquid mixture. My nephew and niece barely drank the first gulp and clammed their mouths shut. They refused to drink any more. I saved the precious water into a container and gave it to my cousin. She raised her neck a little higher and asked, "What is the commotion out there about?"

"Oh, there was a corpse of a woman floating toward our boat."

"Really? Does it look like a Vietnamese?"

"Yes, she dressed like a Vietnamese," I nodded. "Looked like she was dead for a few days. Her body bloated badly."

"May the Merciful Buddha bring peace to her soul," Hằng closed her eyes. "May the Merciful Buddha save us from this fate."

Suddenly, we heard Sơn yelling from the deck, "The corpse is following our boat! It's following our boat!"

I left my cousin and came up to the deck. Sơn, the captain, the boat owner, and several other people were up there gesticulating at the white shape floating at the rear of the stern. It was the most eerie and strangest thing I had ever seen. Our boat was moving fairly fast and should have been quite far away from the corpse in just minutes. Yet, after the corpse drifted to the rear of the boat, it somehow managed to maintain the same distance from the boat for the next two hours. There were no physical explanations that could make any sense.

As the news of the corpse following our boat reached the main cavity, it sparked off intense speculations about the cause of this strange phenomenon. The superstitious people theorized that the woman had died such a terrible death that her soul could not have salvation. The ghost of the woman must be trying to follow our boat to the shore of freedom. As superstitious as it was, it quickly gained acceptance from most people. Those people who couldn't accept this explanation were nevertheless stumped. They couldn't come up with anything to explain this supernatural occurrence.

Finally, the boat owner, Đang, made an altar and found some fruit as an offering to the soul of the dead woman. Soon after, the sound of prayers filled the main cabin. People sat up to pray for the salvation of the woman's soul and ask her spirit to leave us alone. The sound of prayers, the smell of incense, and the woman's corpse following our boat all created a scene that was so surreal it was scary. I was not as superstitious as other people on the boat. Nevertheless the whole thing made my hair stand on end.

I closed my eyes to sleep, but couldn't. It was not until two hours later that the corpse floated away from our boat. As the mechanic announced the news, everyone let out a sigh of relief.

At noon, Tuyết distributed her half-cooked rice. I got a slightly larger share than most other people, half a bowl. Tuyết apologized profusely for the nearly inedible rice. She claimed it was the best she could do because there was not enough firewood and the rocking motion of the boat made it difficult to cook. As bad as the rice tasted, I finished it within a few minutes. The rice pot was scraped clean before I finished. It was all I was going to get today.

The meal didn't relieve the hunger. Instead, it served to remind me I was still very hungry. I huddled in the corner of the boat, trying to sleep and to save every ounce of energy I knew I would need later.

There was no other unusual event for the rest of the day. I repeated the routine of throwing water out of the window for three more shifts. Every time I finished, I thought I would soon drop dead. Amazingly, I was able to work through my shifts without fainting. I never knew I had so much endurance for pain, hunger and thirst. The difference between night and day started to blur. Every time I finished my shift, I passed out until my partner woke me up for our next shift.

The sea remained calm for the next three days. The scene around us seemed not to change an iota. We didn't see any other boat or sight of land. The rice supply, firewood, and water were steadily depleted to dangerously low levels. The cook told us that the rice would not last us for four more days. The water ration, very meager to start with, was reduced. Everyone now got only three-quarters of a cup per day. The men who worked to keep the boat from sinking got twice the amount of water, which was barely enough to keep their throats from burning.

By the fifth day, I concluded that we were going to die. It was now obvious we were hopelessly lost at sea, as the captain, the crewmen and the boat owner had many arguments among themselves about which direction we should head. The hunger and the painful soreness of my body didn't bother me as much as the thirst. My saliva, which substituted for water for the past three days, had run dry. I seriously thought about saving my urine in a cup to drink. I found an empty cup and hid it in my coat. The problem was I couldn't urinate at all. So much for the plan.

The plight of the people in the main cabin was even worse. They had less water than I did since they didn't have to work. My nephew and niece, who never left the cabin except when they had to shit or urinate, stopped crying by the second day. They, their mother, and everyone else lay half submerged in water. The 70-year-old lady, who had no one to take care of her, was paralyzed after the storm. Her nephew was one of the men working to throw the water out. He hardly had any time to rest and look after his wife, who was extremely sick. The old lady couldn't move at all, and no one was willing nor had the energy to take her up to the deck when she needed to relieve herself. She ended up shitting and urinating while lying paralyzed. Within two days, the water in the cavity was fully polluted by human waste. Every time I looked down at the cabin, I could see many pieces of feces floating around. People simply pushed them away as the waste floated toward them. The smell in the cavity was incredibly awful. I was glad I had a spot in the engine room instead of having to lie down in the main cavity.

Every moment I was awake, I prayed silently and incessantly to Buddha to save us from the certain death of starvation and thirst. Reason told me it was just a matter of time before all of us were going to drop dead, one by one. I probably would be one of the first, because the work was taking its toll on my battered body. Yet, deep down inside, some irrational faith in God told me not to give up hope. It was this faith in God, this will to live, that gave me the strength to pick myself up again every time my partner woke me up for the brutal labor.

God must have heard our prayers. Early on the morning of the sixth day, it rained for an hour. Everyone who still had some energy grabbed every container they could find to collect the rainwater. I was quick enough to collect four large cups. I never knew rainwater could taste so good. After satisfying my thirst, I brought the cups to my cousin and her children. The rain barely lasted long enough for everyone to get a cup or two. The crewmen were also able to collect five gallons of water to save for the rest of the journey.

On the seventh day, the optimism of the previous day faded quickly as the food started to run low. The share of rice everyone got became a little smaller. After the thirst was satisfied, the hunger became more dominant. I tried hard to not think of food, but found it was impossible to get the thought out of my mind.

We started seeing some ships on the horizon but could not get close to them. At noon, we came close to a very large ship. As we approached it, I could see the word "Skyline" painted on the side of the ship. The people on my boat became extremely excited. Here was our chance to be picked up to safety.

The captain gathered some white rags, and stood on the roof of the boat signaling SOS to the big ship. I didn't know if the people on the large ship saw us or not. It was almost impossible for them not to see. Nevertheless, the ship nonchalantly passed by our boat without stopping. The size of the ship was about fifty times the size of our boat, and the waves created by its movement nearly turned our boat over.

As the big ship disappeared into the horizon, dejection and desperation were written on everyone's face. There went our hope for rescue. There was no way the sailors on that ship could not see us and not recognize that our situation was desperate. I finally brought myself to the realization that these people didn't want

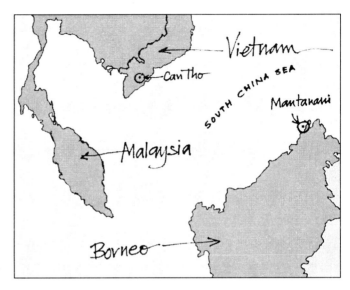

Map of the journey: We planned to sail south from Can Tho around the tip of Vietnam and southwest to the Malaysian peninsula. Instead, our boat was blown so far off course that we wound up on a tiny island, Pulau Mantanani, off the coast of Malaysian Borneo, nearly 1,000 miles east of our target. (Reproduced from Volume 60, no. 2, of the *Stanford Business Magazine*. Copyright 1991 by the Board of Trustees of the Leland Stanford Junior University. All rights reserved.)

to be burdened with us, the wretched Vietnamese refugees. They were willing to leave us to die on our own rather than take us in.

Instead of thinking about the incident any further, I went back to sleep. When all else failed, I always tried to conserve my energy.

On the morning of the eighth day, I was surprised that I was alive at all. My body felt as if someone had taken many needles and pierced every muscle and nerve I had. Most people had given up hope. Many were lying very still, quietly praying for a painless death. The atmosphere in the boat was extremely depressing.

As I worked through my shifts, my arms felt as if they lost all sensation. There were no words I could find to describe the pain I felt just from raising my arms.

In the afternoon, the captain ran down to the cabin and excitedly told everyone that he was able to see what he thought was an island. He had the help of the binoculars to find it. It was the first good news we had heard in the whole week. I strained my eyes to look in the direction the captain was pointing to, but could see nothing. No one else could make out anything either. Then, it was getting dark quickly. Nevertheless, the captain insisted he saw land and would turn the boat to that direction. He estimated it would take another eight hours before we got there. No one argued with him. Everyone was trying to conserve their last ounces of energy. While they were skeptical of the captain's sighting, they were too tired to argue or to object to the new course.

As usual, I went to sleep as soon as I finished my shifts. I wasn't in a hurry to find out whether the captain was right or not. I was more concerned about whether or not I would open my eyes for the next round of torturous work.

On the morning of the ninth day, the excited cries of people woke me up from my deep slumber. The first word I heard was "Land!" As if I had just taken a magic pill, I rose quickly and ran to the deck to take a look.

It was no illusion, no hallucination. There it was, a green island just a few miles away. There were many tall trees on the island. I couldn't see any sign of people living on it yet. There were many submerged rocks in the area. The captain guided our floating tub around the island to find a place it could come in and land. By now, anyone who still had any energy had come on the deck, watching nervously. It was still very dangerous. If the captain made a wrong move, the boat could hit a submerged rock and the boat would sink. We were a good few miles from the shore. Given the physical conditions we were in, there was little chance that anyone could make it ashore alive.

As our boat made its way to the other side of the island, we spotted two fishing boats. There were several dark men with only their shorts on standing on the fishing boats. The fishermen must have seen us too. One of the boats made its way toward us while the other one went toward the island. When the fishing boat came near ours, one of the fishermen signaled us for someone to come on their boat. The captain, who surprisingly had some strength left, jumped into the water and swam over.

The fishermen pulled Dần up to their boat. Standing on our deck, I could see they were trying to communicate by sign language. It was not long before the captain swam back to our boat. The smile on his face told us everything we needed to know. We were saved at last!

The fishermen were Malaysians. They told the captain they would lead us to the island. After nine days wandering aimlessly at sea, somehow we ended up in the place we wanted to be. And we couldn't find land a day sooner. Our food, water and fuel would not last us beyond today.

We followed the fishermen's boat toward the shore. In half an hour, we pulled up to a small wooden pier. There were many natives on the beach looking at us as our boat came in. The fishermen on the other boat must have told the villagers of our presence.

As we set foot on the beach, the villagers brought us biscuits and plenty of water. I had never imagined these people could be so nice. As I sipped the water, I looked at the sky and silently thanked God for saving our lives.

After I had eaten and drunk, I went toward the sea and washed myself. A villager laughed and gave me a mirror. Looking in the mirror, I was horrified. I couldn't recognize myself. My face, neck, head and body were thoroughly blackened by nine straight days of exposure to the smoke from the exhaust pipe. It took me three days to clean all the carbon deposits and grease from my body.

I found a coconut tree and sat with my back leaning against its trunk. The ocean breeze blew my long hair over my face. My whole body was still in pain, but the pain just didn't matter anymore. I closed my eyes and said a thousand silent thanks to the Merciful Buddha, God, or whatever name that we mortals called the omnipotent Creator. To the day I die, I will never forget this journey. For now, I just lay still and enjoyed the cool breeze that soothed my battered body. It felt so good to be alive.

# 16

# The Days of Waiting

After we landed, the Malaysian villagers notified the Red Cross office in Kotakinabalu, a city an hour away from the island. The next day, the Red Cross came to bring us food and clothes. Later they also brought in raw building materials and hired the villagers to build a camp on the far side of the island.

I was told by one of the people who could speak English and had talked with the Red Cross officials that we were very lucky to land on this island in Eastern Malaysia, Pulau Mantanani. If we had missed this island and continued southward, the next land we might find would have been Australia, which was another month away. If we had missed Pulau Mantanani, no one would have been alive to reach Australia.

Despite the journey's incredible conditions, no one died. The Malaysian villagers helped us to move the sick passengers ashore. Most of the men were able to walk on their own. The children were also remarkably resilient. Most of them quickly recovered their energy once they came on shore.

Many women, including my cousin Hằng, were very sick after the nine-day ordeal. In addition, my cousin's sprained ankle hadn't healed properly. The 70-year-old woman was in the most critical condition. She had hardly anything to eat and drink in the past nine days. She was unconscious when people put her on the stretcher to take her ashore.

Once they took a look at the conditions of the refugees, the Red Cross officials decided to take the sick women and their children to a hospital in Kotakinabalu for treatment. The 70-year-old lady was taken to a separate hospital. She never returned to the island. I never knew whether she survived or died.

My cousin Hằng and her three-year-old son, Thái Dương, were among the people taken to the hospital. Suddenly, my cousin Bình and I, two young boys of fifteen and eighteen, found ourselves having to take care of our niece, one-year-old Tú Quỳnh. For the next two weeks, when her mother was away, her two unfortunate uncles tried many different ways, to no avail, to silence her uninterrupted crying.

When the Red Cross officials came, just about all the men on the boat, whether or not they understood English, crowded around these officials. They pushed and shoved each other to be the one to tell the story of our journey. Frustrated, the Red Cross officials finally asked these men to step back, and insisted they would only speak to a delegation representing the group that could speak and understand English.

After long, contentious arguments among the men, the representatives were finally selected. The delegation consisted of Mr. Đang, the boat owner; Ali, the Indian-Vietnamese who had shirked from the hard work of keeping the boat afloat; and two other men who spoke and understood English moderately.

While many people privately despised Ali for his lazy selfishness, they now tried to kiss up to him as he was the only person who could speak English fluently. All communication and requests for help to the Red Cross officials went through him. Ali himself appeared to enjoy his newfound power and popularity immensely. As the de facto leader because no one else really understood English, Ali ordered other people to do all the hard labor and excused himself from having to even lift a finger.

Within a few days, a big Red Cross ship with building materials, food, and clothing supplies came to the island. The additional food and clothes was the supply for our group for the whole month, until the next supply ship came. The delegation of four that spoke with the Red Cross officials now found itself to be the Community Leadership Committee.

The committee's toughest job was to figure out how to distribute the supplies to everyone's satisfaction. After the ordeal of the journey, where they nearly died of thirst and hunger, most people wanted to grab as many of the supplies for themselves as they could. Further, the escapees still remembered the boat owner's false promise that the boat was "well-stocked" with food, water, and fuel. Now that he was a member of the leadership delegation, his assurances that every family would receive its fair share of the supplies didn't sound convincing.

As the men crowded around the supplies to wait for their share, many arguments and near fist fights broke out. Mr. Thành, the self-proclaimed martial arts instructor, threatened to beat up other men for wanting to take "items that fairly should be given to his needier children." Other men, some of whom were ex-soldiers, were not less belligerent. They started grabbing whatever they could use as weapons and challenged Thành to fight. The scene of these ragged grown men getting ready to beat each other up over a few cans of powdered milk or canned foods was both comical and ridiculous.

Fortunately, the leadership group was able to prevent the fights. They had to push the men away from each other. Then, announcing that they would seek advice from the Red Cross officials on how to distribute the goods, they disbanded the group and started conferring among themselves.

The group finally came up with ways to distribute the first shipment of goods to their fellow escapees. Children would get slightly more than adults, and each family had to wait its turn before it could come to get its supplies. While no one was completely satisfied and many people continued to complain loudly, the leadership group was at least able to prevent the violence and embarrassment for all of us. Yet, the heated arguments over supply distribution flared up again every month when the shipment came.

Our refugee camp was a big wooden building with a straw roof. The building was located on an empty beach on the island, one mile away from the Malaysian village. The building was barely large enough to accommodate the 60 people from our boat. It was subdivided into many small rooms, each to accommodate a family. Two large kerosene lamps were hung on the rafters and were lit only at night. These lamps were the only source of artificial light. There was no electricity for the building.

The rooms were separated by bamboo dividers, draped with small blankets to provide some token privacy. Each room was just a tiny rectangular space of two meters by three meters. The small area was the space for a typical family of five. In the tiny space, each family crammed all its material possessions and somehow carved out some sleeping space.

Despite the cramped space, everyone was happy to finally have a roof over their heads. While waiting for the building to be built, we had all slept on the beach or under the bottom of the raised platform wooden houses of the Malaysian villagers. Every morning, I woke up finding sand in my face or ants and other insects crawling all over my body. The building finally gave us some protection from the elements and the insects.

The next seven months of our lives were spent on this tropical island. Were it not for the uncertainty of our resettlement prospects, the time spent here would have been a wonderful vacation in paradise. We did not have to struggle daily for survival like in Vietnam. The Red Cross provided sufficient canned foods and rice for the whole community. The labor we had to do was not excessive or difficult. For the first time in my life, I found that I had more time on my hands than I knew what to do with.

After two weeks in the hospital, my cousin Hằng and her son Thái Dương were brought back to the island. The two weeks in the hospital did them wonders. My cousin's sprained ankle had healed and Thái Dương looked much healthier than when he first came off the boat.

With my cousin back, my life became a lot easier. Now, I didn't have to worry about taking care of little Tú Quỳnh. Also, our little family now had a much better cook. We no longer had to eat just steamed rice with canned meats.

Soon, we got an unexpected benefit. The captain, Mr. Dần, asked Hằng to help cook meals for him and his eight-year-old boy. In return, he would teach me and Bình English and give us physical training. When Hằng agreed to the deal, neither she nor the captain realized the benefit would last me for a long time.

The captain was the only man on the boat I respected. A former South Vietnamese navy officer, he had spent three years in a re-education camp. He was lucky to be released after only three years. When he came back to Saigon, the boat owner, Mr. Đang, came to him with a deal. If he agreed to drive the boat to escape from Vietnam, Mr. Đang would gave him two spaces. The captain tried to bargain for three spaces, so that he could take both his wife and son along, but Mr. Đang wouldn't budge. Finally, the captain ended up taking only his son with him and had to leave his wife behind in Vietnam.

A quiet and dignified man, Mr. Dần did not join the other men in the pushing or arguments when it came to receiving the supplies from the Red Cross. Despite knowing English fairly well, he also did not bother to get on the leadership committee or follow the Red Cross officials around when they came. He kept to himself and spent his time teaching and taking care of his son. I often saw him taking solitary walk along the beach at night.

True to his word, after Hằng agreed to the deal, Mr. Dần started training Bình and me. Every day at dawn, he woke us up for a two-mile swim. Rain or shine, and even on the coldest days, he would be up before anyone else in the camp. He did not accept any excuses nor allow us to sleep in even for one minute. After warming up on the beach, we plunged into the cold water of the Pacific Ocean and swam from our building to a pier in the Malaysian village half a mile away. Every day, my cousin and I swam the same distance, with Mr. Dần by our side all the way. Day by day, he pushed us to go at a faster pace until we could not go any faster. The daily swim gradually made us stronger. After the first month, I no longer dreaded plunging into cold water so early in the morning.

We began to have a daily routine for our activities. After the swim, Mr. Dần, Bình, and I went together to fetch water, gather firewood, or wash clothes. By the time we finished our chores, Hằng would have breakfast ready. After breakfast, we settled down for a two-hour English lesson before having lunch. Then, we would have the afternoon to lounge around.

Mr. Dần took whatever books or materials he could use to teach us. While my English pronunciation did not improve much over the next six months, Mr. Dần helped me to increase my English vocabulary substantially. Through the months, I developed a close relationship with this former navy officer. While my parents were not there, Mr. Dần was the only adult who gave me encouragement and direction in these uncertain days of waiting.

After the initial excitement of the first few weeks of settling on this Malaysian island, loneliness and homesickness started to overwhelm me most of my waking moments. Many evenings, I walked alone along the beach or the woods behind our building, thinking about my parents and brothers. I had written a letter to my mother as soon as I landed, and asked the Red Cross people to send it to Vietnam. My cousin Hằng had also written a letter to her family when she was in the hospital. By now, my parents and my brothers would know that I was alive. But they would have little or no way to send letters to me. Beyond telling my family that I was alive, there was little else I could tell them. Not knowing enough English and anything about applications for resettlement, I could only trust that my cousin Hằng would know what to do to get us admitted to the great country of America.

I wondered how my mother handled taking care of my brothers now. How much longer would my father last in the re-education camps that were designed to strip away all the shreds of pride and dignity of the proud former officers and soldiers of South Vietnam? Then, would the local "Yellow Dogs" get suspicious and give my mother trouble? What would they do to her now that two of her sons were missing?

My thoughts often wandered to my friends who were still in school. By now, Thái would have figured out that I had left the country. Would he carry out his plan to get Mr. Nghiên to let him back in school? Would he include my name as one of the culprits of the desecration of Ho Chi Minh's pictures? If he did, I wouldn't mind. I might never see Thái or anyone from Vũng Tàu, my city, again in my life. It had been only a few weeks, but Thái and my other friends already belonged to a part of my past that I could never go back to.

Occasionally, I thought about Trang. I regretted not having the chance to tell her goodbye nor to tell her that she was on my mind for a long time. Now that we might never see each other again, maybe it was better that way. Time would pass, and day by day, Trang, Thái , and all my friends would gradually fade away in my memory. Perhaps, I would never forget them. But I also knew that with the passing of each day, I would lose a precious little memory of the turbulent childhood that we shared together. For now, I was just trying to hold on to these memories for as long as I could.

On one solitary walk along the beach at night, I found the captain, Dần, strolling by himself. He asked me to join him. We walked along quietly, deep in our own thoughts. After a while, I broke the silence. "Uncle Dần, what will you do when you get to America?"

The captain stopped, looked out to the sea before answering "Well, I don't know yet. I may go back to school to get a degree, or I may join a merchant ship. It's hard to know what you will do, when you don't yet know what will be there."

"Will you try to get your wife over?"

"Of course I will. Whatever it takes. My son and I miss her very much."

"I miss my parents, too, Uncle Dần."

The captain sighed. "I understand. It is tough for one so young like you to go through this. Being alone here, then in another country. It's tough, too, for an old man like me. Whether you are old or young, it's tough to be alone."

"You have your son, Uncle Dần. I don't have anybody, other than my cousins, niece, and nephew. But we are not that close. I don't know how to deal with this feeling of sadness alone. I don't know where I am going, how I'll get there, and what for. If I get somewhere, whom will I share it with? All the people who mean something to me are now an ocean away. I will probably never see them again. Sometimes, I just wonder if this escape is worth it."

"I understand," Mr. Dần nodded. "It is not easy for me to be alone, either. I just had a lot of practice at it. I was alone until I nearly turned 30. I didn't marry until then. Work, military duties, there were so many things that demanded my time. Many times, I had the same questions you have. You don't have to escape from Vietnam and be away from your family to face that."

The captain paused to collect his thoughts then continued "Some-times, I looked at the people who married early and thought how won-derful and happy they must feel. But you know what? As I grow older and see more, I realize that these people are not all that happy. They may not be lonely at the beginning, but they didn't get to do a lot of things they wanted. Then they get frustrated, unhappy, and sometimes even estranged from the people they lived with. It's a different kind of loneliness, and it eats away at your soul later, son."

We were not the only people catching a cool ocean breeze tonight. A young couple holding hand went by us. I recognized them as two lovers from our camp. Walking along the beach, they seemed so perfect together.

"Look at them, Uncle Dần," I pointed at the couple. "They seem so happy together. How can anyone ever see any roots of unhappiness in that?"

"You can't tell just by looking." Dần shook his head. "But I can tell you an analogy. We human beings are like pieces of jade. The pieces that get polished and cut would be brilliant and beautiful. The pieces that don't will be dull and ordinary. The polishing and cutting of the jade are like the hard work, discipline, and sacrifices we go through. Loneliness is part of it, too. They are painful, but they will make us stronger and better. Peo-ple who avoid the hard work, sacrifices, and seek pleasures too early will be ordinary. You will never hear anything of importance from them. Son, if you want to go far in life, you should be prepared to pay the price. Hard work and self-discipline are the minimum requirements. But more than that, loneliness will be part of the package, too. To go somewhere, you need determination. Early companionship and pleasures can only distract you and make you soft. As for people like that couple there, you can't tell how happy they are or will be just by the look of it. Life is long, and if the base of the house you build is weak, it will not last you."

I ran my hands through my tousled hair and looked up at the sky, whispering my response. "But Uncle Dần, why do I want to be anything but just a happy, ordinary person? I want happiness, just like anyone else. I want a happy home, with my dad, my mom, my brothers, and me together. It is a simple dream, with a family of my own with people who will care and love me. What is wrong with that, Uncle Dần?"

The captain looked into my eyes. "You may say it, because it makes you feel normal or ordinary. But you are not ordinary. I have not known you very long, but I have taught you a month. I have worked with many soldiers and sailors before too. Sometimes, I came across a man with a deep burning fire in his heart, wanting so bad to be able to rise and show the world how good he could be. Those men are very special people. Some of them make it and do something great. Many don't. But it is their passion to succeed that always makes me remember them."

"You have the same fire in your eyes as these people I knew. You probably know you have this fire in your gut, but you haven't come to terms with it. It is this quality that will make you go far, but it will also make you lonely, until you find someone who can understand you and live with it. Your simple dream of a happy home is not that simple for people like you and me. We can never go back to our happy homes of the past. The Communist government has taken care of that. We can only go forward to build a new beginning. Only we cannot take shortcuts. Don't take the shortcuts. If deep in your heart you want it bad enough, someday you will make your dream come true. But you need to be patient and build a long-lasting foundation for it."

I was surprised to hear Dần saying that he had such a high opinion of me. It took me a while before I could ask him. "Thank you for believing in me, Uncle Dần. But I still don't understand what you mean by not taking shortcuts."

"What I mean is that when you get to America, you must learn as much and go as far as you can. Learn to live with your loneliness until you can go no further. Don't get into relationship early. Only when you are happy with yourself, with what you accomplish, then you can be happy with a woman in your life. That's the price you pay if you want to achieve your dream."

"Thanks, Uncle Dần," I smiled. "I'll try to remember your advice. But we all have our own fate. What we plan may not be what God's will is."

"Yes, but we can influence our own fate to a certain extent, too. Just remember not to blame God or fate for our own stupidity."

We laughed and got up to walk again. When I went to sleep that night, the conversation with Mr. Dần lingered in my mind for a long time.

By the second month, the UNHCR (United Nations High Commissioner for Refugees) representatives came to process our group for resettlement. We were very fortunate to have escaped at a time when the exodus of Vietnamese refugees became an international crisis. Several hundreds of thousands of Vietnamese boat people overloaded refugee camps in the neighboring countries of Hong Kong, Indonesia, Malaysia, Philippines, Singapore, and Thailand. These countries threatened to turn refugee boats back to sea and repatriate those who were already in camps, unless Western nations took in more refugees and accelerate the process of resettlement.

Fortunately, the Western nations responded positively to the crisis. Countries like the United States, Canada, Australia, and Great Britain increased their admissions of refugees substantially. The United States alone admitted more than 100,000 Vietnamese refugees in 1978. It was this wide-open-door policy that allowed us to come to America. If we were to escape ten years later, we would have languished away in the refugee camps of Southeast Asia and eventually be repatriated to Vietnam.

By the fifth month, some families got accepted for resettlement. They were soon moved from the island to Kotakinabalu, then onward to Kuala Lumpur before going to their final destination. By the beginning of the sixth month, half of the people on our boat had already left the island. Mr. Dần and his son had also left by this time. After five months of studying with Mr. Dần, I had become attached to him. He had been the father figure to me in the camp. I could only bid him and his son goodbye, and asked him to write to me if he could. For his part, Mr. Dần reminded me to keep the fire in my belly burning. I never saw him again.

By November 1978, my cousin's family and some other families and I were the last people to leave. When we left, the Red Cross officials allowed the Malaysian villagers to dismantle the building we had lived in the past six months. No Vietnamese refugees would ever live in this little camp again.

# 17

# Epilogue — After the Rain

After a two-day stay in the city of Kotakinabalu, my cousin's family and I were flown to a staging refugee camp in Kuala Lumpur. There were already a few thousand other Vietnamese refugees living in the place, a huge compound fenced with barbed wire. Quarantined in the place for several weeks, I did not get to see anything else in the Malaysian capital until the day I departed.

The camp was the final stopping point in Malaysia for refugees who were on their way to their countries of resettlement. The longest time one expected to stay here was about two months. There would be a few final health and paper checks before we could expect to leave for America. Weeks before, my cousin Hằng had filled out resettlement applications provided by the Red Cross. Now, we waited nervously for our turn to go through the last formalities. After seven months living in limbo, we couldn't wait to start a new life.

Within a week, we were called up for our health check. After a few days, we got the results. The health results for my cousin Bình, Hằng, and her children, Thái Dương and Tú Quỳnh, were fine. They would be flying in the second week from Malaysia to the United States, ultimately arriving in San Diego, California. My checkup, for some reason, was not good, despite the fact that I was feeling better than I had felt in the past three years. The health officers suspected that I contracted tuberculosis. Thus, while my cousin's family could leave for the U.S., I had to stay back in the camp. The health examiner, through interpreters, told me I would have to go through another examination in a month.

A view of the entrance to the Đống Đa complex today. The old military complex has been bulldozed and replaced with new government office buildings.

As my cousin's family departed from the camp for the airport, I felt a sense of ultimate loneliness. Everyone in my camp had left for their countries of resettlement. At fifteen, I was now really alone in a crowded, noisy camp with thousands of strangers. My cousin Hằng couldn't do anything more, other than give me the address and phone contact of the family that sponsored us. The immigration officer, through an interpreter, told me not to worry. They would take care of making sure I got reunited with my cousin's family when it came my turn to go to America. For now, there was nothing I could do other than eat, take some medication, and wait for the next physical checkup.

Fortunately, I was given a clean bill of health on the next checkup. The health officer told me there was no more sign of tuberculosis infection. He even thought they might have made the wrong diagnosis previously, causing me to stay an extra month. Nevertheless, I was too happy to complain. After a month of sleeping alone on a hammock, I was very anxious to leave the place.

From Kuala Lumpur, I was put on a plane leaving for San Francisco, with a short layover in Hong Kong. Arriving in San Francisco, I was led

The entrance to the old Vietnamese cemetery across from my home on Lê Lợi Street. the cemetery is abandoned today and is inhabited by trash pickers.

by a social worker to a plane bound for San Diego, where I was reunited with my cousin's family.

When I began my new life in America on January 7, 1979, I thought I had passed the hardest time in my life. While I could see many challenges ahead, learning English, getting back to school, and learning how to live without my parents, I thought nothing could compare to the hardships I endured in Vietnam. I had gone through the toughest trials a young man could expect to get at an early age. I had faced my fear in the perilous escape from Vietnam. In my darkest days, I had always told myself that "After the rain, the sky will be bright again." The stormy days in my life, I thought, were now far behind.

However, the road of life, as my father warned me years before, would never be easy. Since my parents were not with me, I became a foster child under the care of my cousin Hằng. With my living expenses taken care of by social service agencies, I got the opportunity to go to high school, first in San Diego, then Orange County, when my cousin's family moved there. I excelled in school, learned English quickly, and escaped ESL (English as a Second Language) classes within six months. Not contented with just studying, I worked after school, taking jobs in fast-food restaurants and gas stations. I spent some of the money to improve my wardrobe from donated, ragged Goodwill clothes to something that my schoolmates would not laugh at and immediately pick me out as one of the "FOBs" (Fresh Off the Boat). The rest, I sent home to help my mother in Vietnam.

In 1980, my mother managed to arrange for my last younger brothers to escape from Vietnam. After a year in a refugee camp, they were reunited with me in California. My mother stayed and waited until my father was released from the re-education camp. When he came home in late 1981, my parents made three attempted escapes from Vietnam. Each time they failed and barely avoided capture.

In the fall of 1982, I entered the University of California, Irvine, as a freshman. I was beaming with confidence, having won two scholarships that virtually paid for my college education. Then, a month later, I received a letter from Uncle Tín, informing me that my parents had made it out to sea on a boat, in September 1982. He told me to expect a telegram or a letter from my parents soon if they made it to a country of asylum. Suddenly, my outlook on life changed from hopeful optimism to sleepless, nervous anxiety.

For a year, I came home daily looking for the telegram or the letter that would tell me my parents were safe. It never came. Instead, several letters from Uncle Tín brought more bad news. He did not hear anything from my parents. Neither did the families of people escaping on the same boat hear anything from their loved ones. My uncle heard there was a storm in the South China Sea after my parents escaped. Perhaps my parents and their fellow escapees just got stranded in some remote islands in the Pacific, my uncle tried to comfort me. Not wanting to believe the worst, I went along with the pretension. It was totally illogical for me, who had gone through the horror of drifting in the vast ocean, to trust the assurance of my uncle, who might know, but never experienced for himself the horrifying dangers.

For four years, I lived in anguish and loneliness, searching for every lead on the whereabouts of my parents. The sorrow made me become an angry young man. I developed a perpetual scowl, a harsh stare that deterred people from getting close. Even my brothers and I grew apart. We were all stubborn, independent young men, who would not listen to one another. We all dealt with our loss in our own way, afraid to show our vulnerability. Thus, all we shared was silence.

It was not until 1986 that I came to accept my parents were lost to me forever. After four years, my brothers and I had a Buddhist ceremony to pray for my parents' peace in heaven. My pain from losing my parents would not go away, but it gradually subsided over the years.

From then on, my life took a turn for the better. In 1986, I graduated with an electrical engineering degree from the University of California, Irvine. Then, I went to work for an aerospace company, Rockwell International, as a design engineer. For four years, I toiled in boredom and obscurity, working on outdated, 30-year-old technology. I couldn't see a way up or out of my dead-end job, let alone finding a way to go back to Vietnam. In 1989, I got my master's degree in electrical engineering, but still couldn't see any promotion or advancement in sight. Frustrated, I decided to leave the technical field and studied to get into business school. In early 1990, I hit the jackpot and got admitted to three top-tier business schools, Harvard, Northwestern, and Stanford. Wanting to stay in California, I enrolled in the Stanford MBA program.

Going to Stanford marked another turning point in my life. At the end of my first year in business school, I met my future wife, Mỹ Linh, through introduction by a friend. After a year of dating, we were married when I graduated from the Stanford business school in 1992.

One week after the wedding, we packed our precious few belongings into my car, and drove across the U.S. from California to Cincinnati. Within two weeks, I was married, moved to a new city, and started a new job with a U.S. consumer products company. For the next two years, we lived in this cold, dreary city, thousands of miles away from our families and friends.

We endured the cold and loneliness of Cincinnati for a good reason. I had never forgotten my promise to my father in the re-education camp long ago, the promise to come back to Vietnam one day to do what I could to help my relatives and other people. For more than fifteen years, the promise was always on my mind, though I had no idea how I would fulfill it. It was not until near my graduation from Stanford that I found the way. The company that I interviewed with, and went to work for in Cincinnati, told me it was interested in getting into Vietnam. When it did, I would be given the chance to go and help to start up the company. But first things first. I must spend a few years to learn the business and the company's ways of doing thing in its headquarters before I could head overseas.

By early 1994, our perseverance paid off. In February 1994, President Clinton lifted a long-standing trade embargo on Vietnam. Seizing the long-awaited opportunity, many American companies, including mine, rushed in to establish a presence in the country. After years of preparation and waiting, I was sent to the Philippines for one more training stop. By March 1995, I finally went back to Vietnam after seventeen years. When I left, I was a ragged boy. When I returned, I was a marketing manager for a powerful American company taking its first plunge in Vietnam.

For three years, from 1995 through 1997, my wife and I lived in and traveled throughout Vietnam. Our experiences and the stories we witnessed taught us how Vietnam changed, and in many ways, did not change, versus what I knew twenty years before.

My return to Vietnam marked a full circle of my life's odyssey, which began on that fateful day of April 30, 1975. On the same day in 1995, I rode a motorbike back to my old hometown, Vũng Tàu, the first time I was back since my escape. On my return, I found some old friends, including Trang, who still lived in the city. The reunions brought me many bittersweet realizations, including the dawning understanding that I had changed so much in the years living outside Vietnam. While I shared a past with my old friends, we had nothing in common in the present and the future. When I left Vũng Tàu, I felt like a foreigner in my own homeland.

Today, when I reflect upon all the events that had happened to me, I cannot help wondering if God has planned everything in our lives—and why. Why wasn't my family deported to Vietnam's New Economic Zones? Why was my life spared—but not my parents' lives—in the midst of the terrible storm of the South China Sea? Why couldn't my mother escape with us? Why did my parents have to escape? If they had not escaped, I eventually could have sponsored them to come to the United States. There are many other whys that I will never be able to find answers for.

The tragedies and tribulations I experienced have given me a unique perspective on life. Most important are the characteristics that I developed from those experiences: the will to survive, no matter how desperate and hopeless the situation; the humility to understand and sympathize with those who are less fortunate; and the willingness to pay for everything I get in life.

Twenty years before, if someone told me that I, a fifteen-year-old orphan fresh off the boat from Vietnam, would make it as far as I have today, getting a great education from a respected school like Stanford University and becoming a successful professional, I would have thought the person a lunatic. Yet, while those achievements seemed improbable twenty years ago, today I no longer give them much thought. Only in a free country like the United States could I advance so far. But that was only half of the story. Without the infinite love and sacrifice of my parents, I wouldn't be alive today. To me, my success is a result of, and a tribute to, the irrepressible human spirit and the sacrifice of my parents.

# Index

An Lộc 8
American 13, 14, 16; Congress 12;
    GIs 7, 97; imperialist 47, 55, 62, 96,
    108, 127, 152, 161–162; journalists
    13, 14; press 13, 14; public 13; pup-
    pets 13; soldiers 18, 65; warships 20,
    57
Anh Ba 77
Anh Văn (English) 56
anti–Communist 38, 104
anti-revolutionary 26, 54, 113, 120–124,
    146, 161, 166
Army of the Republic of Vietnam
    (ARVN) 6, 11, 12, 13, 17, 18, 20, 24,
    27, 40, 44, 56, 57, 60, 98, 105, 110;
    officer 58; soldiers 8, 19, 114; uni-
    forms 19
Australia 176, 212, 219

B40 rocket 18
ba mươi (thirty) 61
Bà Rịa 169
Bãi Trước beach 19, 20
Bàn Cờ 5
Bến Đá 20
Bến Đình 14, 152
Bình Ngô Đại Cáo 144, 157
Bình Trị Thiên 8, 17
boat people 219
Buddhism 19, 33, 44, 181, 197, 198, 203,
    205, 208; ceremony 224; philosophy
    24, 25; prayer 185, 198; temple 156

California 221, 224, 225
Cambodia 163, 164, 166, 167, 168, 169, 183
Cần Thơ 185–186, 191, 208
Canada 219
Cao Thắng Technical College 6
cáp duồn (beheading) 164
Central Highland 12
Central Vietnam 18, 165
Cháu Ngoan Bác Hồ (Good Children of
    Uncle Ho) 106, 107, 109, 112, 113, 121,
    145
Châu Thành High School 56, 60, 62,
    65, 71
Chi Đội (sub-branch) 61, 71, 72, 76, 78,
    110, 112, 113
China 9, 27, 54, 86; army 91; Chinese-
    Vietnamese 174–175
Chính Luận 11
Chính Phủ Cách Mạng Lâm Thời
    (Provisional Revolutionary Govern-
    ment) 69, 115
chó vàng (yellow dogs) 48, 148, 177,
    193, 216
CIA 29
Cincinnati, Ohio 1, 225
Clinton, President Bill 225
cơ sở quốc doanh (government owned
    stores) 86
Communism 2, 4, 5, 7–9, 11, 16–18, 26,
    28–30, 33–34, 39, 43, 47, 52, 55, 57,
    61, 64, 79, 80, 81, 83, 96–98, 100–101,
    105–106, 109, 110, 113, 116, 125, 129,

138, 145, 154, 162, 165, 174, 200, 204;
agent 69; army 164; assassins 6;
cadres 8, 9, 26, 61, 115, 138; government 40, 46, 49–52, 54, 85, 86, 98,
112, 141, 142, 158, 180, 219; indoctrination 1; offensive 11, 12, 17, 18, 105,
165; Party 6, 8, 9, 26, 49, 56, 60, 62,
63, 65, 75, 80, 86, 104, 109, 112, 114,
115, 139, 140, 145, 148, 150, 152, 161,
166, 170; Party members 91, 95, 128,
148, 152, 162, 165–166; Party plenum
107, 139; policy 52, 86; propaganda
14, 53, 86, 99; regime 5, 95, 165; revolution 75; rule 1; soldiers 20, 38, 175;
spy 119, 122–124, 147, 149; troops 15,
17, 18; youths 61
Côn Sơn 81, 190
Confucianism 1, 5, 33
Công An Hải Quân (Coastal Patrol
police) 148
criticism and self criticism 96
Cuba 54
currency change 142; *see also* currency
conversion
currency conversion 50–52, 85

de Lattre de Tassigny, Jean 77
"Đêm qua em mơ gặp Bác Hồ" (Last
night I dreamed of Uncle Ho) 65–67,
116–119
Đố Vui Để Học (Trivia pursuit) 73–74,
112
"Đoàn Quân Việt Nam đi" (The March
of the Vietnamese Army) 66
Đoàn Thanh Niên Cộng Sản Hồ Chí
Minh (The Young Ho Chi Minh
Communist League) 60–63, 65, 70,
166
Đội Thiếu Niên Tiền Phong Hồ Chí
Minh (The Ho Chi Minh Avant
Garde Youth) 60–64, 71, 72, 106–108,
111–113, 139, 145
Đống Đa Officer Apartment Complex
19, 20, 21, 43, 222
Dương Văn Minh, General 15, 16

East Cloud Ice Factory 44
Easter Offensive 4, 17, 18, 105, 165
Edison, Thomas 102
"enlightenment of socialism" 161
ESL (English as a Second Language) 223

famine of 1945 11
First Indochina War 5, 8
FOBs (Fresh Off the Boat) 224
French 8, 62; cemetery 42, 43; colonial-
ists 6, 77, 81; government 42; soldiers
42; nationals 42

Geneva Accord 4
Giải Phóng Quân (Liberation Army)
18, 47, 48
Great Britain 219
Gulf of Siam 174, 182

Hải Phòng 5
Harvard University 225
Highway 1 18
Ho Chi Minh 17, 48–50, 53, 65, 67, 74,
80, 86, 97, 109, 112, 170–171, 185, 191,
216
Hồ Quí Ly 27
Hồ Tôn Hiến 26
Hòa Bình (Pacific) Hotel 19
Hoạn Thư 26
Học tài thi lý lịch (Study with talents,
take exam with background) 98, 100,
107
Học Tập Tốt, Lao Động Tốt (Study
well, Labor hard) 57, 107, 162
Hong Kong 219, 222

ideological enlightenment 63
Indian-Vietnamese 191, 197, 201, 213
Indonesia 219

Japanese 6, 11
Jesus 197, 198
Junior Military Academy (Trường
Thiếu Sinh Quân) 16

Kế Hoạch Nhỏ (Small Plan) 108, 111,
113, 151
Khmer Rouge 163–165, 168–169
Kim Trọng 25
*Kim Vân Kiều* 24
Kotakinabalu 212, 220, 221
Kuala Lumpur 220–222

Lambretta 38
Land Reform 5, 9
Laos 8
Lê Dynasty 25

Lê Hồng Phong 81
Lê Lợi, King 27
Lê Lợi Street 31, 42, 45, 223
Liên Đội (branch) 71
Lincoln, Abraham 102
Long Khánh 156, 178
Lực Lượng Công An (Public Security
  Force) 47
lý lịch (background) 63
Lý Thường Kiệt Street 158

Malaysia 190, 193, 196, 204, 212, 219;
  capital 221; fishermen 210; peninsula
  209; Borneo 209; village 214; villagers
  212, 214, 215, 220
Mặt Trận Giải Phóng Quốc Gia
  (National Liberation Front) 69, 115
Mekong Delta 163–164, 169–170, 176,
  185, 191
Mekong River 164, 190, 191, 193
Ming Dynasty 27
Mùa Hè Đỏ Lửa ("The Summer of
  Fiery Red Fire") 4

Nam Định 4, 5, 6
Navarre, Henri 77
Ngụy Quân (Illegitimate Army) 19, 40,
  128, 162, 164
Ngụy Quyền (Illegitimate officials) 19
Nguyễn Ái Quốc 77
Nguyễn Du 24, 25, 26
Nguyễn Dynasty 4–5
Nguyễn Phi Khanh 26, 27
Nguyễn Sinh Cung 77
Nguyễn Tất Thành 77
Nguyễn Thị Minh Khai 80, 81
Nguyễn Trãi 26, 27, 28, 144
Nguyễn Văn Thiệu, President 12, 14, 29
Nha Trang 13
Nhất Quỷ, Nhì Ma, Thứ Ba Học Trò
  (First is the Devil, Second is the
  Ghost, and Third are the Students)
  64
Ninh Kiều pier 191
Nixon, President Richard 13
North Vietnam 4, 5, 9, 22, 31, 47, 48,
  86, 90, 115, 116, 129, 180–181; authors
  104; classmates 115, 116, 118, 120, 121,
  122, 124, 125, 127; kids 115, 116, 118,
  120, 121, 122, 124, 125, 127; party
  members 95, 110, 152; refugees 100,
110; spy 116; students 56, 58, 116, 118,
  120, 121, 122, 124, 125, 127; teachers
  56, 58, 90, 100, 126, 161
North Vietnamese Army (NVA) 3, 11,
  12, 13, 14, 15, 19, 23, 27, 38, 47, 58;
  soldiers 13, 17, 18, 48, 111
Northwestern University 225

Orange County 223

Pacific Ocean 215, 224
Paris negotiation 13
People's Army of Viet Nam (PAVN) 77,
  146, 164, 168
People's Committee 19, 23, 36, 46, 47,
  49, 55, 69, 141, 148, 163, 168
People's Courts 9
phản động (rebellious) 47, 65, 70, 116–
  117, 120, 122, 146
Pháp Văn (French) 56
Philippines 219, 225
Phù Đổng 117–118
phường (ward) 46, 142
Pol Pot 164
political enlightenment 28, 61, 62, 96,
  120, 124, 152
Procter & Gamble 1
Pulau Mantanani, island 209, 212

Quan Thế Âm Bồ Tát (the Merciful
  Buddha) 185, 206, 211
Quang Trung, Emperor 91

Red Cross 212, 214–216, 221; officials
  212–215, 220
re-education camp 28, 57, 156, 167, 178
Republic of Vietnam (also see South
  Vietnam) 50
Rockwell International 225

Saigon 5, 7, 12, 13, 14, 15, 75, 83, 110,
  113, 139, 140, 176, 180, 185, 191, 194
Salan, Raoul 77
San Diego 221, 223
San Francisco 222
security agents 46–51, 54, 85, 140, 141,
  148, 169, 185, 187–189
Singapore 176, 219
Socialist Paradise 90, 95, 166, 180
Socialist Republic of Vietnam 50, 54,
  56, 109

SOS 208
South China Sea 1, 176, 190, 200, 204, 224, 226
South Korea 14
South Vietnam 4, 5, 7, 12, 14, 24, 36, 40, 47, 48, 51, 54, 59, 61, 65, 69, 83, 85, 97, 108, 110, 114, 115, 140, 163, 167, 200, 216; armed forces 64, 69, 140; army 4, 13; authors 104; cities 47–48, 140; currency 50–52; draft dodgers 47; generals 12; government 7, 15, 16, 18, 28, 29, 46, 50, 57, 58, 64, 69, 96, 115, 127, 138, 165; lackeys 47, 108, 127, 161–162; militia 47; money 50–52; navy 191, 215; newspapers 54; officials 23, 26, 28, 47, 64, 69; people 29, 47, 61, 127, 140; politicians 28; puppets 13; soldiers 28, 47, 216; teachers 90, 100, 104
Southeast Asia 220
Soviet Union 54, 86
Stanford: *Business Magazine* 1, 209; MBA 1, 225; University 1, 209, 226
Suzuki motorcycle 38

tactical evacuation 12
tactical withdrawals 14
Tây Ninh 168–169
Tây Sơn Dynasty 25
Tết Offensive 4
Thai pirates 174, 182
Thailand 219
Thủ Đức Military Academy 6
Tin Sáng 11
Trần Dynasty 163
Trần Hưng Đạo Street 19
Trần Nguyên Hãn High School 24, 25

Trần Văn Hương, Vice President 12
Trường Sơn 117
Trường Thánh Giu Se (The St. Joseph High School) 56, 58–60, 65
*Truyện Kiều* (*Tale of Kiều*) 24, 26
Tú Bà 26
tư bản mại sản (capitalists) 50, 51, 142

Uncle Ho 48, 50, 57, 61, 68, 73, 74, 77, 79, 81, 86, 107, 118, 120, 145, 148, 152, 161, 166, 170, 177, 191; *see also* Ho Chi Minh
UNHCR (United Nations High Commission on Refugees) 219
United States 219–221, 226
University of California, Irvine 224, 225

Viet Cong 6, 59, 61
Vietnam Nationalist Party 6, 29
Vietnam War 6, 7, 139, 165, 166
Vietnamese Communist Party 48, 49, 56, 62, 69, 73, 79, 81; *see also* Communist Party
Vietnamese refugees 219, 220, 221
Vùng Kinh Tế Mới (The New Economic Zones) 139–141, 226
Vũng Tàu 3, 4, 7, 13, 14, 15, 18, 24, 36, 42, 44–46, 57, 65, 69, 75, 85, 86, 109, 110, 114, 119, 140, 141, 164, 175, 178, 185, 193, 216, 226; High School 55, 56, 59
Vương Thúy Kiều 24, 25
Vương Viên Ngoại 26

*We Want to Live* (*Chúng Tôi Muốn Sống*) 8, 9